What Does the Lord Require?

What Does the Lord Require?

HOW AMERICAN CHRISTIANS

THINK ABOUT ECONOMIC JUSTICE

Stephen Hart

New York   Oxford
OXFORD UNIVERSITY PRESS
1992

Oxford University Press

Oxford   New York   Toronto
Delhi   Bombay   Calcutta   Madras   Karachi
Kuala Lumpur   Singapore   Hong Kong   Tokyo
Nairobi   Dar es Salaam   Cape Town
Melbourne   Auckland

and associated companies in
Berlin   Ibadan

Copyright © 1992 by Stephen Hart

Published by Oxford University Press, Inc.
200 Madison Avenue, New York, NY 10016

Oxford is a registered trademark of Oxford University Press

Library of Congress Cataloging-in-Publication Data
Hart, Stephen, 1946–
What does the Lord require? : how American Christians think about economic justice /
Stephen Hart.
p.   cm. Includes bibliographical references and index.
ISBN 0-19-506762-2
1. Christianity and justice--United States.   2. Christians—United
States—Attitudes.   3. Social justice.   I. Title.
BR115.J8H37   1992
261.8'5'0973—dc20   91-30834

1   3   5   7   9   8   6   4   2

Printed in the United States of America
on acid-free paper

To Gail and Charlie,
who have supported and encouraged me
in life and this enterprise
through good times and bad

PREFACE

This book is an attempt to understand the varied ways in which grass-roots Christians in the United States use religious faith to help them think and talk about economic justice issues. The conclusions I have reached are based on about fifty in-depth interviews with Christians of many different political and religious stripes. My hope is that the understanding I have arrived at will be helpful for several different kinds of people:

- For people concerned with social justice questions, especially those situated left of the political center, whatever their religious commitments (or lack thereof). Since nine out of ten Americans identify themselves as Christians, no movement seeking major social change in the United States is likely to succeed unless it comes to grips with the implications of Christian faith for American politics.
- For members of religious communities, and the ministers, seminary faculty and students, church leaders, and staff who serve them. Such people will learn more about the state of mind of rank-and-file Christians, and may, I hope, use this understanding to make useful dialogue on social issues within the church more likely and the church's voice and mission more *effectively* faithful.
- For scholars, teachers, and students interested in the relations between religion and politics. I hope they will discover here approaches, perspectives, ideas, and findings that can assist them in their own study and research. Chapters 7 and 8 are especially addressed to these readers.

Any reader will soon realize that I fit into all three of these categories. My own values and beliefs will be apparent, and have certainly motivated me to write this book and to carry out the research underlying it. I do not believe that research can be neutral or above the fray; one's particular values and social position necessarily influence one's point of view. Nonetheless, this book is first and foremost an attempt to *understand:* to grasp how people think in a way that gives full credit to the cogency of their views and the life-affirming motivations, the care and concern, they bring to the world around them. One need not agree with the conclusions other people draw; however, to have much chance (and perhaps even much right) to change their ways of thinking and speaking, one needs to engage in dialogue based on or aiming toward this kind of understanding.

A focus on understanding rather than judging was made easier for me by the fact that I became attached to almost all my respondents. Not all are well educated or politically sophisticated, not all are consistent or systematic, and certainly many hold religious or political views I disagree with personally, but I found almost all of them personally appealing and many quite thoughtful. Most are struggling to make sense of a complex world and to be faithful Christians within it, and I learned a great deal from them. By the end of the research, I was much more convinced even than I had been when I embarked on it of the power—for both good and ill, but I believe more good than ill—of Christian faith.

Milwaukee   S. H.
January 1992

ACKNOWLEDGMENTS

A great many people have contributed to this project over the years it has been in progress. The most important are the respondents, who gave freely of their time and mental effort, and often bared their souls, to help a stranger who came into their homes to ask them about topics that were sometimes new to them. My attachment to these people goes beyond the rational, and I will always be grateful to them for sharing so much of their lives and thinking.

As with any writer, I owe unredeemable debts to writers who have preceded me. I am especially aware of the help I have received from the thinking of writers on the political left concerned with culture, and of scholars studying religion from within the tradition stemming from Max Weber. Two of my teachers at Berkeley, Charles Glock and Robert Bellah, were the source of many of the theoretical ideas and methodological strategies I have used in this study.

I was inspired to undertake this study by these two teachers, and by Victor Lidz and W. Russell Neuman. Three able interviewers—Theresa Moser, Jeffrey Johnson, and Rolando Juarez—complemented my efforts and skills, and a series of typists, transcript editors, and content analysts, particularly Patricia Vandervort and Hilary Roberts, helped me in the steps between raw tapes and a usable form of the data.

Various organizations also helped along the way. The Survey Research Center at the University of California at Berkeley, through the good offices of William Nicholls and Charles Glock, provided me with office space, equipment, and access to the respondents. The United Presbyterian Church—now merged into the Presbyterian Church (USA)—and the National Science Foundation provided grants to cover the significant out-of-pocket expenses of the project. The former Lutheran Church in America, by the decision of Leonard Sibley, allowed me to use continuing education time to do the crucial early writing of the manuscript; I was also lucky enough to have help from our unit's capable word-processing specialist, Dorothy Oscar. The Evangelical Lutheran Church in America provided a three-month sabbatical during which I wrote the last three chapters.

Large numbers of my friends and colleagues, as time went on, were drafted into reading the manuscript, giving me enormously useful ideas and suggestions; these include Paul Buhle, Mary Ann Clawson, Richard Elphick, Richard Fernandez, Charles Glock, Frank Griswold, Benton Johnson, Roger Johnson, Michael Norman, Richard Ohmann, William Placher, Douglas Porpora, Michael Rogin, Leonard Sibley, Guy Swanson, Ann Swidler, R. Stephen Warner, Marlie Wasserman, and anonymous reviewers for publishing houses. My editor at Oxford University Press, Cynthia Read, helped especially in deciding how to revise the most intractable chapters, and has been a model of efficiency and speed, for which I have been extremely grateful. In an act of great friendship, Roberta Schott provided meticulous and speedy proofreading.

My greatest debts are to Charles Glock, who has gone far beyond the duties of a thesis adviser in ways touching many parts of my life, and to my wife Gail Radford, who has been part of—and affected by—this project from the very beginning, and even read the penultimate draft of every chapter with enormous care at a point when she was under pressure in her own professional life. These two have truly touched me with a piece of God's free grace.

CONTENTS

Practical Conclusions

What Does the Lord Require?

What does the Lord require of you
but to do justice, and to love kindness,
and to walk humbly with your God?

Micah 6:8

Introduction

Faith and Economic Life

Many Americans have strong feelings about the connection between religion and politics. Jerry Falwell and Pat Robertson see the source of many social evils in humanism and disbelief. They are sure that real Christian faith will naturally lead people to support their right-of-center agenda on all issues, including economic ones. Many secular leftists agree with this analysis, although not with the political goals of the Christian Right. They, too, think that Christian faith—or at least, the theologically "traditionalist" kind found among evangelicals and fundamentalists—is naturally allied with political conservatism.

Both of these perspectives assume that the correct religious views (which for secularists would be atheism or at least a modernist theology) will help produce correct political views. Another frequent assumption is the opposite: that religion is essentially irrelevant to American politics. In this view, Americans may be superficially religious, but when push comes to shove they are rather materialistic and individualistic, and make their political decisions based on self-interest. The majority of pollsters and students of voting patterns, proceeding on this assumption, pay little attention to religion.

All these assumptions have some truth (and, of course, can be developed in far more complex and sophisticated ways than just presented). The evidence linking religious traditionalism to conservative views on social and political issues connected with sexuality is strong. Social class variables have done better than religious ones at explaining how people vote and how they react to economic issues. That Americans often think in individualistic and materialistic ways—one of the conclusions reached by sociologist Robert Bellah and four colleagues in their recent book *Habits of the Heart*[1]—is undeniable.

Nonetheless, there is something different, equally true, and in some respects more illuminating to be said about the capacities Americans have for ethical thinking, and for connecting religious faith to economic life. Consider these paradoxes: religion and politics are the two forbidden topics for polite discussion, yet constantly discussed; critics attack Americans at some moments for being concerned only with their self-interest, and at other moments for being too moralistic; religious perspectives are sometimes seen as pure window dressing, but at other times attacked for having all too great an impact on politics. The United States appears to be at once the most and least religious nation in the world, a nation where ethically based politics can be powerful and where politics can be the pursuit of the crudest self-interest. Social-movement organizations with strong religious constituencies work for goals as varied as eradicating pornography and housing the homeless. Sometimes the same person may even manifest two (or more) of these varied tendencies. If we are to make sense of these phenomena, we need to approach what people say and how they think in a way sensitive to the diverse and competing ways of understanding Christian faith that coexist in the United States.

The fact is that religious leaders and movements frequently speak to economic issues. When they do, it becomes clear that their understandings of faith and its social implications are far from uniform. Pope John Paul II and the American Catholic bishops commit their somewhat left-of-center visions of social justice to writing and commend them to Catholics; Jimmy Carter and many local religious activists around the country work to create better housing; José Miranda writes that the biblical message is demonstrably communistic. Meanwhile the Catholic theologian Michael Novak articulates a religious rationale for what he calls democratic capitalism, and conservative evangelical leaders such as Robertson and Falwell speak of American-style private enterprise as the system best conforming to their understandings of faith. Whatever the merits of these divergent views, clearly Christians are, in fact, capable of finding remarkably diverse readings of their religious traditions and texts. How faith should inform economic life is not determined once and for all by the internal logic of Christian tradition but is a subject of debate.

This is evidently true of religious leaders and movements, and I will argue, on the basis of in-depth interviews with a diverse group of Christian church members, that it is equally true of rank-and-file Christians. Both economic conservatives and economic liberals can take legitimate comfort in faith; we will see that there are strong grounds in indisputably authentic strands of Christian tradition for a variety of stances toward economic life. Christians are far from united with regard to the implications of faith for economic life, and are struggling with one another (and inside themselves) to define the social role Christianity will play. There is, at least at this point, no clear winner in this struggle (although my interviews indicate a few advantages for the liberal side), and the liberal and conservative uses of faith often cancel each other out politically. That does not mean that faith is irrelevant but, rather, that Christians draw varying conclusions for economic life from their faith, and that the implications of faith for economic issues will be determined by human effort and intention, and by the current cultural context, not by the inherent qualities of texts or ideas. Given this situation, the question of whether Christianity is a liberal or conservative force is unanswerable and uninteresting. The key question, instead, is how and why Christians come to their varying social interpretations of faith.

When we examine the thinking of grass-roots Christians, we also discover that the theological and denominational differences most obvious to journalistic and scholarly observers—the differences between theological modernists and traditionalists—are quite unimportant in how people articulate their economic views. The resources within Christian faith that people draw on to ground economically conservative views—and equally the ones used to ground economically liberal views—are common to all kinds of Christians. Furthermore, I will present strong evidence that there is in fact no relationship between theological conservatism and conservatism on economic issues. (Pope John Paul II gives a hint of this, with his combination of quite conservative theology and moderately left-of-center views on economic issues.) The situation with regard to the differences between Protestants and Catholics is less clear; the basic themes used by both kinds of Christians are similar, but Catholics do tend to relate faith to economic issues in a somewhat more liberal way than Protestants.

A variety of observers—Robert Bellah, Alisdair MacIntyre, Jeffrey Stout, Stanley Hauerwas, Christopher Lasch, among others—have commented on the resources Americans bring to ethical reasoning. Some argue that the loss of older ethical languages has left American thinking quite impoverished, and others that the diversity and secularity of much ethical thinking is actually a strength. I am convinced, contrary to both these views, that more survives from older modes of ethical thinking than is generally recognized, and that this has a variety of consequences, assisting both liberals and conservatives, supporting both passivity and activism. I found my respondents frequently addressing economic issues on the basis of religiously based ethical principles going far beyond individual self-interest—sometimes to support a sense of the importance of public concerns and at other times to support individual choice as the central criterion of a good economic order. Even theological modernists, I will argue, often show signs of thinking in ways that are significantly "otherworldly." When people—whether traditionalists, modernists, or even secular humanists—do think in otherworldly ways, furthermore, this is not just a source of conservatism or quiescence in their thinking about economic issues. It often helps them counter the strong individualistic strands in American culture and the relativism about economic decisions incarnate in the market, and encourages them to imagine and work for a better economic order. Thus Christian faith, despite the hopes of secularists and the fears of those who see faith as increasingly privatized, is still contributing to public discourse.

These issues are significant not only for possibilities for ethical discourse but also for social transformation in the United States, the ways in which such a transformation might come about, and the approach those seeking change might best employ. Given how attached most Americans are to Christian faith, any transformation for which loss of faith is a precondition is unlikely to occur. In the past decade or so, thinkers to the left of the political center (especially historians) have been paying increasing attention to the ways in which "traditional" forms of culture in the United States— religion, moral ideas, commitments to families, ethnic solidarities, and the like—can help as well as hinder struggles for economic justice. The role of Christian faith is a key case in point. Without assuming that ideas direct historical events, or ignoring the many difficulties Christian faith can present to the efforts of social change activists, we need to understand, as I will argue, that American Christians still retain a significant capacity to understand faith in a way that is potentially more of an aid than an obstacle to social change.

The varying social interpretations of faith held by grass-roots Christians also bear on concerns many have about the life of the church: Why are Christians so divided as to whether and how faith can be related to economic issues? What are the obstacles to more Christians connecting their faith to realms of life beyond church—work, politics, community life, and so on? Why are denominational statements on social issues mostly ignored, and why do they so deeply disturb many of the lay members who do notice them? Is there a gulf between left-leaning clergy or denominational leaders and a conservative laity? Some of these issues crosscut differences between left and right. For instance, the same arguments used in the 1960s to oppose church civil rights activism are now heard in opposition to the Catholic bishops' activism around abortion; both forms of activism seem like moralistic meddling to people who disagree with them. That implies that the bases of left-wing and right-wing activism, or the connections between faith and quite diverse political views, have things in common. When I point this out to activists on either side, I encounter considerable discomfort, which indicates that neither side has entirely come to grips with the ambiguities in its stance and in the guidance given by Christian faith.

The Focus and Approach of This Book

These are some of the issues to be explored in this book. It may already be clear that the focus here will be on "ordinary" Christians, rather than movements, leaders, intellectuals, or denominational structures and statements.

The assumptions behind this focus are that leaders only sometimes and partially represent their constituencies, and that the thinking of ordinary Americans is very important for the future of this country. Out of this concern, I engaged forty-seven people with a broad variety of religious and political perspectives—Catholics, evangelicals, and mainline Protestants; political conservatives, liberals, and radicals—in discussions of their religious faith, their views on economic issues, and the connections between their religious and political views.

People who give speeches or publish their ideas are listened to with care, and their views are often analyzed in a way sensitive to their ambiguity and complexity. To give grass-roots Christians the same opportunity, the discussions with the respondents were lengthy and intense—typically about three hours, divided between two sessions—and the interviews were transcribed verbatim. Each person's thinking is thus documented in a transcript about the length of two chapters in this book.[2]

The ideas these people express make it possible to understand how and why ordinary Christians come to their varying understandings of faith, appropriating the resources found in Christian traditions to help them think and speak about economic issues. As we proceed, we will disentangle the strands of faith Christians use to think about economic life, and the way they use these strands to ground both conservative and liberal views on economic issues.

By "economic" (or "economic justice") issues, I mean the political questions that arise in the United States about how economic life should be organized. These include:

- What kind of economic order would best promote justice, community, and well-being?
- What kind and degree of equality should we seek?
- Who should make decisions about the use of economic resources?
- What should be the balance between individual self-determination and common decision making in economic life?
- How should we try to bring a better economic order into existence?

These questions are complex and controversial, and have been central issues in American political debate since at least the New Deal. Americans address them not just on the basis of their interests and their ideas about what is technically feasible but also of their ultimate values and views of reality (views, for instance, about human nature). It will come as no surprise that the main focus here is on the broader values and views of reality people use when thinking about economic life, since this is where faith has a role to play.[3]

Theologians and ethicists also treat economic issues, but their purposes are primarily *prescriptive:* to articulate what they see as a faithfully Christian stance on economic issues and ethical principles applicable to economic life, to persuade others, and to motivate people to take personal responsibility for acting on their convictions. The focus of this study, on the other hand, is primarily *descriptive:* to understand, on the basis of empirical evidence, how people actually think, rather than to determine how they ought to think. I am no relativist, and hold definite views on many of the issues to be addressed; this book, and the research on which it is based, were motivated by my own passions and perplexities as a Christian and an activist. Nonetheless, my hope is that the description presented here will be convincing to people with varied political and religious perspectives. At various points, and particularly in the final chapter, I will describe some ways in which I hope my analysis might influence the thinking and actions of various constituencies.

The People Interviewed for This Study

Who are the respondents, and where did they come from? Thirty-seven of them were chosen, in a way designed to maximize religious, political, and socioeconomic diversity, from two random samples of church members previously drawn for public opinion surveys. These are the "regular" respondents. The other ten were located through my network of contacts, three (chosen to represent varying perspectives) from African-American churches, and seven to represent "extreme types"—one Quaker, and one socialist and one extreme conservative from each of the mainline Protestant, evangelical Protestant, and Catholic camps. (Information on exactly how the respondents were chosen, along with other details of the methods used in the study, can be found in the appendix.)

The respondents represent many different perspectives and walks of life. Among the regular respondents, for instance, are found Catholics, Nazarenes, Jehovah's Witnesses, Presbyterians, Methodists, Lutherans, an Episcopalian, Baptists, a member of the Assemblies of God and another from the Missionary Alliance, and several people belonging to independent evangelical congregations. Politically, they range from socialists to Reagan-style conservatives. Some are manual workers with little schooling and modest incomes, while a few have post-graduate degrees and several are quite affluent. Four of the respondents are African-American and three Latino or Latina. At the time of their interviews, they ranged in age from twenty to seventy-eight. Given the diversity of this group and the way it was chosen, any perspective that has much following among American Christians is likely to be held by at least one of these people.

The information about the respondents provided here is unaltered, except that I have given pseudonyms to the respondents whom I quote repeatedly. I have tried to respect the individuality and voice of these people: all the respondents mentioned in the book are actual, specific persons, not composites or types, and what I have quoted are their exact words, with only the most minor editing.

We will start with seven particular people and how they link faith to their views on economic issues. Thus the organizing principle for chapter 1 is the *individual,* whose views are described as a more or less coherent whole. The people profiled in this chapter—all of whom come from the "regular" group of respondents—provide good examples of the key ways in which faith grounds economic views among American Christians. This will provide a basis for subsequent chapters, where we will focus on recurring themes, seeing how a variety of respondents address a series of key issues about faith and its relationship to economic life.

Individuals

1

How Seven Christians Think about Economic Life

David Jenkins: An Individualistic Nazarene

"We have too much law," says David Jenkins, "and too little human re-lationship. We're too much involved with laws, like we are with our money." This is David's basic premise when he talks about every kind of social and political issue, and it is an ethical perspective with deep religious roots.

How does David apply this premise to economic life? For one thing, he says, "people have thrown away their ability to reason because they let all this ridiculous legislation do their thinking for them." For another, the development of social welfare programs "has changed our whole social structure. Before they started, when we saw the hungry, we would feed them. Now, we don't take care of each other, because we figure the gov-ernment's going to do it." In short, laws stunt our development as caring, intelligent beings who make choices and are personally involved with each other.

Many conservatives want to maximize individual freedom in economic life, but want to uphold authority and limit choices with regard to sexuality and reproduction; many liberals hold the reverse combination of views. David, however, is consistently on the side of individual freedom. He is not sure having police makes us safer, doesn't think it matters much what we do sexually, and wants people to be free to decide whether to have an abortion. (David shows us, by this combination of views, that people do not always combine their political views in packages corresponding to conven-tional ideas about what it means to be "liberal" or "conservative"; for instance, a person can reasonably hold conservative views on economic issues and liberal ones on abortion, or vice versa. Still less, as we will see repeat-edly, should one assume that there is any connection between *theological* and *economic* conservativism or liberalism.)

It is not by accident that David pairs laws and money as two key things with which we are too involved. Both laws and money are objective, external, and material; they motivate us, in part, by appeals to our physical or economic self-interest. Both are forces that can influence us to do the right thing, but not necessarily to have the right intention. Laws reduce our freedom, and involvement with money does, too; it's fine to enjoy a comfortable life, David thinks, but you lose your capacity to make free choices about the best way to live your life if you make decisions on the basis of striving for money.

It is already clear that David is worlds apart from both those who argue for a totally free market economy on the grounds that this will be efficient and make us all prosperous, and those who believe that it is good to pursue one's self-interest wholeheartedly, limited only by law. He backs Ronald Reagan's economic perspective, but worries that Reagan doesn't have "a real strong sympathy for his fellow man." David's goals are freedom and caring relationships, not affluence. And freedom, for him, is first of all the spiritual freedom to follow whatever call one receives from God—without being distracted by attachment to material wealth, or by institutional arrangements that diminish one's sense of responsibility to others—rather than freedom from government constraint.

Where does this perspective come from? David's consistent individualism might seem like the social philosophy of an upper-class sophisticate—in some ways, it even resembles the libertarian "playboy philosophy" of Hugh Hefner—but its roots are very different. The son of a railroad worker stationed in Kansas, David has had two years of college and six children. He suffers from seizures, and has never tried very hard to get ahead. As a result, he says, "I've been in a financial crisis all my life." When interviewed (at fifty-six years old) he lived partly on a disability pension and partly by getting an apartment rent-free in return for working as a building manager.

David belongs to the Church of the Nazarene, part of what is usually considered the theologically traditionalist or conservative wing of Protestantism. In this wing are usually classed the Assemblies of God, pentecostal and holiness groups, the Churches of Christ (not to be confused with the United Church of Christ), Southern (and most other) Baptists, and most of the small denominations and independent congregations in the United States. Most of these groups would call themselves "fundamentalist" or "evangelical." The modernist or theologically liberal wing, on the other hand, includes what are often called the "mainline" or "mainstream" denominations: Episcopalians; most kinds of Presbyterians, Lutherans, and Methodists; some Baptist groups, the United Church of Christ ("congregationalist" churches mostly belong to this denomination), and several smaller groups. The nature of the differences between these two wings is not easy to specify, especially since there are major theological differences within each. Members of traditionalist denominations tend to believe that the Bible is totally normative for Christian faith and life, and should be read literally; that it is very important to convert people to an explicit commitment to Jesus Christ as their Lord and Savior; and that conversion is a particular kind of experience or event, often referred to as being "born again." Members of mainline denominations tend to read the Bible less literally, give it varying amounts of authority, are unwilling to engage personally in evangelistic activities, and are usually queasy about claims that people need to undergo conversion in order to be right with God.[1]

David's religious life is different from that of most members of mainline denominations. When he was six years old, he attended a camp meeting and had an intense religious experience—although what he seems to remember most vividly is an intense storm blowing the tents down, and his excitement running through the storm with a large African-American man. He wanted to be baptized in a river, following Jesus' example, and got his way even though his minister tried to talk him out of it. (His parents were unchurched Methodists who became religiously involved—as Nazarenes— after David's conversion.) He remembers many details of his baptism; ever since then, he has felt a strong sense of being "called" by God, not to any ordained ministry but to carrying out God's work in the world. Using traditional evangelical terms to express a sense of conversion, he says that he was blind but now he sees. He goes to church three times a week and prays frequently; sometimes, but very selectively, he prays for what he needs, and he feels that he has always gotten a positive answer, particularly at a time when his son was in grave danger in Vietnam. When telling of these experiences in the interview, he was moved toward tears, but not embarrassed. An active volunteer in his church, he has started a ministry on his own initiative, taking tapes of sermons and worship services and playing them to people who cannot come to church because of age or ill health.

David is very articulate about his faith, and even though the questions did not directly ask him to state a theological perspective, many elements of his theology came out in the conversation. He is a Bible-believing Christian, but he never raises the issue of biblical literalism or authority. Instead, he talks about prayer and faith. Sounding like a Lutheran talking about the primacy of faith and grace over works, he says that "morals aren't necessarily the criteria"; the key thing is to trust in God and to "pray and lean on faith and [God's] vital promises." This relationship is highly personal, direct, and inward; organizations and even behavior are not very important.

David's sense of God's power, closeness, and trustworthiness, of the degree to which God can be spoken to and intervenes in our lives, is stronger than most mainline Protestants report, but in other ways David's religious perspective seems quite "modernist." For instance, he explicitly distances himself from his denomination's position that one has to believe in Jesus to be saved. "My personal conviction," he says, is that "anybody that dedicates their life to being guided by the divine spirit, whatever they want to call him," can be saved. Another example is his view that "everybody that dedicates their life to Christ, whether formalized as ministers or not, has a definite call to God, and laymen shouldn't feel any less called than they expect of their ministers." This call is mainly acted out in secular activities rather than church work, and David believes that how you act in your business dealings is more important than your sexual behavior. Some of these statements express a point of view similar to the one that has developed in the "ministry of the laity" movement within mainline denominations. A third example of David's "modernist" tendencies is his view that psychology and philosophy are ways to deepen the life of faith, rather than enemies.

All of his opinions—on religion, ethics, economic issues, abortion, and so forth—are strongly colored by a basic perspective, deeply rooted in Christian tradition, that could be called "voluntarism." For instance, he doesn't believe in evangelizing by "knocking on doors" or "altering other people's faith." Instead, he hopes that he sets an example that people will emulate. He is "inclined to let people go their own way" in deciding how to live, unless they're harming others. Sexual behavior in itself isn't very important ethically—"What's rubbing a little flesh together?"—but if one intends to hurt another person by what one does sexually, then serious issues arise. This is a good example of the primacy David gives to subjective intention over objective behavior in making ethical judgments. Furthermore, he believes that God will often give him what he prays for even when that is not what is best for him. In other words, he thinks that God, too, is a voluntarist—a being more committed to our freedom of action than to our welfare.

In his church, David prefers to do things spontaneously that strike him as useful or necessary rather than hold a formal position or office. The church, in any case, is secondary: "[As] I understand the concept of Christianity, my personal belief is that it is a relationship that a person has directly with God, and that his church affiliation is on the same level as an affiliation you might have with a fraternal organization like the Kiwanis Club. It gives you dignity and happiness to be affiliated with people that think about the same as you do, but it can't represent your personal belief any more than being a Democrat or Republican." As a person in the evangelical tradition, he has "a personal working relationship with Christ." Clearly, however, that relationship is just a particular form of what he sees as the core of any way of being religious or finding meaning in one's life: having your own relationship with whatever you consider sacred, chosen by yourself and essentially independent of any organization or institution. Churches are essentially *means;* they have no value aside from how they help their members in their religious lives. But because he gets a great deal from his church, he values it highly.

When David equates the Kiwanis Club, his church, and political parties, we can see how the voluntaristic principle colors his views in every aspect of life. It is first of all a religious principle, in that his intense, personal religious experiences give him meaning and guidance in his life, and he cares far more about spiritual life than about any political or even ethical issue. But it also resonates through all his views on economic and political questions. He supports private enterprise, wants to minimize regulation of both businesses and individuals, and in principle prefers private charity to public social welfare programs. However, in practice he doesn't favor cutting back existing welfare programs, since he believes that people's charitable impulses have already been largely destroyed.

The pattern we see in David—conservative economic views grounded in a desire to maximize individual choice—is a key way in which Christian faith can serve to support conservative politics. It is strongly and authentically rooted in important Christian traditions, and entirely compatible with David's appealing personality and caring approach to life.

One more point needs to be stressed about David's economic conservatism. His real interest, in opposing government intervention, is in the broader issue of how social forces can undermine voluntary choice and seduce us into placing our reliance on external, "material" things like laws and money. The social force he focuses on most is government, but occasionally he speaks of others. For instance, he thinks that automobile insurance undermines our sense of responsibility for not hurting people and helping out when we do, and makes us litigious—too interested in winning our case, and too little interested in what is fair. And he criticizes the hunger for money that in his view motivates many businesses not to take enough care for how they may be hurting people.

David is economically conservative, but he is also conservative in a somewhat different way: in his way of looking at the role of individuals within our society. "Politically," he says, "I feel real annoyed that everybody gets involved with trying to straighten one another out." This is an annoyance that liberals often feel when confronted with the Moral Majority, but it cuts both ways: in the 1950s and 1960s, some Southerners saw civil rights work in this way. Tolerance for cultural diversity is one thing, but it is quite another to say that we should not engage in discussion with people who have different values with the intention of persuading them to act differently, or of achieving better agreement on common values by which to organize our life together. David sounds here as if he adopts this more extreme view.

This view and many others that bear on the possibility of making social change come out of David's voluntaristic sentiments. Above all, he opposes any means of trying to achieve social goals—even goals he approves of— that is coercive. He defines coercion broadly, to include almost anything done in an organized fashion rather than by individuals making their decisions separately. "I don't like picket lines," he says; "I don't like the concept of intimidating people into things. I think people should be reasoned with, not intimidated." He regards demonstrations as coercive; petitions, on the other hand, are a means of political expression that does respect individual choice. Injustices should be corrected by the voluntary actions of individuals, and not by coercive laws. For instance, he is against racial discrimination in housing, but if we didn't rely so much on laws, he says, in the case of a discriminating landlord "other people would realize that his way of doing things was bad and nasty, and the natural failure to support him and want to live in his houses would take care of that."

In general, though, he is not very interested in even non-coercive methods of righting *societal* wrongs. He prefers to "deal with people on an individual basis," helping them and making them more happy. Christians should be involved in changing society for the better, he says, "by living an exemplary life," and churches should be socially or politically active only to protect religious liberty and their interests as organizations. In all of these opinions, he seems to take the view, implicitly, that a good society is one in which individuals have caring relationships and meaning in their lives. The way we get there is by setting a good example, by caring for others, and perhaps by persuasion. Good institutions are not important, either as characteristics of a good society or as means to create and maintain one. This is what could be called an "atomistic" view of a good society and of how we might get there.

In addition to voluntarism, there is another theme running through many of David's views that might be called "non-materialism." He is not against accepting the "little fleshy satisfactions God gives us"; he points to the nice apartment he lives in as an example of what he enjoys. But he frequently talks about love of money as a danger, and—as we have seen—connects this to reliance on laws and government. These views, perhaps combined with the fact that he has not experienced or seen much real economic suffering, lead him not to be very interested in questions about inequality or social justice. And because so many political disputes have to do with economic or material questions, he has a second reason (beyond his dislike of the coercive power of government) to be uninterested in politics.

David's focus on the world of one-to-one relationships means that ideas that other people use to ground quite radical politics do not have the same meaning for him. For instance, his way of thinking about his call to ministry— a call that applies mostly to life outside church walls—leads him to value serving the world. Some Christians take this to mean that we all bear some responsibility for the quality of our social institutions. But this potential is not realized in David's thinking; for him, our responsibility begins and ends with our direct contribution to the well-being of people we meet face to face and the example we set for others. To take another example, David believes in thinking independently, constructing a systematic view of the world, and acting out of conscience. These are bedrock convictions for any radical, but for David they have only private implications.

Taken together, David's views separate religious values from any criteria for a good *society* beyond the principle of maximizing individual choice. He wants our economic decisions *as individuals* to be governed by Christian ethical principles. But the only responsibility for practical action on behalf of a good society (however defined) that he assigns to individual Christians is to respect the freedom of others. Personally, he tries hard to live in a caring way in his face-to-face interactions, but even that is not a responsibility he feels is binding on others. He appears to give no responsibility whatsoever to the church. These views make it hard to articulate any substantive ethical framework for measuring our life together as a whole society; Christian ethics, in essence, apply only to private life, and need to be constructed and applied separately by each person. Social change takes place only through the accumulation of individual decisions.

David values practical life, and wants us to find spiritual meaning within it, but for him, such meaning is a purely individual and internal phenomenon. Thus, spiritual concerns are very separate from material ones; the individual has little to do with those aspects of our lives going beyond person-to-person dealings, and inner intentions are very different from practical outcomes. In each duality, the first element is taken to be far more important and in some sense more "real." These dualities, which David adopts for essentially religious reasons, make him unlikely to have much impact on the world, even for conservative purposes.

Catherine Kennedy: A Social Democratic Catholic

When Catherine Kennedy was asked what relationship she saw between her faith and her social and political values, she said, "They're all kind of tied up." In the Sixties, she wanted to go to the South to do civil rights work. "Was that," she asks, "a political value—having equal opportunity for Blacks—or was it that essentially they were my brothers?" For her there is no clear separation between religious and social concerns. She is happy to see the church take up social issues, in addition to serving people in need. In her view, "If the church gets involved in racial equality, to me that's a part of Christianity; the church has a *responsibility*" to work on this.

Catherine thinks very differently from David Jenkins. Her faith is explicitly connected to a vision of a good society—a vision that focuses on compassion and equality rather than on maximizing individual choice. We might say that she has a "substantive" vision of social justice, whereas David focuses on the "procedural" issue of freedom. His view of life is at least as coherent as Catherine's, but she makes or favors many more connections than he does: between church and society, individual and society, individual and church, religious and political values. Both want a society in which people will care for each other more than now, but for David the only kind of caring that matters is that which happens when a freely acting individual helps another specific individual, whereas Catherine is interested in having caring *institutions* and in the actual help received by those who need it. With regard to helping the needy, David focuses on the moral state of the giver, Catherine on the material state of the receiver. David has a rich and so-phisticated way of thinking about faith, but one that cuts off many connec-tions between faith and political life. Catherine's faith perspective is simpler, but it has much richer connections to the social world, partly because it gives much more attention to ethics and behavior.

Catherine, who was sixty-five years old when interviewed, comes out of a highly traditional Irish Catholic background, and is the daughter of a skilled blue-collar worker. She describes herself as religiously conservative, and this is true in some ways. She attends mass at least weekly, has generally followed church rules (confession at least yearly, Friday abstinence until the rules were changed, and so forth), and answered a series of religious belief questions with the conventionally orthodox answers. In traditional fashion, she prays to her mother who is already in heaven and has better access to God than she has.

But there is another side to her background and religious thinking. Her father was not Catholic and had been divorced, and so her parents' marriage was not recognized by the church. When she was ten years old and her mother was gravely ill, a "cranky Irish Catholic priest" refused to administer last rites unless her mother promised to leave her "life of sin"—that is, her husband. She did so, and later married another man—this time with the church's blessing, since it regarded her first marriage as void. Catherine's father had been waiting in hopes that her mother would return to him, but at this point he gave up and soon remarried. Catherine's parents continued to love each other as well as their new mates, and she remained close to both parents; still, this was hard on her. This experience left Catherine unready to accept church authority uncritically. For instance, although she goes to confession as required, she thinks the priests performing this rite mostly have little to offer her. Even more radically, she believes that the church should bless the unions of gay people. Her own life, too, has had some unconventional aspects for a person of her generation. After high school she went to normal school, taught in a rural school for several years, and then married and became a housewife. When nearly forty years old she entered college as an undergraduate, ultimately got a master's degree in social work, and has worked ever since for a Catholic agency.

She describes her religious life in terms very different from David's: she speaks a little of beliefs, a lot about the church, even more about the ethical meaning of "performing your religion," and not at all about trust or faith in David's sense. She describes her faith as not having changed very much, and there is no sense of conversion in her religious history; she is truly a once-born person. Nonetheless, she welcomes the changes that have come to the church since the Second Vatican Council in the 1960s—such as the mass in English, more Scripture readings and a greater variety of musical styles in worship, more openness to modern culture, loosening of traditional Catholic rules, and a somewhat more participatory style of governance. She has also become increasingly independent of the church in how she thinks about ethical matters.

What does it mean to "perform your religion"? For her, this has occasionally implied following traditional sexual rules, and it influenced her choice to become a social worker. Most of all, however, it implies "accepting everyone as your brother, whether they're doing what I approve of or not; whether they're different from me or not"; not "just Christians," and not just (as with David) people one meets face to face. Her key ethical and religious premise, running through all her statements about her faith and about social and political issues, is what could be called "universalistic love."

This point of view is not based primarily on ideas about freedom or tolerance. Rather, the point is to act like "a kind and loving God," who cares for every human being regardless of weaknesses and deserts. God loves us unconditionally, and that is the model we are supposed to follow in our relations with others. The universalism in this premise is that all differences among us—of race, class, gender, nationality, even talent—are unimportant in God's sight: we are all of equal value to God, and should be to each other. In addition to acting these principles out in our personal lives, we should try to see that our society lives up to them.

For Catherine, these premises imply views on economic issues close to those of European social democracy. If "socialism [means] everybody getting an equal chance" to have a life free from want and to enjoy possibilities for recreation and education, she favors it, but she doesn't want "government owning things." Asked about a series of social welfare programs, in almost every case she wanted them expanded to meet needs more effectively. She feels that America does not live up to its promise of equality and opportunity for all, that many people are treated unfairly. (As a social worker, she must frequently meet people in need or trouble, and this may contribute to her sense of the need for more social justice.)

Voluntaristic themes are far from absent in Catherine's thinking on religious and ethical issues. We have seen that she does not look to the church for guidance on ethical issues at this point in her life. She believes that different decisions on abortion and homosexuality can be right for different people, and favors tolerance for people of varying lifestyles. But she does not fear collective action, as David does, or much mind the fact that such action inevitably has some degree of coerciveness. Equality of services to all kinds of people may require "imposing from the top down." "I don't mind paying taxes," she says, "if the services are good—and equal," and she makes practically no complaints about bureaucracy or big government.

What explains the difference between her and David, in terms of how commitment to freedom of individual conscience—which they share—influences ideas about economic life, and about the right way to go about improving human life? Part of the difference has to do with how Catherine *describes* the world: she believes that social forces beyond our control have a major influence over our lives. She tends to blame institutions more than individuals for the wrongs of the world: "Our institutions work to allow people with faults of character to operate in an underhanded way." "There should be safeguards," she says, "to prevent" corruption and abuse of authority by government officials.

These positions stem partly from the influence of the perspective of contemporary social science, but they also seem deeply Catholic; they express beliefs but also involve values; they are a mixture of the secular and the religious. Catherine is not a simpleminded optimist, basing her liberal views on the idea that human nature is infinitely improvable; instead, assuming that human nature is a somewhat fixed mixture of good and ill, she wishes to improve the institutional structures that channel it so that people in fact behave relatively well. This is the function of institutions: not just to maintain order or a framework within which people can act voluntarily but to affect our conduct.

Intention, or the state of our hearts, is important, but how we actually behave is at least equally important. On ethical questions, Catherine is often "situational," but she never focuses solely on intention. Intention and action do not even always have to coincide. To David, the combination of not believing that the church's system of confession is reasonable but following church rules anyway would seem strange or even hypocritical, but Catherine perceives no discrepancy. In a sense, she is more worldly than David, but this is partly because she comes out of a religious milieu that is older and in some ways less "modern" than Protestantism. This milieu, compared with David's, gives more value to ritual—a public and external or "material" form of action, even though invested with spiritual meaning—and more importance to institutions, as compared with the direct relationship of each individual with God. Contrary to what some proponents of "modernity" might expect, it is to a large degree because she is—in this respect—less "modern" than David that she is more liberal and more interested in political and social issues.

Joseph Krieger: A Corporatist, Centrist Catholic

When Joseph Krieger thinks about life, the first thing that seems to come into his mind is the value of hard work. "What you work for, you appreciate," he says, but actually he is at least as interested in the work as the reward. He has urged his sons to "get into something where you can put your whole self in it, something meaningful, where you're helping people." But whatever your work is, it should be "dedicated to God," and even "the most menial thing," if done well, will give you a sense of satisfaction and help "gain you eternal bliss when you pass on." His mother is surely in heaven, since she worked so hard. Thus work is a way to heaven. It is also a model for the other things that lead to heaven: "What you do in treating your fellow man day in and day out, that's what's going to help when they take account of it upstairs." Lutherans and Calvinists of earlier centuries would have called this "works-mongering": thinking that you can earn salvation. Joseph's God, however, seems to believe in the work ethic just as much as Joseph.

Personal experiences, as well as religious faith, have led Joseph to this point of view. He is the same age as Catherine Kennedy but comes from a "strict" German Catholic family and grew up in a midwestern city. His early life was not easy, for his father died when Joseph was ten years old. From then on, he worked while attending school and serving an apprenticeship to become a printer, helping his mother (who did domestic work) keep the family afloat. He was so appreciated by a small printing firm that hired him part-time while he was in the Navy that he was able to negotiate for the chance to buy into the firm in return for coming to work for it when he was discharged. He eventually became the owner, and had just retired when interviewed. A warm and unpretentious as well as upright person, he seems to be well liked by employees, those he does business with, and even his competitors. Given his happiness in his work life, and his success in the face of difficult conditions, it is not surprising that he believes so strongly in work, and is convinced that in America, "[as nowhere] else in the world, you can really lift yourself up by the bootstraps if you're willing to work."

This last statement clearly has conservative overtones. Another conservative theme is that "we should be a little more self-reliant; people in minority groups sometimes tend to think that everything should be handed to them." We have to try to prevent people from becoming "shiftless" or "lackadaisical" and avoid undermining their "initiative." This requires that both private charity and public social welfare programs be very carefully run.

Joseph is also conservative in that he thinks economic inequality is natural and God-ordained. "I never did believe that people in the truest sense are equal. In the eyes of God, all men are created equal, but some just don't have the ambition that others have, and some of them don't have the intelligence, so we're always going to have different strata."

This is only half the story, however. Joseph is a liberal in many important ways. He is a Democrat liberal enough to have voted for George McGovern, says the tax system unfairly favors the rich, and wants ours to be a society with more sharing. He happily runs a union shop and has made major and successful efforts to recruit African-Americans and other people of color as printers in his shop. In fact, he returns over and over again to the need for racial justice.

How does all of this cohere? To understand, we have to look at his faith and connection to the church. Like Catherine, he is a Catholic who has never doubted his faith, but his perspective is more systematic and articulated in more detail than hers, and he accepts the church's authority without any of the reservations she expresses. The tone of his speech is more religiously traditional than hers, with explicit references to heaven and eternal life, and frequent use of biblical phrases. Like her, however, he speaks with much more passion and personal conviction about the church and about ethics (in fact, his definition of what it means to be a Christian is entirely ethical) than about spiritual, experiential, or theological dimensions of faith. He has always been deeply involved in the church, attended parochial school as a matter of course—"we never gave too much thought to it; it was a way of life"—and still attends mass several times a week. He has deeply absorbed the social teachings of the church, and can articulate them clearly, correctly, and in some detail—despite not having much formal education. To a large extent, the connections he makes between faith and politics are not ones he has constructed on his own or even absorbed unconsciously from his religious and cultural environment but explicitly those of the church.

What are the church's social teachings? Of course, there is not just one Catholic social perspective, and church teachings have changed over time. Joseph's views reflect Catholic teachings of the first half of this century, well before the Second Vatican Council and more recent developments such as the theology of liberation.[2] The social perspective he absorbed emphasized a combination of social justice and harmony, to be achieved through responsible corporations, moderate unionism, and some kind of social welfare state. It was anti-communist and defended private property—but only some of its prerogatives. It was against what it saw as materialism and derogation of human dignity both under communism and under unrestrained capitalism. It was against revolution and rebellion but in favor of using the power of the state to bring about changes in social conditions. The prototypical early papal statement of this perspective is the widely influential encyclical of Leo XIII, *Rerum Novarum,* issued in 1891; Joseph referred to Pope Leo explicitly during the interview and has his perspective right, although there is no sign that he has read the encyclical. In the United States, more specific and somewhat more radical interpretations were given to the same basic approach, for instance in the 1920 "Bishops' Program of Social Reconstruction" drafted by John A. Ryan. Pope John Paul II's teachings today, despite some differences, are in a similar spirit.[3]

How does Joseph express these ideas? He brings up the idea of social justice on his own initiative. "As a Catholic," he says, "I feel strongly about social justice, and believe that we who have had an opportunity to live a good life have an obligation to share some of that." (Note the phrase "as a Catholic," indicating that he is speaking not just for himself but also for an institution; very few Protestants would ever use a parallel phrase with regard to their views of social justice.) Then he goes on to give a more substantive image of social justice: "Basically, Christianity is love of God and neighbor," and the key point is how you carry that out in "your daily living." This "depends on what you're doing. If a person is working for somebody, then his Christian duty is to do the best job he can and give his boss a full day's work. For the boss, social justice demands that he pay a living wage and respect the dignity of his workers," and help them if he can. If a person is in business, the duty is to be honest and fair, and content oneself with a reasonable profit.

All of these statements refer to what the British historian E. P. Thompson calls a "moral economy": a desire to have an economic order in which our relationships are regulated by human feelings and needs and by ethical principles rather than by market forces or technical factors. Images of socialism refer to a hoped-for moral economy in the future, but many times moral economies are idealized images of a society one believes existed in the past—images that are used to oppose what are felt to be oppressive forces within the present economic order. Joseph's vision is of this kind; basically, it envisages a *pre-capitalist* economic order. In such a society, there would be inequality, but people of higher and lower station would be bound together by mutual obligations. These obligations go against single-mindedly pursuing one's self-interest.

There are points of connection between this perspective and David Jenkins's, but other points where they disagree. One principal difference is that for Joseph, these obligations are not discovered by each individual separately, examining his or her conscience, but publicly defined by laws and institutions. Furthermore, they are to be enforced by whatever degree of coercion is necessary to make people adhere to them. In other words, Joseph, unlike David, does not think voluntaristically; he has a substantive and collective vision of a just society. This vision is not nearly as liberal as Catherine Kennedy's, in that he does not favor as expansive a welfare state, is more interested in self-reliance, and objects to social conflict and claims of "rights" that she endorses. But his vision and Catherine's are equally Catholic, and his is actually less individualistic. He is somewhat conservative, but in a different way and for different reasons than David: David is conservative for the sake of the individual, Joseph for the sake of the community.

Even if the church did not espouse these perspectives, Joseph might well reach them on his own. His starting premise is anti-materialistic (and similar to one of David's): comfort is fine but "accumulation" is not important; one's main goal should be to save one's soul, which for him primarily means to act ethically. His ethical view is basically that one should be upright and honest, work hard, and "spend your whole life trying to help your neighbor as much as possible when misfortune or sickness befalls him." This last view expresses the ethic of love, and it has the same kind of implications that we saw with Catherine.

Furthermore, he is not much interested in issues of freedom of action.

For instance, he is very upset that the Catholic high school his son attended taught that it is not a mortal sin to miss mass. He would like abortion to be made illegal, and favors restraints on pornography. People are weak, but not basically bad, and need help and constraints in order to fulfill their potential and contribute to the community. This came out, in a personal context, with regard to the ancient Catholic rule against eating meat on Fridays. He describes a sense of loss when the rule was lifted. He felt that the rule set Catholics apart from others in a good way; on Friday nights at restaurants, when friends ordered steak and he ordered fish, he might be kidded a little but he felt respect behind it. When he expressed these feelings to a cousin who was a bishop, his cousin suggested that he could benefit from continuing Friday abstinence as a personal discipline. Joseph reports, however, that "the spirit was willing but the flesh was weak," and soon he was eating meat on Fridays. Thus rules, for Joseph, are not chafing constraints but supports for what is best within each of us.

The combination of Joseph's allegiance to the ethic of love with his lack of any strong concern for individual choice constitutes a personal perspective highly compatible with the social perspective he articulates. Individual responsibility is socially useful, he thinks, and this requires a degree of economic liberty, but unlike David he does not give liberty enormous value for its own sake. Thus, his non-voluntaristic perspective gives support for both liberal and conservative economic views. (In the non-economic realm, it has more clearly conservative implications.)

How does Joseph think about the responsibility of the individual and of the church, the means to be used to achieve social change, and the relationship between faith and social issues? He is quite active in community affairs and to some extent in politics, out of a sense of duty to the community, and thinks everyone should be active. He provides a polling place in his house, has attended political meetings, writes letters, and is active in a homeowners' association and on the board of a community college.

Joseph wholeheartedly supports the church in its taking an active role in social and political issues, although he also supports separation of church and state. Showing his allegiance to the teaching function of the church, he says that it had a great impact when "Pope Leo came out with the encyclical about how the average working man should be entitled to a fair wage." This happened before Joseph was born, but he describes it as if it were a contemporary event. At a more practical and local level, he defended the priest of his parish when people got upset over his bringing in a speaker against a state ballot proposition that would have made fair housing laws unconstitutional. The opponents said, "That's politics," but in his view, "There's a case of social justice; I think it was warranted." He is proud that the church has been active with social welfare programs of its own "in a lot of areas, along with encouraging social justice in programs of the government."

There is one way in which Joseph is not so favorable to means by which many seek to make social change: he dislikes "demands" by groups who feel they are not being treated fairly. His vision is of social harmony and of love put into action by institutions, not of justice achieved through struggle; he desires to dampen conflict. Also, he thinks in terms of hierarchy, and so he looks mainly to the authorities—not to individuals asserting their "rights"—as the way to achieve social justice. He thinks workers are "entitled" to decent wages, and probably to the protection of unions, but overall he uses the language of rights quite sparingly. In short, his views partake deeply of the corporatism and paternalism of some Catholic social philosophy.

By paternalism, I mean a perspective in which the interests of those lower in a hierarchy are expected to be taken care of by the benevolence of their superiors rather than through their own empowerment, rights, or struggles. Corporatism, to be discussed more thoroughly later, means a conception of society as similar to a body, with each part having a special function and making a distinctive contribution to the whole; in such a vision, we are all interdependent, and the interests of the whole are far more important than the interests of any part. By contrast, the language of rights often asserts what are taken to be the legitimate interests of individuals against those of the community or its leaders; as we will see, this language can have both liberal and conservative implications.

Joseph brings faith and political views together more fully than do the vast majority of Americans. Unlike many of the respondents, he sees no reason to be cautious in drawing conclusions about any social or political issue on the basis of ethical principles derived from faith, or in basing public policy on such principles. He is not talking about a theocracy, religious intolerance, or making this a "Christian" country in the sense favored by some in the Christian Right; it is not religious faith and practice that he wants embodied in politics but a set of ethical principles. He derives these principles from faith, but the tradition of Catholic natural-law thought regards these principles as accessible through reason and conscience to non-Catholics and even non-Christians, and every indication is that Joseph agrees. Nonetheless, he is very different from David Jenkins and many other respondents in seeing his faith and ethical perspective as equally applicable to material and spiritual issues, to concerns public as much as private, collective as much as individual.

Susan Wainwright: A Presbyterian in Conflict

David Jenkins, Catherine Kennedy, and Joseph Krieger have different points of view, but each of their perspectives is very coherent—even though they are all rank-and-file church members and only Catherine has had much formal education. Susan Wainwright, on the contrary, seems pulled in several different directions, although she is well educated and holds the responsible position of clerk of session in the Presbyterian congregation to which she belongs.

On one side, she understands and basically accepts an activist and economically liberal way of interpreting Christian faith. She has just been reading the gospel according to Luke—a text with fairly explicit social content—in a Bible study group, and it is apparent to her that "to loosen the shackles and free the oppressed are things that we should be doing." In her words: "Faith can't be separate from our lives. The inner life is important, too, but in terms of making our lives count for something it has to be in relationship to our fellow human beings, working for justice, freedom or equality, and all these things. It seems to me that if you read the gospels it's pretty obvious that a lot of these things need to be done."

In other words, the message of liberation in Scripture is not just *spiritual* liberation: liberation from sin, from being separated from God, or even from the psychological categories that have partly taken the place of these older terms in some contemporary churches: freedom from guilt, anxiety, lack of a sense of one's worth, or lack of meaning in one's life. Nor is it just talking about liberty of conscience, or even the kind of liberty of choice David Jenkins focuses on. Rather, the Bible is also talking about practical—and in certain ways "material" or political—liberation from oppression, hunger, want, powerlessness, and so forth. In this perspective, Christians are supposed to take an active part in struggling for social justice. (This view is expressed most radically in liberation theology, and Susan seems to be influenced by some ideas that can be found in this theological current, but she never refers to it or expresses ideas unique to it.) Susan also thinks the church as an organization should be active, and mostly approves of national Presbyterian social action programs. She especially wants her local congregation—a downtown church with a relatively elderly membership—to minister more actively to the needs of members and others who live nearby.

Of course, the views just described are compatible with quite varied opinions about economic issues. Some of Susan's views are liberal, and others conservative. On the liberal side, she is convinced that many African-Americans and poor people do not have equal opportunity, she would like to restrict inheritance of wealth, and even favors a guaranteed annual income. When she explains this view, she talks in ways that show the influence of her social interpretation of Christian faith: "No one should starve, no one should go hungry, nobody should be deprived of the right to be healthy; extreme poverty is unjust."

But Susan has another way of thinking that operates simultaneously. A lifelong Republican, she thinks taxes are too high and is concerned about keeping government spending in check. She thinks "a person has a right to earn as much money as he can, if he does it legally, so that initiative, ambition and creativity can pay off." None of these positions resonates much with how she describes her faith, nor does she connect any of her conservative positions to faith, in the way she does her liberal ones. But they do seem congruent with her background and situation in life. She is the child of a lawyer and grandchild of a state supreme court judge, from midwestern WASP stock, with a family history of consistent Republicanism. After college, she worked for a few years, got a teaching credential, and taught high school for two years before getting married. Her husband is a successful, self-employed professional who works out of their home, and at thirty-eight years old (at the time of the interview) she lives in a stylish and expensive house that she and her husband have spent the past three years improving and remodeling. Her two children, her husband, and volunteer activities (at church, in local politics, and at her children's private school) occupy her time rather fully. Our interview was carried on amid continual interruptions from phone calls and her family.

The nature of her faith perspective, and its role in her life, did not emerge very clearly in the interview. She is well educated and interested in religious issues intellectually, and has had some college courses on religion, although she has not been able to carry this interest forward much. When she was nineteen years old, she spent a year in Scotland and encountered a number of people who connected faith to life in a way that moved her. She has been immersed in the milieu of the church ever since, and yet her statements about her religious and ethical beliefs are somewhat vague and disconnected from her feelings, experiences, and activities. She herself seems to feel that her spiritual life is arid and that the church is not feeding her in the ways she currently needs. She describes herself as at once hungering for change— she would like a more active spiritual life, perhaps even an exploration of the power of the Holy Spirit—and frightened of it, worrying that it will not be intellectually respectable and (perhaps) that it will engage uncomfortably powerful emotions. The core of her religious life, for now, appears to lie primarily in the work she does to sustain her congregation, and the relationships with other members (many of whom she sees more than just on Sundays) she has built up over the years. Most of her friends, in fact, seem to be members of her congregation.

She has also been quite active politically, working as a volunteer in a recent municipal campaign. But her activism does not seem much connected to her faith—even though she speaks of how faith should be a source of activity in the world. Rather, as she describes it, it comes out of family tradition, out of enjoying political work, and out of a kind of feminist concern—the candidate she worked for was a woman, and this interested her in the campaign.

Furthermore, in some ways she wants to separate faith from life. This comes out in her views about the social role of the church; on many issues she prefers that the church not take a position. With regard to busing schoolchildren for integration, for instance, she says, "I don't see that as a religious issue; I think the government can handle that without the church. I think people have a right to equal opportunity and equal education, but I think it's more of a civic issue than a church issue."

Separation between faith and life comes out even more strongly, however, when she describes the conflicts between various themes in her thinking—conflicts of which she is well aware, and that seem to cause her considerable pain. Over and over again, she says that faith shows her a direction she does not want to take. This is true in her personal religious life, as we saw a moment ago. Most of her statements about conflicting ideas, however, have to do with balancing the claims of a call to social concern—which she definitely feels—against what fits conveniently into her life. When I asked her what current issues had a strong moral element, she said one was farm-worker unionization, but "I just put that out of my mind when it crosses my path because somehow it seems pretty far removed from me. I just can't figure that all out; that's head in sand, I know." After saying that poverty largely results from a mixture of lack of equal opportunity, poor education, and poor upbringing, she adds—apparently speaking only half her heart—"I fail to feel responsible for every person who doesn't have what I have." When asked about the relationship between her faith and her social and political values, she said, "I see a conflict there, between wanting the best for humanity, for all the children of God, and wanting nice things, liking luxury. Knowing there are so many poor in the world, I feel guilty about that, I've read about it, and once in a while I worry about it extra hard, then I sort of put it out of my mind." After saying that faith involves working for justice, she went on to say, "But I'm not always interested in doing that." Thus, she is aware of the contradictory pulls in her life. In her thinking, in sum, Christian faith has basically liberal economic implications—for much the same reasons as in Catherine Kennedy's thinking—but they have little chance to blossom.[4]

Linda Watson: A Populist Evangelical

Linda Watson feels God's presence in her life in an immediate and intense way. As a young child, all on her own, she joined a Salvation Army church and prayed every week that her parents (who were unchurched) would join. When they did, "that was truly a big reward for me because God had really heard my prayers." At seven years old, she dedicated herself to God; she rededicated herself twenty years later, at a Billy Graham crusade. At Christmastime, as a child, she would collect money, ringing a bell in time-honored Salvation Army fashion. She would feel God's presence in the ring resonating through her whole body, and bring in more money than anyone else. Although there have been some periods when she attended church irregularly, she has never lost this sense of God's closeness.

When interviewed, she was thirty-seven years old and had gone through many problems in her life: marriage to an alcoholic, separation and divorce, a child with emotional difficulties, and now staying afloat on a combination of wages from a poorly paying (even though full-time) job as a school aide, unemployment benefits during vacation periods, and Aid for Families with Dependent Children (AFDC, or "welfare") payments. Through all of this, she feels, God made sure that too many problems never occurred at once. "The Lord just knew that I couldn't have dealt with it at that time, so he didn't do that to me." (Notice the directness and intimacy of this language. Few mainline Protestants would talk in this way. This is one of the characteristic differences in the languages of these two religious camps.) At one point during her marriage she had to struggle with "feeling not worthy of having God's love," but has never doubted that she would be saved. She goes to church—nowadays at a Missionary Alliance church—but churches seem hardly more essential for her than for David Jenkins. When she needs guidance, she gets it from prayer or the Bible—means of direct, personal communication with God—rather than from the church. Her faith, then, is largely based on direct experience of God's presence in her life. It also involves a clearly articulated ethical perspective, one that she directly relates to economic issues.

Politically, Linda is at least as far left as Catherine Kennedy. She does not think people have equal opportunity to get ahead and says, "There needs to be a closer gap between rich and poor." She wants more jobs to be created, proposing a four-day work week as one way of getting there. She thinks our society should provide for everyone's basic needs, and is "thankful" to be receiving unemployment insurance. She has no problem with restricting businesses, and no great attachment to private enterprise. A registered Democrat, she regularly votes for liberal candidates. Her perspective might be called populist, in that she's on the side of "Joe Blow" or the "underdog"; she doesn't like politicians who seem to care mostly about the rich and powerful, or businesses that make money at the expense of people who are weak.

These views make sense in terms of where Linda is in our class system, but they are also deeply grounded in her view of the kind of ethics and society Christian faith should imply. In describing her ethical perspective, she says, "I'm not trying to say I'm trying to be Christ-like, because we never can. But we can do the things that he would want us to do: to be loving and giving, and considerate of other people." This is a standard formulation of the ethic of love: that we should love one another as Christ loved us. For Linda, this ethic has clear social implications. When we started discussing economic issues—a few days after the session in which we had discussed matters of faith and ethics—she immediately said, "Everybody is struggling to get ahead. In the process, they've lost this thing of brotherly love. What we're about as far as I'm concerned, what Christ was put on this earth to teach us, is brotherly love." Competition, then, goes contrary to Christian ethics. To be a Christian, one should "be giving, giving of yourself." Therefore she is concerned with "whether we are a caring type nation—that's a part of my philosophy and my faith, being a caring type person."

All these statements reflect the value of love. Linda (like Catherine) also uses the universalistic elements of Christian tradition. "Everyone," she says, "regardless of physical or mental capabilities, is still human" and therefore has a right to certain things—which for Linda include the kinds of things provided by a welfare state.

These links are quite explicit. In addition, there is a kind of resonance between her populist sentiments and her religious belief that "the meek shall inherit the earth." She thinks of herself as a somewhat weak person, not very able to be economically independent, and she knows that this makes her an "outcast" in our society's terms. And yet, these characteristics seem linked, as she talks about herself, to what she values in herself: being a generous and giving person. Thus, she is weak, but the kind of person who might inherit the Kingdom; she does not greatly value a society like ours, which mostly rewards those who assert themselves aggressively. In this way of thinking, she draws on ancient religious traditions: the rejection and reversal of the world's standards of value classically expressed in the Sermon on the Mount (Luke 6:20–49 or Matthew 5:3–7:27) or the *Magnificat* (Luke 1:46–55).

As a person of traditionalist religious beliefs, she is not nearly as relativistic as most Americans. She makes value judgments about our society, and finds it wanting. The fact that she draws fairly specific ethical principles from faith is a resource for liberal-to-radical economic views. Another such resource is that although she is religiously voluntaristic, favoring freedom of religious choice, she is not highly voluntaristic in her view of society (although she is pro-choice about abortion as a legal issue). Since she shares a lot religiously with David Jenkins, this indicates that his thoroughgoing voluntarism is not the only possible interpretation of an evangelical faith or of a religious perspective that values individual conscience. She does not conceive of a good society just in terms of how people relate on a one-to-one basis but also in terms of how our institutions work. David may feel just as strongly that it is important for us to take care of one another, but in Linda's way of thinking this value has quite different implications. For Linda, further-more, Christian ethical standards imply that we have a duty to be "concerned for our fellow man," and therefore "to be involved" with public issues. She feels overwhelmed by what it takes to keep her head above water, and feels that she is not doing much, but actually she has been more politically active than average, attending a rally for a municipal candidate, participating in a protest demonstration, and talking about current issues with co-workers at her school.

Linda shows how love and universalism can ground liberal politics in a theologically traditionalist Protestant. Basically, these core values are the same for Christians of different kinds, and have the same ethical implications. Her way of linking faith to politics, for instance, is quite similar to Catherine's, despite major differences in religious background and belief. Whether a person is theologically traditionalist or modernist, Protestant or Catholic, in short, matters much less than how much emphasis a person gives the values of love and universalism, and how—if at all—they are applied to issues beyond those each of us faces as an individual.

Richard Schenk: A Methodist Individualist

"The less government, the better, in economics." This is Richard Schenk's guiding principle when he talks about any economic issue. "Government involvement should be kept at a minimum," he thinks, partly because it is wasteful, diverting "money into non-productive work," but mostly because it infringes on our freedom. He sees socialism as "government involvement in personal affairs," implying that economic decisions are "personal" or private matters. He is concerned that "dependence tends to weaken initiative if not destroy it," and favors "self-reliance." He firmly believes that self-reliance will work: "a person can still get ahead pretty well." As one might expect, he is a Republican.

Richard's experiences are consistent with these views. After growing up in Montana in a blue-collar family, he went to college on a scholarship, acquired an M.A. degree, and now, at fifty-five years old, teaches social studies in a suburban high school. It is a story of upward mobility, and must have demanded great self-discipline and self-reliance. Richard works hard, and seems to feel that he does a good job, but he does not get great satisfaction out of his work; he finds that he can't have the same effect on his students he was able to have ten years earlier. He was married for twenty-two years, but was divorced five years before the interview, and regards himself as having made "a *lot* of mistakes" in his family life; he takes full responsibility for its not having turned out very well. Some of his fondest memories, on the other hand, are of his involvement as a teenager in the rituals of the Order of DeMolay (a youth branch of the Masons).

Richard's views on economic questions are part of his systematic and consistent concern to limit government control—and all other forms of imposed authority—and strengthen individual autonomy. "We're overburdened with laws," he says, and he constantly uses the term *control* to refer to what he most disagrees with. In his view, the "fundamental freedom" that he has as an American is the "right to do" anything that doesn't "infringe on others' rights."

Along with freedom, Richard says, comes "responsibility." He repeatedly speaks of the importance of self-discipline and self-reliance. Speaking of his teaching, he says, "I like a situation where I can leave a class, and then come back in and find that if anything they're better when I'm gone than when I'm there—not out of subservience or fear, but because that's the way they operate. Then the heavy hand of control isn't there, and the best situation is the one that has the least control. That government is best which governs least." Elsewhere, he speaks of how people ought to obey traffic laws for their own sake, rather than because they're afraid of being caught, and do "a good job, not because you get overtime or someone forces you or because society says it is the thing to do, but just because that's the thing to do." He wants to be self-reliant psychologically, too. At one point, he says, he discussed some personal problems he was having with the minister of his church, but he emphasizes that he went only to get "insight that might lead a person to help himself; I don't expect any help."

Richard's religious perspective is cut from the same mold. He is a Methodist, and likes the latitude there is for local churches in his denomination to vary widely. His religious beliefs are vague and his spiritual life seems almost nonexistent—like Susan Wainwright, but to an even greater degree. The difference is that he does not feel any of this as a lack. He has never had a conversion experience, does not believe in trying to convert people, and dislikes emotional forms of religion—apparently because he thinks of freedom as making rational, unconstrained choices. Religion is a realm of private freedom, a place to do as you wish, just like private property.

God, for Richard, is far away, and has little to do with our lives: "I don't see any divine hand watching over me." Clearly God, too, values self-reliance. He criticizes himself because his interest in religion, through most of his life, has been too "external." Think of the comparisons with David Jenkins. Richard is a theological modernist (for instance, he does not read the Bible literally), while David is a traditionalist. Richard does not experience God or the supernatural as an important part of ordinary life, and talks in Christian terms much less frequently and fluently than David. Yet his use of the term *external* carries the same basic religious message: the priority of internal intention over external behavior, and of what are considered spiritual motivations (felt to be internal) over material ones (felt to be external). Furthermore, Richard and David are quite similar in how they use voluntaristic ways of thinking to ground a conservative view of economic life.

This grounding is explicit for Richard, just as for David. Richard sees "a fairly close relationship" between his religious convictions and his social and political values: "My political attitude—less control and so on, where possible—goes along with those religious beliefs." To him, the Golden Rule implies that "people have to appreciate the fact that the responsibility is theirs to do something if they see something wrong," and if people realize this, there can be relatively little law enforcement. An ideal society in Christian terms "would be much more voluntary than it is today." As he listens (in church) to the story of Jesus' life, the main impression he gets is that

Jesus went through a lot of suffering in the course of "the work that he did. I'm impressed by that; it makes you think, okay, buster, other people haven't had it easy, so don't expect a soft road." Thus Jesus is a model of self-reliance.

Richard thinks we need to do better at cooperating with and helping each other. But he hopes this can come about through voluntary means, and so these aspirations end up supporting conservative rather than liberal proposals. Consumers, he says, can force a company to be more responsive to human needs by becoming more educated and refusing, as individuals, to buy substandard products. (However, he is against boycotts.) Employers, similarly, realize more than in the past that treating employees decently "will affect production favorably." In other words, the best way to bring about social change is by appeals to rational self-interest or pressure brought by individuals acting separately. When he talks about social welfare programs, he says that what really appeals to him is what he understands to be the Mormon system: that everyone's basic needs are taken care of, primarily by providing jobs, but in any case "voluntarily," within the Mormon community.

In short, he, like David, hopes for a community in which people voluntarily take one another's needs into account better than they do now. Unlike David, but like many secular advocates of the free market, he relies primarily on rational self-interest and contractual relationships—between producers and consumers, employers and workers—to bring this about. In a sense, Richard is more worldly than David: more interested in economic theories, more concerned with what will make our economy more productive, more willing to use coercive means when voluntary ones break down, and more interested in current political issues. Much more than David, or indeed than many academic or journalistic free-market theorists, he emphasizes self-discipline and internalized restraints, not only as key prerequisites for the voluntary society he hopes for but also as important ends in themselves.

Victor Santiago: A Liberal but Separatist Jehovah's Witness

"I am no part of this world," says Victor Santiago, and he means it. Everything about his faith, life, and view of the social world is geared toward keeping him apart from the diabolical forces found in human life as we know it now, and toward preparing himself for the better Kingdom that is soon to come. In rejecting the world rather totally, Victor draws on classical Christian themes, and his perspective, while somewhat unusual among Christians in the United States today—even among religious traditionalists—is in many ways quite orthodox historically.

Victor is a Jehovah's Witness, and spends several nights a week at meetings in addition to daily door-to-door work and personal study. Perhaps because of this strong involvement, he has extremely consistent and systematic views, even though he was only twenty-one years old when interviewed, and has not had much formal education. More than any of the previous six people (including Joseph Krieger, who most resembles him in this regard) he articulates an organizational as well as an individual perspective. That perspective is complex and worthy of study in its own right; for the purposes of understanding Victor's social analysis, the central ideas are a strongly apocalyptic view, in which the end of the present world is expected to be soon and dramatic; a strong sense of the depravity of life as we know it, with special emphasis on warfare, racism, moral decay, and poverty; and a highly disciplined way of life for adherents, including ethical standards, a high level of organizational involvement, and incessant evangelistic work.

Victor was born in the United States, as was his father (who is also a Witness), and has little connection to relatives in Mexico; his environment, then, is American. His father is a forklift operator, and he is a construction worker. This station in life seems entirely satisfactory to him. Over and over Victor emphasizes the importance of rejecting worldly standards of value, and he seems quite accurate in saying that he is "not a materialistic pursuer." He hopes to learn more about his trade but has no interest in becoming a contractor himself; he thinks "there will always be room for Indians and for workers; there are too many chiefs and not enough Indians in the world today." He describes this value as "humility," and quotes Scripture— "Whoever exalts himself will be humbled; whoever humbles himself will be exalted"—when he talks about it. Many intelligent and well-educated people, he says, "are so intelligent they don't even understand the basic things of life." Here again, he contrasts different standards of value: on the scale that really matters, people are often in the reverse position from the one they occupy on the scales used in the world, such as wealth, education, and power. These themes are reminiscent of the ones Linda Watson used as part of a populist perspective, and they ground similar political views in his thinking.

To be separate from the world also means avoiding idolatry; that is, not worshipping anything that is not God. He feels that Catholics especially violate this commandment, and also draws more political conclusions: that a Christian should not pledge allegiance to the United States or its flag, or fight in any human wars. Christians should not even set up leaders, or give too much respect to any human, and for that reason the Witnesses have no paid clergy.

In some ways, Victor is like most evangelical or theologically conservative Protestants, but in other ways not. Although he never uses the phrase, he is "twice-born"; when he was growing up, he says, "my heart was into this world," but gradually he came "into the truth" and decided to be baptized. He accepts Jesus as his savior, believes that supernatural forces (especially the devil) invade the world regularly, and feels that God is close to him and watches over him but he has never had—and does not value—an "emotional" experience; he thinks of his conversion as a kind of learning experience.

His perspective is in some ways voluntaristic, but never relativistic. It is important that each person make his or her own voluntary decision about what to believe and how to live. Only God passes judgment—Victor would refuse to serve on a jury—but that doesn't mean there is much doubt about what God wants of us and what judgments God will make. "I don't like to put down other people's religion, but the way I feel, facts are facts. Either the Bible says one thing, or it doesn't." In making decisions about how to live, "you're going to have to decide for yourself what's right and wrong for you, and he's going to have to decide whether you're serving him rightly or wrongly." (Another, older, Jehovah's Witness shows the tension this can produce; he was desperately afraid that his children might make the wrong choice and be damned, yet he felt that he could not interfere, that they had to make their choice on their own, in their own time.)

When Victor starts discussing economic questions, he has the same clear sense of right and wrong, and the conclusions he reaches are similar to those of the liberal wing of the Democratic party. Universalistic love is the basic value, just as for Catherine Kennedy. He speaks strongly against discrimination (he has experienced some, as a Chicano) and is proud of the racial and ethnic diversity found among the Witnesses: "We're all different types and nationalities and love each other just the same." He condemns competition in every context: sports, getting ahead economically, and the arms and space races between the United States and the Soviet Union. We need to help each other more, and reduce inequality: "God didn't [intend] man to allow some to starve and some to be rich."

When more specific issues come up, Victor's views are equally liberal. He is in favor of continuing or expanding every social welfare program we discussed; helping people in need by such programs is "a God-given responsibility." He would like to see money now being spent on the arms race used to meet human needs, and wants our country to send food or money to wherever there is hunger—even to the Soviet Union. In other words, even though Victor tries to be separate from the world and is hostile to government whenever it tries to get respect that is due only to God, he has no problems about using government programs as a way to carry out Christian ethical principles. In this way, he is very different from David Jenkins.

But when we come to issues about public participation and making social change, Victor's faith has more conservative implications. To reject the world and try to avoid idolatry can have radical implications. It can give people courage to risk suffering as they struggle for social justice. It can be a reason to be suspicious of established authority, and help a Christian conclude that only a reconstruction of our society from the roots up will do. (The word *radical* comes from the Latin *radix,* meaning root.) It can protect one against the relativism of the marketplace, or lead people to resist the military draft. Some of these possibilities can be seen in Victor's thinking, but the main implication he draws from rejecting the world is quite different: that he ought not to be involved in trying to change the world.

This does not mean that religion and other parts of life are separated: "My faith is a way of life; everything is influenced by it." Or, to put the paradox bluntly: "My faith governs my life, including my political opinions and everything," but "I try to keep politics out of my life completely."

This paradox is possible because Victor has a very specific view of what God wants him to do with his life. After expressing views on a variety of political issues (for instance, public social welfare programs and laws against discrimination—both of which he favors), he goes on: "But I will not take action. That is not for me to do. My government is in Jesus Christ; he is the king of my government. I only exist here in the world to preach God's word, to try to gain understanding and everlasting life, and to save people from the world's distress that's going to come down pretty soon." This limited view also comes out in discussing laws. "We comply with man's laws until they conflict with God's." This conflict occurs when one is asked to serve in the armed forces, but not, it appears, when laws promote or sustain social injustice. Unlike David, Victor isn't against laws, but he won't do anything to make them better. Even when they are against God's laws, he will disobey them but not work to change them.

All of these views are strongly influenced by Victor's firm conviction that as humans we are incapable of making any significant improvement in our social order, and that God will soon bring our sad story to an end. "Man looks to me like he's going to destroy himself pretty soon. He's had almost six thousand years where he said, 'I can rule myself,' and he hasn't shown anything. That's why I don't vote: I don't see man solving the problems of the world." There is hope, but not within human history or by human effort: "We believe that soon, as it says in Daniel, it'll be a new kingdom, a new government, that will rule, but not here on earth." The implications he draws are the opposite of Jerry Falwell's; Falwell uses apocalyptic imagery in support of the arms race, while Victor uses similar imagery as part of a perspective deeply opposed to the arms race. Nonetheless, the left-of-center views he holds are largely made politically irrelevant by his view of history. He draws conclusions from his faith in much the same way as Linda Watson, but like David—although in a different way, and for different reasons—he eschews public involvement.

The seven people whose thinking has just been described are in one sense not typical: they are among the most articulate of the people I interviewed; and (except for Susan Wainwright) they express their views more consistently and systematically than most, applying a single set of premises to a wide variety of subjects.

But the themes they express are not idiosyncratic; there is a little of each of them in most Christians, and—due to the enormous influence Christianity has had on American secular culture—in other Americans as well. These seven people were chosen because they express more clearly than others recurring themes found over and over among all the forty-seven respondents for the study. These themes include a voluntaristic perspective on faith, ethics, and politics; the ethical ideal of Christian love; the principle of universalism; ideas of a "moral economy"; corporatistic images of society; the idea that faith should guide every aspect of life; religious (and other) reasons for separating faith from politics; the idea of a reversal of values; religious bases for valuing self-reliance; and rejection of the world. All these themes will be treated in depth in subsequent chapters.

Some of the religious differences among these seven people are also worthy of attention. In some cases, what is striking is that these differences are *not* linked to political differences. Take, for instance, some pairs of people who are very dissimilar religiously. Despite their religious differences, David Jenkins and Richard Schenk are very alike, not just in their political outlook but in how they ground it in faith. Similarly, Catherine Kennedy, Susan Wainwright, and Linda Watson (for some purposes we might include Victor Santiago, as well) are very different religiously, but ground political opinions in faith in similar ways (although Susan does not make as many connections and holds conservative economic views grounded in non-Christian frameworks, and Victor's connections are never acted upon). Clearly, how "traditional" a Christian is theologically is not the key issue for understanding that person's politics.

On the other hand, there are other religious differences that clearly *are* politically significant. Joseph Krieger's Catholic traditionalism is connected with his lack of relativism—which in turn helps ground the liberal aspects of his economic views—but also with his dislike of conflict and self-assertion. The two Catholics have less voluntaristic views of economic life than the five Protestants. The two respondents who most radically reject the world— Victor Santiago and David Jenkins—are the least interested in structural change. The ones who most emphasize the values of love and universalism— Catherine Kennedy and Linda Watson—are the most "leftist" politically. Such religious and political similarities and differences provide clues we will follow up in the coming chapters.

Faith Perspectives

2

Building Blocks
in Christian Faith

When I looked at how the people I interviewed related faith to economic
issues, I found that five basic tendencies within Christianity—which I will
call voluntarism, universalism, love, thisworldliness, and otherworldliness—
were used over and over again. These five tendencies could be termed
"building blocks," for Christians "assemble" them in varying combinations
when they "construct" their views on economic life. They are not mutually
contradictory; any serious Christian—Catholic, evangelical, or mainline
Protestant—has some commitment to all of them. The relative emphasis
and political interpretations of these themes, however, vary widely.

We have seen examples of each of these themes within the thinking of
one or more of the people introduced in the last chapter. Now we will look
at each one separately, as it is found in the thinking of all the respondents.
Of the five themes, voluntarism is the most complex, and so it will be taken
up first and treated at greatest length.

Voluntarism

Voluntarism is the strand within Christian tradition that focuses on the direct
relationship between God and each person as a centered, coherent, freely
acting individual. At root a theological perspective, it has many implications
for ethical views, political opinions, and ways of seeing the church.

Theologically, voluntarism emphasizes the basic Christian premise that
being right with God (or saved, or justified) is a problem that faces each
one of us individually. This problem confronts us particularly in the interior,
voluntary, seemingly private part of our life that is often felt to define our
individuality. Outward observances are not enough: to be right with God,
our intentions, our hearts, have to be in the right place. This emphasis on

the relationship of each individual to God has been central to Christianity from the very beginning, and increasingly dominant since the Reformation.

Voluntarism is especially powerful when combined with what is sometimes called "the Protestant principle"—although many Catholics accept it, too. This principle (derived primarily from the strand of otherworldliness within Christianity) says that we should place our allegiance only in God, avoiding the "idolatry" of treating the things of this world as if they were sacred. In other words, we should not make an ultimate commitment to things deserving only a provisional commitment. At the extreme (as in some of Paul Tillich's writings) this principle means that all laws, ideas, institutions, and writings—even the church, inherited creeds, and the Bible—are only more or less perfect witnesses to God, not sacred in themselves. If this is so, then we are very much alone in our relationship with God, since we cannot place complete trust in any source of guidance outside ourselves about how we should live or what we should believe. (Our own perceptions, of course, are also imperfect, but they are all we have.) Even views that do not go this far can be quite voluntaristic. For instance, those who take the Bible as the supreme authority generally believe that each person can understand it and use it as a personal tool for understanding reality and making decisions. Since in fact people come to varying conclusions about what the Bible is saying to us, focusing on the Bible gives the individual great authority.

David Jenkins and Richard Schenk, among the seven people whose views we examined in the last chapter, are the clearest examples of how voluntaristic views can permeate every aspect of a person's thinking. The similarities between this aspect of their thinking shows how little (for some purposes) the division between evangelical and "modernist" Protestants matters. In general, the evangelicals I interviewed tend to speak of individual conversion experiences and of having an intensely personal relationship with Jesus Christ; as one puts it, "Your faith is a very, very personal thing; that's probably the main part of it, your communication one-to-one with him." The mainline Protestants speak more of their autonomy in making decisions about what to believe, or about coming to a sense of personal ownership of their faith and ethical commitments. Paradigmatically, Phyllis MacIntyre, an engineer in her mid-twenties who is very active in her Presbyterian congregation, describes how around seventh grade "I started claiming my faith as my own." (As a woman in a highly male-dominated profession, she has claimed her occupational choice as her own, as well.) The Catholics, when they speak in voluntaristic terms, tend to focus on their independence of the church, how they can be right with God while not following church rules or accepting all church teachings. We have seen such ideas in Catherine Kennedy, but they can be found among much less educated and more culturally or economically conservative people as well. For instance, an elderly, theologically conservative Chicana says that she "used to believe everything, but when I grew up, I questioned; I didn't believe in confession anymore.

... I find myself talking to God in my mind, and I ask for his help," instead of asking the saints, as she used to do. To take another example, "Things are no longer black and white; you have to rely on your own conscience," says an economically conservative Catholic. But the fundamental premises and—as we will see later—the implications for social and political opinions do not seem significantly different in these three branches of Christianity. And almost all the people I interviewed speak in voluntaristic terms at least occasionally.

Ethical Implications

Ethical views are an important link between faith and politics. They relate faith to issues about how humans should act, and obviously this can have implications for our sense of our own responsibilities, and also for our views about how human life should be organized. In what sense, though, are ethical perspectives "religious"? When we look at the thinking of people with a systematic worldview—for instance, all the people considered in chapter 1 except Susan Wainwright—the connections between faith and ethics are crystal clear. Sometimes they are not so clear, however, especially because ethical perspectives originally based in Judaism and Christianity have become part of our common ethical culture, available to everyone. Ordinary observation, as well as more systematic studies such as *Habits of the Heart*,[1] indicate that the ethical perspectives that many respondents ground in voluntarism as a religious framework are very widely diffused in American culture.

The starting point for ethical voluntarism is a focus on intention and conscience. If we are to be coherent selves, our actions have to be determined by internal, personal motives, and we have to have a "conscience" capable of resisting the outside world when it conflicts with inner standards. Furthermore, only action done out of a desire to do what is right—not action done from fear of punishment, desire for social approval, or even fear of hell—pleases God. We all have to follow our individual conscience, our own best light on what is right; laws cannot be more than a general guide. (This does not necessarily mean that laws are useless or evil, but just that ethics and law are taken to be very different and separate from each other—a view also found in legal philosophy, within the perspective known as legal positivism.)

In other words, one important aspect of ethical voluntarism is a perspective on how one goes about making ethical decisions. Over and over, the people I interviewed emphasize the internal, subjective side of this process; only the least voluntaristic have much to say about the external, institutional or "objective" side. This emphasis takes various forms.

Perhaps the most traditional is the view that we have to follow God against the pressures and even laws of the world around us. Victor Santiago thinks in this way when he resists the draft (he is of draft age). Jennifer Habib, a late adolescent who belongs to the Assemblies of God, uses the same idea when she resists the sexual norms she sees among her peers and her boyfriend's advances, saying, "Look, you're number two," while "the Lord [is] number one." In these cases, people who are not at all relativistic nonetheless affirm the importance of individual conscience as something to set against the world and its standards. Each person has to follow conscience, in order to act in accordance with objectively true ethical standards that the world does not accept. In other words, it is because the world is sinful that one has to have a strong conscience and follow it; the goal of following conscience is to have a better chance of doing what is objectively right. This kind of voluntarism has no relativistic or subjectivistic implications, as we can see in Victor Santiago's statement (quoted in chapter 1) that each person has to decide what is right or wrong, but God will judge whether we decided correctly.

In other cases, the goal is not the same, and the focus on the role of conscience in the process of ethical decision making does not assert absolute standards or access to God as the legitimation for following internal rather than external standards. In David Jenkins's thinking, as for many other respondents, the fundamental reason for an emphasis on conscience is that this is the internal, voluntary factor in ethical decision making, and that only an internally directed, voluntary decision is of religious value.

For instance, we find an evangelical saying of a good friend's abortion, "It was something between her and her conscience and God." She does not necessarily approve of the decision itself, but she does approve of making the decision autonomously. Catholics and mainline Protestants talk in similar terms, as when a committed Catholic says that homosexuals must decide for themselves whether what they are doing is right or wrong, or in the statement quoted earlier on how things are no longer black and white. Several Catholics raised before the Second Vatican Council describe long and difficult processes by which they came to feel able to assert their own consciences against church teachings, for instance about birth control. Their assertion of voluntarism is hard-won, compared with the reflexive voluntarism of most Protestants.

Often respondents speak as if other people's values were their own business, as if it would be a kind of invasion of privacy to disagree with their ethical choices, pass judgment, or even call upon them to explain and defend their choices. Such assumptions are widespread in America; people who do insist on passing ethical judgments are often pejoratively termed "moralistic" or "self-righteous." Similar views are widespread among my church member respondents. As a Catholic respondent put it, speaking of abortion, "I think it's a matter of your own personal feelings." A young Catholic puts it more broadly: "I am in no position to either make judgments on people or to tell people how to run their lives." Respondent after respondent spoke of how it is good not to be "judgmental." William Westfield, a fifty-year-old Quaker—and hence heir to one of the most voluntaristic branches of Christianity—has been involved in a variety of social change movements: "I'm not inclined," he says, "to be judgmental about other people, but unlike a lot of other relativists I know, I think there is a real place for conscience and for trying to live by whatever light one is given."

Such views are not confined to liberals. George Hoffman—a very conservative, middle-aged accountant—says, "I've got to minimize to the extent possible that sense of self-righteousness which says, if I think it's right for me, then everybody ought to do it." Or as Susan Wainwright puts it, "I make an effort to try to be less judgmental—to live my life in accordance with my beliefs but not condemn other people because they don't do it the way I do." Even a middle-aged woman who belongs to the Evangelical Covenant Church and holds conservative views on both economic and non-economic issues takes a similar position; she thinks "a lot of things [smoking, drinking, and so on] are just dependent upon your relationship with the Lord. Some things along that line I definitely feel are wrong, but I cannot say they're wrong for other people."

Statements like the ones just quoted could be interpreted in several ways. The Quaker William Westfield seems to believe that all action based on the light of conscience is valid; this could be a relativistic position, or alternatively he may be assuming that each person's light is God-given or based on something ethically objective. Or consider an evangelical who told me, "I've gotten to the point where I feel what's right for me could be wrong for someone else, or what is wrong for me could be very right for another person." Is she saying that under the different circumstances of another person's life, the same ethical principles might lead to different conclusions, or that the principles themselves are relative? When people speak of how bad it is to be judgmental, they may be saying merely that full knowledge of the facts of another person's situation and of the considerations that person has in mind when making a choice—knowledge that is not normally available to others—is a prerequisite for making a responsible evaluation of that person's choices. Or they may be asserting that some traditional or proposed ethical rules in the simple forms in which they are often expressed ("homosexual activity is wrong"; "abortion is murder"; and the like) need to be applied in a way sensitive to variations in human characteristics, needs, and situations. Or they may be saying something stronger: that ethical decision making is inherently a purely internal or subjective process, with very little accountability to any community or possibility of meaningful discussion. At the extreme, they may be saying that all ethical decisions, rules, and even principles are valid only in relation to sets of values that persons or groups choose to fit their preferences and needs, and thus have no objective validity. Value judgments, in such a view, are merely "matters of opinion," as opposed to factual or scientific questions with regard to which one might reasonably aspire to find an objective or agreed-upon answer. Religious believers tend to hold that even though it is hard to know about God, or to reach agreement about what God wants or is like, there still *is* an objective divine reality whose existence does not depend on our say-so. At their strongest, the views about ethical reasoning the respondents ground in voluntarism tend toward the position that ethical judgments are not only hard to make and to agree on but also perhaps *do* depend on our say-so. This tendency could be called ethical relativism.[2]

Most likely, the implicit ethical theories of the respondents who make the kind of statements I have been quoting are ambiguous and variable: these Christians are capable of talking like relativists at one moment and asserting absolutes at another. What is clear is that they put great emphasis on the factors in ethical decision making that are highly specific to the actor and situation, and accessible only to the actor: particular feelings toward and relationships with others; personal needs, circumstances, and personality characteristics; intentions; a "relationship to the Lord"; or the promptings of conscience. The result is to promote tolerance but also to define things in such a way that dialogue about ethical judgments can take place only with difficulty. Furthermore, they put such stress on the obligation to follow one's conscience or personal feelings about what is right, as opposed to any other criteria for making good ethical decisions, that ethical decision making becomes in practice an essentially subjective process.

Such conclusions may have been no part of the intention of even the radical wing of the Reformation, but one can hear echoes of the speech of the radical reformers in the respondents' statements. In this country, the antinomian tradition and others that emphasize the subjective side of ethical decision making have exerted a strong influence. Originally, in the Reformation period, an antinomian was a person who believed that the Holy Spirit dwells within a justified person, who is therefore free from having to follow externally defined rules. Anne Hutchinson was considered an antinomian, as were the Quakers; Roger Williams held views that similarly undermined external authority. These people were exiled by the Puritans and "lost" their struggles, in one sense, and yet today probably more Americans are in sympathy with the ethical implications of their positions than with the ethical theory of the people who vanquished them at the time. An emphasis on the workings of the Holy Spirit is important religiously today in groups as diverse as pentecostal and holiness denominations (including the Nazarenes and Assemblies of God), charismatic movements within the Episcopal and Roman Catholic churches, and of course the Quakers. But the ethical influence of antinomianism and similar Christian perspectives is far more widespread than this specifically religious influence. Americans are relativistic and subjectivistic in their ethical thinking, not so much because of the often overrated influence of secular humanism, or even of more obviously self-centered and materialistic secular perspectives—"winning through intimidation" and the like—but because potentials for this kind of thinking are inherent in the core of Christian tradition, and were released by the Reformation. The Jehovah's Witnesses can maintain the tension between rejecting relativism and affirming freedom of conscience, but most Americans, in affirming the primacy of conscience, have also incorporated a significant degree of relativism and subjectivism in their ideas about ethical decision making.

Implications for Churches and Organizations

Voluntaristic views, when applied in a thoroughgoing way to churches, can easily lead to conclusions like the ones reached by David Jenkins: that "church affiliation is on the same level as an affiliation you might have with a fraternal organization like the Kiwanis Club," and is parallel to "being a Democrat or Republican." What this means is that the church, like other organizations, is seen entirely as a *means* to help people attain their individual ends. This does not necessarily imply that people's ends are materialistic or self-seeking; an organization may be a means to improve spiritual life or make the world a better place. Indeed, people may be very committed to their organizations. But it is the individual member who creates the ends, and the organization is valued only as long as it helps fulfill them. This "privatized" perspective on churches and organizations deeply affects all Protestant churches and seems to be beginning to affect the Roman Catholic Church as well. It has implications for religious life, and also for how people relate to political organizations and other institutions.[3] Radical organizations, in particular, suffer when members either make very weak commitments to them, or are ready to split the organization whenever any serious disagreement arises. Like relativistic ideas about ethics, this kind of privatism is not just or even mainly the result of the influence of secular forces on churches and other organizations. It is one logical outgrowth of the ways in which the Reformation changed the relationship between member and church, and of the voluntaristic tendency within Christianity.

Voluntarism and Modernity

Voluntaristic thinking appears modern and rational in spirit because it accords with the cultural preferences and practical demands of modern life, with democracy, and with the Enlightenment goal of setting us free to think independently of the constraints of tradition and authority. It is corrosive of traditional religious authority, institutions, and ethical standards. Yet voluntaristic ways of thinking first emerged not as the result of a secular critique of religious thinking but as an internal development within religious traditions. This development occurred and became culturally influential long before the Industrial Revolution, the Enlightenment, or democratic revolutions. Indeed, a whole tradition of historical research has argued that the voluntaristic strand of Christianity was a *precondition* for these other developments.[4] Whether or not one accepts this argument, the respondents show us how easily voluntaristic sentiments can mesh with a variety of religious sentiments and lifestyle choices, from traditionalist to modernist, and that even the most extreme forms of voluntaristic thinking can be linked to traditional strands within Christian tradition. They show us how strong a specifically Christian impetus toward voluntarism remains today, and how little voluntaristic thinking depends on a culturally modernist worldview.

We should note, too, that voluntarism, whether religiously based or not, depends on a quite problematic (which is not to say invalid) mental step that could easily be called a leap of faith. This is a belief that there is an internal essence of the individual that can be called "conscience," enabling us to make truly ethical decisions independent of the social environment, and endowing us with the capacity to construct a centered self that can be constant across the myriad social situations and structures (and their pressures) we experience in our lives.

Now we will take a briefer look at the other four building blocks.

Universalism

Universalism is a fundamental Christian principle, encapsulated in St. Paul's formula that "there is no longer Jew or Greek, there is no longer slave or free, there is no longer male or female; for all of you are one in Christ Jesus" (Galatians 3:28). The possibility of being a Christian, and of being saved, is universal, not limited by any line of human division—nationality, ethnicity, gender, kinship, or class position. We are all equally children of God, with the same religious potential, and God cares for each of us equally. Our religious loyalty to one another is based on a common relationship to God, and on common religious beliefs and commitments, not on kinship, ethnicity, or the like. In fact, as Jesus makes clear, religious loyalty can be opposed to other loyalties: "I have not come to bring peace, but a sword, . . . to set a man against his father, and a daughter against her mother. . . . Whoever loves father or mother more than me is not worthy of me" (Matthew 10:34–37).

This point of view is based on some of the same premises as voluntarism. What might be called "intermediary" structures—institutions and groups— are relatively unimportant compared with our direct relationship with God. In Christianity, as in Islam and Buddhism (and some versions of Judaism and Hinduism), we relate to the sacred realm as individuals, independent of our group memberships. Belonging to any particular ethnic group or social category (perhaps even any church) cannot put us right with God, for each of us has to make peace with God on our own, as an individual. But in universalistic thinking, as compared with voluntarism, the focus is more on the fact that every human being is a beloved child of God, with all the dignity due this status, and the idea that we owe one another a universal dignity and respect, based on our fundamental equality in the sight of God. (This should not be confused with the theological doctrine sometimes called "universalism": the idea that God intends to save every human being, contrary to the Calvinist idea that only a small group—God's elect—will be saved.)

We have already seen many expressions of universalism, as in Catherine Kennedy's view that all people are her "brothers," and Susan Wainwright's, Joseph Krieger's, and Linda Watson's statements that all of us are children of God and should be helped if need arises. Almost all the respondents, of every political stripe, enunciate this principle in one way or another. Philomena Jackson, an African-American evangelical in her fifties, states it in classical terms: "I know that with Jesus Christ we're just one, there's no Black, White, Caucasian or anything else. In front of the cross we're all equal, and I'm glad about that." In another respondent's words, we should show "love for other people whether we know them or not." The principle of universalism constantly challenges Christians with the example of the Good Samaritan: the member of a despised outgroup who took care of a person in need. (Jesus explicitly used the example of the Samaritan to help his followers understand universalistically who our "neighbor" is.) As we look at the principle of Christian love, we have to keep in mind that universalism defines the scope within which love is supposed to work.

Universalism has a modern and rational quality; it focuses on a spiritual and in that sense abstract and impersonal basis for loyalty, as opposed to the loyalties we have because we belong to a particular group, and there has been a historical tendency in Western society away from what are sometimes called "primordial" or "particularistic" ways of organizing social life. But we should also keep in mind that universalism asserts the importance of a characteristic we are born with—being a child of God—rather than one we achieve. Our value and dignity, in other words, is a little like that of a royal heir. In modern, democratic societies, we tend to think that we should not pay attention to the characteristics people are born with—gender, race, aristocratic or common family background—but only to their personal accomplishments. Universalism is a democratic principle, in that it gives the same status to everyone, but in relying on birth rather than achievement it is not fully "modern." Furthermore, universalism is based on a non-rational assertion that in some fundamental sense we are all equal, an assertion that flies in the face of the obvious ways in which we often appear to be far from equal.

This basic premise, like voluntarism, has close cousins in the world of secular thinking. The secular Jewish sociologist Emile Durkheim's vision of an individualism based on the sacredness of the human person is one example, and the idea of citizenship as a universal status carrying many rights and privileges is another. Karl Marx's vision of solidarity cutting across national lines, and eventually destroying lines of class division, also partakes of universalism (and of a secular equivalent to the value of Christian love).[5]

What are the implications of universalism? At a minimum, our equality before God means some kind of spiritual "equality of opportunity" in which we have equal chances of being saved or right with God. For many respondents, it also means valuing a church that treats different kinds of people alike, trying to bridge the gaps that divide humans. Victor Santiago, for instance, is proud of how well people of different races cooperate among the Witnesses. Ethically, most of the respondents feel that they should try to do the same personally; for instance, that they should not be racist. In this vein, Joseph Krieger talks about being non-discriminatory, and even pursuing a kind of affirmative action policy as an employer. As we will see in chapter 5, universalism can have varied implications when applied to economic policy issues.

Christian Love

The political scientist Michael Walzer argues that American ethical thinking is often stymied either by the "subjectivism" of regarding ethical questions as a purely private matter or by the "objectivism" of dealing with value-laden questions at a purely technical level—that is, in a way that pretends to be neutral about values. These two tendencies make it hard to discuss ethical questions. But he says that we also have capacities that work in the opposite direction. In his view, Americans do, in fact, regularly make ethical judgments and arguments, in ways that often remain unstated or even unconscious but are based on "older moralities, remarkably resistant to cultural or intellectual transformation."[6] Universalism and love are two such moralities, and of the two, it is love that retains the more "old-fashioned" character.

Love is the central principle of Christian ethics. We are to love one another as God loves us: blindly, unconditionally, selflessly, and passionately. We should treat people better than they deserve, dispense grace and mercy rather than strict justice, and return good for evil. This is not a rational form of love, compared even to sexual love or love for our children, let alone the love we have for a respectworthy and faithful friend. The paradigm for this kind of love is God's love for humanity, most obviously expressed in Jesus' willingness to give his life to save us. We are, or can be, reconciled with God, and we are called in turn to reconcile ourselves with one another. This love has a universal quality, not just because of the value of universalism but also because Christian love can only be what it is supposed to be if it is unconditional: it has to reach across boundaries of family, race, nation, and differences of education, interests, and income.

We have already seen several examples of this theme. David Jenkins uses it as he talks about caring on a one-to-one basis for others; Catherine Kennedy uses it to support social welfare programs and racial equality; Linda Watson draws much the same conclusions; Victor Santiago uses it to condemn both individual and national self-seeking; and Joseph Krieger explicitly grounds his comprehensive image of social justice in love of neighbor. Almost all the respondents, in fact, articulate the value of love. Religion, in a typical formulation from a respondent, gives "a man the goal of serving his fellow man." A good society in Christian terms, says another, is one "where people would have concern of the needs of others."

These statements are on the bland side, expressing as they do something non-controversial. There is, in fact, little variation in how people articulate the value of love. But there is a lot in how it is applied. In terms of the church, it often appears in a desire that the church be a place of genuine solidarity—better than the world around it—with little or no conflict. As an ethical principle, the value of love generally supports a concern for taking the needs of others as seriously as our own, something it is always hard for us to do. Therefore the value of love is often used with a somewhat critical tone, as a corrective to the self-seeking, uncaring, or exploitative behavior one sees around. Ideally, all of human life—including our society—would be governed by love. The respondents have strong disagreements about how far we are capable of achieving this, and what practical consequences flow from this mandate. Many confine their hopes for realizing any significant degree of love governance to private spheres such as home and church. Still, most of the respondents feel dissatisfied with the current ethical state of our country, as measured by this standard, and many hope for improvement.

Thisworldliness

Ethical issues—about an enormous range of activities, from business to sex—have always been central to Christianity. Prayer and ritual, although important, are not the totality of a good relationship with God; tangible action is also part of it. As Jesus put it, "Not everyone who says to me, 'Lord, Lord' will enter the kingdom of heaven, but only the one who does the will of my Father in heaven" (Matthew 7:21). The respondents echo this view repeatedly. We have seen how David Jenkins talks about the importance of ministry in daily life, and that Joseph Krieger, Catherine Kennedy, and Linda Watson draw clear conclusions from their faith about how our society should be organized. David Jenkins is talking about person-to-person dealings, the others about broader spheres, but all are talking about applying faith to practical life outside church. Other respondents speak in much the same terms; as one put it, "Jesus talked about your life in relation to other people, that you helped him when you fed the hungry." Michael Butros, one of the Presbyterian respondents, is a good example of these and several other themes we will be concerned with. A public school administrator with left-liberal economic views, he has a strong sense of the importance of living out faith in everyday life. Asked about salvation (*not* ethics or putting faith into practice), he volunteered a model statement of thisworldliness: "Salvation will come about, but it's from the kinds of things that I will be doing every day, in business and whatever kinds of relationships I have in whatever I do with people." Michael's views are echoed by those of an African-American Presbyterian: "I'm not obsessed with the notion of going to heaven; I'm obsessed with the notion that we have to be of service during this life."

There are two key bases in Christian tradition for this point of view. The first is an appreciation of God's work. The world is God's creation, and therefore valuable. In the incarnation of God in Jesus Christ, similarly, "the Word became flesh and lived among us" (John 1:14); that is, God's will was given material form. Just as we are called to love one another as God loved us, so we are called to use our creative energies to produce things of practical value and help carry out God's will, as the Lord's Prayer has it, "on earth as in heaven." The idea of the Kingdom of God embodies a promise that this can and will eventually come about.

All these Christian themes support a view in which the world is regarded as very valuable, and in which loving and caring for creation and trying to mold the world into a shape more pleasing to God are taken to be important parts of the life of faith. Historically, however, many Christians have not emphasized these themes, placing a low value on worldly life, focusing on how much evil there is in the world, and anchoring their hope in life after death or after Christ's return to earth. To this extent, it is correct to say that Christianity was originally a "world-rejecting" religion. But a more positive view of worldly life was always there, too, and is now dominant among almost all kinds of Christians. Among the respondents, only the two Jehovah's Witnesses take a strongly negative view of worldly life. But even they are thisworldly; we have seen that Victor Santiago wants his faith to control every aspect of his life. Despite all the ways in which he is a separatist, he believes strongly in putting faith to work in daily life. How is this possible?

It is possible because there is a second basis for thisworldliness: that God has put us here and wishes us to be active in this world. The world is the *place* for religious activity, even if the world's well-being is not a religiously significant goal. We have to fashion a meaningful and religiously valid life in the midst of the moral complexities and difficulties of practical, daily life. One could say that this is a self-centered and otherworldly view, for it focuses on how we gain religiously by the right kind of practical activities much more than on how the world around us benefits from these activities. But it still calls us to make ordinary activities follow a religiously based ethical standard.

David Jenkins and Victor Santiago are good examples of this second basis for thisworldliness. (David also uses the first to some extent). Both have a strong sense of call and ministry, and of the importance of carrying out faith in their whole lives. But they are not greatly concerned with how this will affect the world, in David's case because he is so focused on intention, in Victor's because he expects the world as we know it to end soon, and has no hope for improvement in the meantime. Joseph Krieger and Catherine Kennedy, at the other end of the spectrum, are strongly concerned with practical outcomes and institutions: that the needy actually be taken care of, that our institutions practice social justice, and so forth. They value activity for "material" reasons, whereas David Jenkins and Victor Santiago value it for more "spiritual" reasons.

(These two bases for thisworldliness are parallel to two key Christian perspectives on work. Traditionally, many Christians emphasized the character of work as a spiritual discipline—even as a way to mortify the flesh—and saw its value mostly in terms of keeping us physically alive while we pursue spiritual well-being. The necessity for work manifested our fallen state, and work had a penitential quality. A more modern view is expressed in John Paul II's 1981 encyclical *Laborem Exercens* [On Human Work].[7] Here, the primary focus is on our partnership with God in creation and on the value of work as an act of love in the world, a contribution to the material well-being of other creatures of God. The modern view of work is connected to the first reason for thisworldliness just described; the traditional view to the second reason.)

Christians generally accept the premise of thisworldliness—usually on both bases described earlier, but at least on the second, more traditional one—but what it means in practice is not so clear. Some use it as a basis for wanting the church to be active in the world rather than just serving its members. Some see it as a reason that Christians should be concerned with the well-being of the whole society in which they live, and this can lead to political activism of either a conservative or a liberal stripe. But others apply their faith only to "religious" life (church, prayer, observances such as grace at table, and so on) and perhaps family life and relations with friends. In the middle, there are those who apply faith to daily life in a variety of contexts, but only to a limited range of issues. For instance, some people would recognize the issue of whether to report on a dishonest co-worker who is a friend as an ethical dilemma on which to bring to bear the resources of faith, but would not so recognize the issue of whether one should support unionization. At the least, however, when Christians think in thisworldly terms, they start thinking about faith in a more wholistic way, as a "Monday" just as much as "Sunday" enterprise.

Otherworldliness

"Otherworldliness" conjures up images of prophets, saints, ascetics, mystics, and monks: people who have rejected the ways of the world in a radical and obvious fashion. This kind of otherworldliness has always been rare and is probably becoming rarer. More subtle forms of otherworldliness, however, have always been fundamental to Christianity, and are still powerful forces. One might think that the only social implication of otherworldliness would be passivity. But this is not so; the historical record is full of ways in which otherworldliness has influenced the social values Christians held and even increased the chances of their taking action. To explore this paradoxical aspect of Christianity, we need to look at some of the traditions that have contributed to the development of the otherworldly strand of Christianity.[8]

Long before the emergence of Christianity, ancient Judaism was quite different from other religions of its period. Jews worshipped a single God who transcended everything on the earth. Yahweh could not be located in rivers, mountains, forests, or seas, and ruled all peoples, not just the Jews. All humans—including kings and priests—were simple mortals, with no sacred status. The First and Second Commandments codified this perspective: nothing and nobody but Yahweh was to be treated as divine. (This is the basis for what I described earlier as the "Protestant principle.") The upshot is that for Judaism the empirical world was much more "secular," and in a sense more separate from God, than it was for other ancient religions. In this limited sense, ancient Judaism was more otherworldly than its contemporaries.[9] In such a religious situation, religious and human loyalties could be at odds, with religious principles used to judge political leaders or customary social and economic practices. Prophets such as Micah and Isaiah show these potentials in action. The world is not rejected, but it *is* relativized—subordinated to God and transcendent values.

Early Christianity, like Buddhism and some versions of Islam and Hinduism, rejected the world more radically. Jesus and his closest followers gave up the amenities and supports of ordinary life: home, occupation, possessions, family, and even a change of clothes. The world and what St. Paul called "the flesh" were counterpoised to heaven and the spirit. As most early Christians saw it, a sphere of life outside ordinary, visible life was much more important and valuable. To attain the rewards of that sphere, one had to reject the rewards, temptations, and standards of earthly, material existence. Jesus advises us to store up treasure in heaven rather than on earth, and tells us that to save our lives we have to lose them (Luke 12:33–34; Mark 8:35). He repeatedly teaches that the values of this world are upside down, and will be reversed in the other world. Themes of reversal can be found in the Sermon on the Mount and the *Magnificat;* another obvious example is the story of Lazarus and the rich man, where the beggar Lazarus goes to heaven while the rich man suffers (Luke 16:19–31). In other words, we are to reject earthly standards of what is good and valuable: wealth, power, and status. The world we know is mostly ruled by evil and death; it is a place of suffering and testing, and will soon come to an end. This is the classical version of otherworldliness, and it is very uncompromising.

What are the implications of this kind of otherworldliness? Most obviously, it separates religious and "secular" values, organizations, and identities. Religious and secular values are so distinct and different that they are at odds with each other. A "church" emerges as an independent organization, and people are members of the church—and "saved" or "damned"— independent of whether they belong to any other collectivity. These separations could be described using the term *dualism*. There is a series of strict oppositions: this world and the other one; the flesh and the spirit; religious and secular values; the church and secular social involvements.

Another implication of world-rejection in this form is that it supports the individualism also inherent in universalism and voluntarism, since each person's religious identity and status is independent of what other groups that person belongs to. A third implication is that this kind of otherworldliness limits the impact of the value of thisworldliness. It makes little sense to work on long-term endeavors aimed at building a better material life for oneself, one's family, or community. One works to survive, and acts rightly because a loving God asks one to, but not to build a better world. Given such a view, thisworldliness is based only on a desire to please God, and is weaker than if creation itself is highly valued.

Few Christians today—even those who consider themselves the most orthodox or Bible-believing—are otherworldly in quite this way. (One can argue that Jesus, also, was not otherworldly in this sense.) Nonetheless, there are important ways in which otherworldliness is still with us. To understand these, we have to consider how more recent Christian thought has re-appropriated classical Christian themes concerning otherworldliness.

In some ways, Reformation worldviews were more dualistic than early Christian (or at least medieval) ones. God was even more separate from the world, in that the sacredness and power of the church and saints were reduced. Calvinists tried to re-establish the independence of the church from political leadership, which had been lost after Constantine. (Early New England, where Calvinists were dominant, is sometimes called a theocracy, but in fact ministers did not wield the power of the state, and civil government did not control the church.) Luther and Calvin were as focused on saving people's souls as was Jesus, and at least as skeptical of the power of goodness in the world.

Nonetheless, in some ways the Reformers were more interested in the world than the medieval church had been. They had a broader concept of ministry than the pre-Reformation church, for instance, emphasizing the "priesthood of all believers" and asserting that every lawful occupation was just as much a divinely given calling as the priesthood. Before the Reformation many Christians (including non-celibates) believed that celibacy was a religiously superior way of life, bringing people who practiced it closer to God than was possible for people living ordinary lives in the world; the Reformers rejected such thinking. Work outside the church, to a greater extent after the Reformation than before, can be a way of doing God's will.

The whole world becomes the place to do God's work, and so in this sense this view is less dualistic; the church loses its privileged and separate place, and everything in the world is both completely secular and potentially of religious concern. Even the ordained ministry is not as separate from ordinary life as before; this is most obvious in the rejection of priestly celibacy. Furthermore, Christ is not expected to return soon, at least not in a way that would make it pointless to start families, plan for the material future, and work to make the world better.[10]

In our day, the language of the Reformation can often seem alien—unless reinterpreted—when it speaks in the tongue of classical otherworldliness. Few people today, for instance, would write religious music expressing a longing for death such as is frequently found in the music of Johann Sebastian Bach or Heinrich Schütz. The devil, as the historian Heiko Oberman has recently reminded us, was present to Luther and most people in his day with an immediacy and concreteness few people experience today; Victor Santiago is the only one of the respondents who has this kind of experience of the devil.[11] The more theologically conservative people I interviewed certainly believe in life after death, and want to be "saved." But with the exception of the Jehovah's Witnesses, most of their energy goes into thinking about how to live spiritually rich and religiously valid lives during their earthly lifetimes. Many of the mainline Protestants, and the less traditional Catholics, are not so sure that there is a life after death, a heaven or a hell.

One more example of the difference between the spirit of the Reformation and contemporary Christianity can be seen in the change in the promises Episcopalians make at baptism. In the old *Book of Common Prayer,* the language of which dates largely from the Reformation, one promised "to renounce . . . the vain pomp and glory of the world, with all covetous desires of the same, and the sinful desires of the flesh."[12] In the new prayer book, published in 1976, one promises to "renounce the evil powers of this world which corrupt and destroy the creatures of God," and "all sinful desires that draw [one] from the love of God."[13] In the new formulation, the condemnation of the world seems less sweeping: it is only the "evil powers" we have to renounce. The idea of sinful desires, on the other hand, is a little broader: we have to look out for "all" of them, not just the desires of the flesh. Seemingly one has to renounce only selected aspects of the world. There is less distrust of our bodies, less equation of the bodily side of existence with evil or secularity—and perhaps more acknowledgment of how "*non*-fleshly" a lot of our sinful desires are!

Where does this leave contemporary Christians with regard to other-worldliness? A few, such as the Jehovah's Witnesses, think in ways that are otherworldly in the classical sense. Others, however, do not, but still try to retain some of the core values of an otherworldly perspective. Above all, they try to maintain the independent, transcendent character of Christian values and churches, and to avoid being controlled by desire for "worldly" things like wealth and power, so that they can freely answer God's call. Christians still try to live "in but not of" the world.

Many still see the world as fundamentally disordered morally, a place that very often rewards and values the wrong things. In such a world, the problem isn't merely that people behave badly but also that the people who behave badly often come out better than those who behave well. Finally, most contemporary Christians are still strongly attached to maintaining the independence of the church from the state, and many strive to keep it free from too close a connection to ethnicity and other "worldly" bases for loyalty.

In some ways, this is a return to the transcendence of ancient Judaism and the first two commandments, but it also shows the influence of the radical world-rejection that originally characterized Christianity. Even today, when Christians put on their "Christian" hat and think about human values, they are skeptical about the pursuit of wealth and power, and about the possibility of achieving fulfillment through purely "material" means. Christians are frequently (perhaps not frequently enough, however) on their guard for signs of becoming too accommodated to, or influenced by, the world. Conservative Christians accuse radical ones of losing the independence and transcendence of Christianity by yielding to the influence of "secular humanism" or "atheistic Marxism." Meanwhile, radical Christians accuse the conservatives of an idolatrous glorification of America, or of confusing Christianity with the ethos of capitalism or the "traditional" family. Serious Christians of all theological and political stripes remain concerned to live in tension with the world. Meanwhile, older dualisms also show great persistence. The desire to keep religious concerns independent of political ones—not just to separate church from state, but also religion from politics, religious from civic issues—still runs deep, and a great many Christians have a hard time thinking of their ministry as extending beyond church and family to work, community involvement, and politics.

The respondents frequently express themes from either the classical version of otherworldliness or the more modern forms just described. This is obvious in the case of Victor Santiago, but his perspective is quite unusual today. The others, however, also show the influence of otherworldliness. David Jenkins speaks strongly of the need to keep one's independence rather than make decisions on the basis of what will get one ahead materially. Joseph Krieger says it does little good to gain material goods if one loses one's soul. Linda Watson talks about a reversal of values in which God will treat the meek better than the powerful. Susan Wainwright, reflecting dualistic ways of thinking that come out of otherworldliness, thinks of church and civic issues as separate arenas.

The key issue, as with all of the values considered in this chapter, is not whether a person is a theological modernist or traditionalist. A person who reads the Bible literally is not, for that reason, either more or less able than a non-literalist to preserve the transcendence of Christian concerns in the face of the world. One might expect belief in heaven and hell to lead people to conclude that they should put their trust in God and doing right rather than in accumulating possessions, but in fact many are able to maintain such religious beliefs alongside values and lifestyles that show scant evidence of transcendence and great attention to accumulation.

What are the implications of the otherworldly strand of Christian tradition for ethical perspectives? The most obvious one is what could be called "non-materialism": an ethical stance that says that if you pursue material well-being beyond a modest level of comfort and security, you are following the wrong direction in life. Like the value of love, this can have quite varied social implications, but is likely to be in some tension with the value of pursuing economic interests. Thinking in otherworldly terms also sometimes leads people to make critical judgments, either about what they see as bad behavior in the economic realm by individuals, manifesting the influence of "the world," or about broader social trends or institutions. In addition, otherworldly thinking still tends to involve many Christians in dualisms between "religious" and "secular" spheres, with economic affairs placed on the "secular" side.

Otherworldliness, like all the themes considered in this chapter, could be said to be non-rational, in that it goes beyond what one could easily justify on the basis of a rational philosophy making reference only to observable events and phenomena, supplemented by the kind of unavoidable assumptions made in natural science. Otherworldliness represents a commitment people make when they experience or desire a relationship to a reality they cannot see. And it creates ethical obligations and values that are not based in practical interests or the bonds we form with people who have similar interests or with whom we are cooperating for mutual advantage. In short, it is another basis for what Walzer would call an "older morality."

Christians vary in the relative weight they give to these five themes. Nonetheless, a Christian ideally is both thisworldly and otherworldly. Ideally, one has a coherent and autonomous set of values and acts voluntarily, out of conscience, but cares deeply about others and respects every person's rights as a child of God. There is a little of each of these in every Christian, and for good reason. Each of these principles is authentically Christian and has deep roots in Christian traditions. Christians may differ about how they should be applied to the social world, but it does not make sense to question people's legitimacy or orthodoxy as Christians when they use any of these principles. Furthermore, these themes are the shared property of all kinds of Christians—Protestants and Catholics, modernists and traditionalists. The language in which they are expressed can be quite different—and of course that is important—but there is a core of shared meaning as well. Quite similar voluntaristic views, for instance, are expressed by Catholics and both mainline and evangelical Protestants. Contrary to stereotypes, evangelical Protestants often have a strong commitment to making their faith this-worldly, and mainline Protestants to retaining its otherworldly quality.

I have called these themes "tendencies" because they are not all explicit principles enunciated by Scripture, creeds, or theologians. Some are: the value of love is an explicit principle within Christian thought; hundreds if not thousands of books have been written to explain it, often starting from the biblical concept of *agape. Voluntarism,* on the other hand, is not a term used by large numbers of Christians. However, it represents a package of ideas that appear together over and over among respondents, and the more voluntaristic respondents are quite aware of the coherence of the various ideas in the package.[14]

These are not the only Christian values and beliefs that can be linked to economic opinions. The idea of the Fall—of deficiencies in human nature and the prevalence of sin—is another. A belief that God is still in control of the world and orders all things (this is often called "Providence") is yet another, as is the belief that God created the world and installed us as its stewards. Other themes come up in one or another of the respondents we examined in chapter 1. Such themes, however, are used to support economic opinions much less often than the five described here.

There are analogs to these themes in secular thinking. Still, they are not just values that Christians happen to hold but part of a faith commitment Christians make, and part of a mode of discourse quite different from science or Enlightenment-style social philosophy. These qualities make a difference to the ways in which Christian faith enters into political dialogue. None of these five themes would be quite the same when removed from a Christian context.

Each of them, finally, has the potential to be used in quite varied ways. Some tend to have more conservative economic implications than others, but each can be used to support both conservative and liberal views on economic issues, and on the issues of public participation and means for change. Therefore, no matter what our political perspective, we are likely to find some implications from each that seem to us good and life-affirming, and others that seem unfortunate.

Issues about
Economic Life

3

Faith and Politics: Integration or Compartmentalization?

Should religion be related to politics? Christians have differing answers to this question, and the differences crosscut the lines between liberals and conservatives. Liberals wish conservative Christians would refrain from trying to get the law to enforce traditional sexual standards, while conservatives are dubious about applying faith to Central America issues. Inversely, Jerry Falwell on the right and many pacifists on the left see a clear and direct relationship between the teachings they find in Scripture and their views about nuclear weapons.

Actually, this is not one but three distinct issues. The most commonly discussed is separation of church and state—prayer in public schools, teaching creationism, and so forth. It has to do with government action in the religious arena. We will not consider this issue here.

The second concerns the propriety of speaking out or taking action on public issues on the part of churches and religious leaders. People outside the church who worry about such actions fear that too much of this may jeopardize the separation of church and state, or transgress boundaries religious leaders and institutions ought to accept if they wish to retain privileges such as exemption from taxation. From the standpoint of church members, the issue concerns the nature and role of the church: What does it exist for, and what is its mission?[1]

The third and by far the most important issue—given the limited power, as organizations, of even the largest churches—has to do with the connections between religious principles and social or political issues, as constructed by individual Christians and discussed within religious communities. The issue here is the extent to which faith ought to affect a Christian's stance toward the social world. Even when we eliminate all questions having to do with the church's taking practical action as an organization or trying to influence people and institutions outside the church, there remains a set of issues Christians do not agree about, concerning the extent and ways in which faith ought to be deployed to help people think and speak about social and political issues.

All of these issues are "meta-issues," in that they raise questions different from, and in a logical sense prior to, any particular, "substantive" political issue. Before Christians advocate that the church take a position either for or against legal abortion, for example, they need to decide whether it is appropriate for the church to be addressing the issue of abortion at all. Many church members object in principle to the church's taking *any* position— even one they agree with personally—on a political issue; other members feel it is vital that the church speak up for important values and try to influence public debate. Before individual Christians consider whether their religious principles are more in accord with capitalism or socialism, with intervention or non-intervention in Central America, they need to decide whether it is legitimate, appropriate, and possible to derive views about economic systems or foreign policy from Christian faith. Many Christians are reluctant to make connections between their own faith and their views on such issues, and disapprove of Christians who do so; others argue that a faith unconnected to social and political issues is incomplete. Christians who make statements of any of these kinds are explicitly addressing meta-issues, not substantive ones.

In principle, one can be liberal, centrist, or conservative on a given substantive issue, independent of whether one believes that faith has anything to say to it. It is inaccurate to describe people as politically "conservative" because they want to keep their faith and political views separate, or want the church to stick to "spiritual" questions. In practice, condemnations of religiously based political action tend to be heard most frequently when the actions in question are taken on behalf of views either to the left or the right of the political mainstream. In principle, moreover, meta-opinions might hold for all social and political issues; in practice, many people think that faith is appropriately connected to some issues but not to others.

Note that we are talking here about people's *opinions* on whether and when to connect faith and politics, not about the degree to which *in fact* they do so. A failure to make connections could have many causes: lack of interest in politics, marginal knowledge of or attachment to any religious framework, lack of exposure (in one's religious upbringing or environment) to the possibility of making connections, low skill or inclination for constructing connections among different aspects of one's thinking, or the presence of competing concerns working at cross-purposes, such as we saw in Susan Wainwright. People who oppose making connections, or define religious and political concerns as "naturally" unrelated, espouse what I term "compartmentalization." Some people are compartmentalized, but others simply fail to make connections. Similarly, one could imagine a person in whose thinking religious and political views were linked but who did not explicitly favor an "integrated" or wholistic faith. In practice, however, the respondents who make connections between faith and economic issues are generally aware of doing so and think that it is a good idea.

The separation between religion and politics for which many Christians argue is part of a web of beliefs that Americans typically hold with regard to separating different spheres of life; for instance, that universities, courts of law, the military, and business enterprises should make their decisions by their own special criteria, and not be influenced by ethical, social, or political criteria other than those specific to their sphere, such as the rule against plagiarism in an academic setting, or against embezzlement in business. One sees such separation in action, for instance, when the governing board of a pension fund says that it cannot refrain from investing in South Africa because this would violate its duty to maximize investment returns. Such separations, it is argued, allow each institution to operate with maximum efficiency—to everyone's benefit—and also support individual freedom. This position expresses a preference for what sociologists call "structural differentiation." This preference would most obviously ground separation of church and state and disapproval of church social action; however, it can also be applied to the connections between religious and political ideas.[2]

Some of the building blocks described in chapter 2 have substantive ethical content, and others are criteria or methods of thinking about Christian faith. The latter group—thisworldliness, otherworldliness, and voluntarism—most influence whether people compartmentalize or integrate faith and politics. Let us begin by looking at how people relate the themes of thisworldliness and otherworldliness to their meta-opinions.

Living In but not Of the World

As we have seen, Christian tradition includes strong elements of both otherworldliness and thisworldliness. Their religious commitments point Christians toward values different from and inevitably partly at odds with the operative values of daily life in our society—such as getting ahead, obtaining the esteem of others, finding fulfillment in love—and taken to have a superior claim on our loyalty. At the same time, Christian teachings often call us to fashion a meaningful and religiously valid life not in withdrawal from the world but amidst the moral complexities of practical, secular life. We are supposed to follow the ways of God, not of the world, but to do this within the terrain the world provides. This is the classical idea of living "in but not of" the world.[3] The two premises it contains are always in tension. The more we try to maximize our purity as beings who are not *of* this world, the greater the danger of not being enough *in* the world. At one extreme, complete withdrawal from the world (like that of a hermit or a cloistered nun or monk), is a way of life open to only a few; it does not generate children, and few people are suited to a life of celibacy, poverty, and obedience. If we make ourselves too pure and separate, we risk having no impact on life around us, in disobedience to God's call to have a mission in the world. On the other hand, to be fully engaged in the world is to risk losing the integrity of our principles. We can easily become so attached to material affluence that we lose the capacity to put other considerations first. Even if we try to put our principles first, we may make so many compromises in the effort to have a practical effect on the world that we lose the distinctiveness of our message and values.

Christians differ in the degree to which they choose to minimize the risk of accommodation or the risk of purism. The classical version of a radically purist position holds that the ideal Christian life is one of maximum withdrawal from the social involvements that enmesh people in material concerns: family, politics, economic life. Traditionally, this means the life of a hermit or a cloistered monk or nun, but it can be pursued in other contexts as well: within utopian communities or subcultures that keep fierce separations in place even though their members deal with others on a day-to-day basis. Among the people I interviewed, the Jehovah's Witnesses are closest to this position. They are probably at least as separated from the world in their attitude toward life as most Catholic priests or members of non-cloistered religious orders, even though they are not celibate, have families, and work at ordinary jobs. At the other end of the spectrum we might place those Christians who emphasize that in order to affect the world they have to speak about ethical and theological questions in language that even non-Christians can understand, appealing to common human experience and standards any reasonable person could accept, and that there is nothing distinctive about the church as opposed to other organizational settings in which one can do God's work. Such Christians wish, like the previous group, to preserve the integrity of their values, but are especially concerned to make sure that they are fully *in* the world.

It is often hard to discern whether a given position is too purist or too accommodative, or strikes the right balance, in part because of divisions among Christians. Is liberation theology a surrender to the ethos of Marxism? Has mainline Protestantism lost the ability to resist contemporary cultural norms as the standard by which to decide what to believe and how to live? Is fundamentalism an idolatry of the ethos of small-town nineteenth-century America? Is a celibate male priesthood the only way for Catholicism to preserve what used to be called a "saving difference" from the world; an expression of non-Christian, patriarchal assumptions, and therefore too much *of* the world; or a form of purism that does not allow the church to be fully *in* the world? Charges of accommodation or purism can be hurled in many directions.

Radical social and political movements (whether of the Left or the Right) face much the same dilemma. They, too, are in tension with the existing social world, and at the same time have a mission within it. Among Marxist-Leninists, the term reserved for those who accommodate themselves too much to the world, losing the integrity of the socialist message, is *right opportunist*. The term for those who make doctrinal purity a fetish and fail to really engage the world is *left sectarian*. In this context, as among Christians, the correct path is not always easy to discern, and charges of deviation from it are easy to make.

Bases for Compartmentalization

The willingness of Christians to connect faith to politics partly depends on their approach to this dilemma. As we saw in the last chapter, one of the possible implications of the otherworldly strand of Christian tradition is dualism: separation of religious from secular concerns. Christians can easily construct a whole series of dualities: between heaven and earth, true values and the values of this world, God and humanity, spirit and body, spiritual and material concerns, life inside and outside the church. This way of using the tradition of otherworldliness, especially when understood in a purist fashion, can support compartmentalization.

At the extreme, one can deny that material life has any importance. In such a vein, one might say that salvation is the only really important concern. The poor are already blessed, because they are less likely to be distracted by attachment to worldly goods. One should not interfere with their spiritual well-being to improve their material state. Claims for economic equality and justice are simply another form of materialism, to be condemned as much as the selfishness of the rich. The most practical deed of love one can do for other people is to bring them to Christ and a faith that will help them win salvation. Universalism is a precept about our spiritual equality but has nothing to say about material life.

Hints of such views are heard occasionally from the respondents. Joseph Krieger and one or two other respondents say things that seem to imply that the equality of universalism is a spiritual equality, and condemn what they consider materialistic claims by the less privileged. (Joseph is in favor of helping the less privileged, but he is hostile to their making claims or asserting rights.) Victor Santiago thinks that his major contribution to the well-being of others is to help them improve their fate in the new Kingdom that will come after Christ returns.

The mainstream of Christian theology, especially since the Reformation, has tended to say that Christians need to be both thisworldly and otherworldly. Correspondingly, the respondents seldom expressed the extreme positions just described. Few church members, furthermore, are world-rejecting in the pre-Reformation sense: few wish to retreat into monastic settings or undertake celibacy. Nonetheless, traditional dualities remain strong, among theological modernists almost as much as among traditionalists.

There is, first, a widespread tendency to think of material and spiritual concerns as very different, and to connect Christian faith only to what is thought of as the "spiritual" realm. Most of the depth-interview respondents are not in fact disengaged from the world, but many sound as if they were when they have their Christian hat on—when they are thinking or speaking in Christian terms. Their interpretation of faith is dualistic in that they give little *religious* importance to material life; the importance they evidently mostly *do* give to economic life comes from other sources. Religion concerns the spiritual, not the material realm; the latter can be important, but it is not a Christian concern. For instance, when I asked a member of the Evangelical Covenant Church what connections she sees between her faith and her political views, she said, "Normally I feel that they should remain pretty much separate." Or as a Baptist puts it, religion concerns "your soul, not all these mundane things. My beliefs in religion have nothing to do with government or political" issues.

Applied to the church, this means that all church social action and advocacy is highly suspect (unless it has to do with "religious" issues: the church's interests as an organization, school prayer, and so on). The church's role in society is to enhance people's *spiritual* well-being, and perhaps their moral consciousness. By doing this, of course, the church will make an important contribution to the well-being of the whole society, but that is a side effect, not the main goal. Susan Wainwright's statement about how busing is a "civic," not a "church" issue, is in this spirit. Similarly, she is not opposed to sermons on social issues, but she is much more interested in ones on "spiritual" subjects. Many respondents condemn church social action, and even discussion of social issues within the church, in stronger terms. A characteristic statement comes from a young Catholic: "I think churches should stay out of politics and stick with teaching moral and religious issues." Jennifer Habib, who belongs to the Assemblies of God, is equally adamant that "the church should not take stands."

Another appropriation of the tradition of otherworldliness is seen in the stance that a Christian must keep a high degree of separation from the world and its values. When Christians opt for trying above all to minimize the risk of accommodation, they separate themselves from politics. Victor Santiago is a paradigm of this possibility. He clearly rejects the values of an economically and militarily competitive society, and wants faith to govern his life. Yet, as he says, "I will not take action; I will not raise organizations; that is not for me to do. My government is in Jesus Christ. I want no part of this world; I am only here in this world for a purpose: to preach God's word." And the purpose of preaching God's word is not to change the world, but to save more people so that they are ready for the moment (which Victor thinks will come "pretty soon") when God returns and destroys the world as we know it. Victor's purism does not keep him from making connections between faith and his vision of a good society, but it blocks any practical application of these connections. The potentials coming from a thisworldly commitment to putting faith into action are nullified.

It is possible to take a less purist position than Victor's, and yet end up with the same separation between faith and politics. A Presbyterian in his mid-sixties shows one such possibility. This man feels that Jimmy Carter was sincere in his commitment to being a Christian, but that this put him in an untenable position. "To be a Christian and a politician at the same time is most difficult, because a Christian cannot compromise himself, and you cannot be a politician without compromising." By compromise, he means the ordinary give-and-take of political negotiation, not selling out in some crude way, as a corrupt or especially opportunistic politician might. To keep one's purity as a Christian requires that one make no compromise with the world, so what is one to do? The political participation an ordinary citizen engages in poses no problems for him—he is happy to vote, sign petitions, and so forth—and he does not say that Christians should eschew deeper involvement. Rather, he seems to be saying partly that the most devoted Christians will stay out of politics (parallel to how the married state, in much pre-Reformation thought, was regarded as respectable but not quite as good as being celibate), and partly that when Christians do get involved they leave their Christian identity behind, putting on another "hat."

The next form of dualism is far less purist, but has very similar implications. This rests on the idea that earthly life and the heavenly Kingdom are organized on very different principles. One version of this idea is that Christian values are too idealistic to offer effective guidance for earthly life, which must be organized instead according to hardheaded, practical principles. (These practical principles may have varying amounts of ethical content. They may refer only to technical efficiency, satisfying constituencies, or advancing national "interests," or they may be based on a secular theory of how some principles of justice can best be advanced.) In other words, Christian values belong to a different kind of language and discourse than the kind one should use when making political decisions or organizing economic life.

As a young member of an independent evangelical fellowship explained it, "The ideal Christian society was tried and it didn't work." Or, according to a Methodist, when the apostles tried to apply Christian principles by holding goods in common, "They came up with a cheater."[4] These people, compared with the Presbyterian who felt that Jimmy Carter could not act as a Christian and a politician simultaneously, show less concern for purity and separation from the world, but they separate the language of faith from that of politics just as thoroughly. The implication they (and several other respondents) draw is that economic life should be governed not by Christian principles but by ones drawn from a naturalistic social analysis based on prudence, self-interest, or minimizing disorder and risk. This position is partly based on thisworldliness—there is a concern here to be practically effective in making economic life better—but also on otherworldliness. The otherworldly component is the view that the gospel is pure and idealistic, saying much about our spiritual lives but nothing about the social, political, and economic world.

Note that the perspective just described is not a necessary implication of believing in the Fall or the reality of sin. Catherine Kennedy seems to feel that if human nature is fixed, this is all the more reason to concentrate on changing institutions. But the three respondents just quoted do not seem to think any significant improvement is possible. Joseph Krieger appears to feel that although any society will be imperfect, we could get closer to the ideal than we are now, and that it makes sense to use the ideal as a measuring rod, a definition of the direction in which we want to move. The respondents we have just been discussing, on the contrary, do not want to define an ideal for economic life—at least, an ideal that can provide any guidance for action—on a Christian basis. They hold opinions on economic issues, and not necessarily conservative ones, but they base them on non-Christian principles.

All the positions just described tend to separate faith from views on any political issue. They apply particularly strongly to economic issues, because these are the ones that are "material" in the most obvious sense. But they also have some application to other political issues, in part because (as David Jenkins so clearly perceives) political life is largely "material" in the kinds of action it entails: laws, regulations, grants, budgets, armies, and the like.

Bases for Integration

Thisworldliness, as we have seen, can be a vague principle, but often it is much more. At the least, this way of thinking tells Christians that the life of faith involves practical activity as much as ritual or prayer, and that the material world is God's creation and therefore of great value. Furthermore, each of us has a responsibility to manifest our relationship to God as we act within the actual, material situations of the world by contributing to the well-being of others. Even the theological traditionalists among the respondents put much more thought and energy into the question of how to live a religiously valid life here and now than into being saved. Such views can be compatible with wanting to separate faith and politics. But when the respondents favor integrating faith and politics, they usually draw on these ideas. When does this happen?

First, it tends to happen when people are deeply attached to the idea that God and their faith should govern every aspect of their being, their views and activities in every area of life. Victor Santiago states this perspective clearly and radically: "Everything has to do with my faith; my faith is a way of life." And when he talks about laws against discrimination, he explicitly refers back to that statement to explain why he favors them. "Faith governs my life," he says, including "my political opinions and everything." Note that this is far from a perspective that reduces faith to social ethics or social action; rather it advocates a wholistic faith, which permeates every part of life, from prayer to social action. (Victor is thus an example both of ideas that integrate and ideas that separate faith and politics; his eschatological assumptions and concern for maximizing separation from the world work in one direction, while his application of faith to every aspect of life, including the material and social, works in the other.)

This perspective militates against traditional Christian dualisms. As Michael Butros, the Presbyterian quoted in chapter 2 as an example of this-worldliness, puts it, "I don't think you can separate political, social, and religious aspects of personhood." This applies not just to our views but also to our activities. Given the basic idea that the Christian life is (among other things) a matter of ethics, many Christians can conclude, with Susan Wainwright, that "faith can't be separate from our lives," and has to be expressed, in part, by "working for justice."

Christians are also likely to favor integration of faith and politics when they decide that material life is religiously significant and should therefore be governed by religious values. If God created the world in all its materiality, and loved it enough to take human, material flesh, in the life of Jesus, then who are we, argue some Christians, to say that we will keep our hands clean of material affairs? Instead, we should try to see that God's will governs the economic sphere just as much as other spheres of life, and apply our faith to economic issues just as to other areas in which human life could stand improvement. Catherine Kennedy is only one of several respondents who speak in these terms. Phyllis MacIntyre, for example, has come to believe that faith has specific implications for food-assistance legislation: that we should make decisions on assistance to other countries based only on the need of recipients, not on foreign policy considerations. Her views are in striking contrast to the respondents quoted earlier who want policy governed by practical, hardheaded, non-Christian considerations. She acknowledges that her proposal may be less "pragmatic"; a minute later, however, referring to a variety of political and ethical issues, she says that "if you truly hold your ethics to be important, the lack of practicality will be the expense for supporting them." This is especially striking given that she thinks of herself—probably correctly, since she is a successful engineer— as an eminently practical person, and that she is a Republican who sympathizes with the foreign policy goals of the administration in power at the time of her interview. Her disagreement is with means, but this puts her at odds with U.S. policy. She recognizes the conflict, indicating that on this issue faith leads her in a direction which—given her own political views— seems impractical but should be taken nonetheless.

Christians who hold all these views are likely to connect faith to their thinking and activities with regard to economic issues. For such Christians, God's will is the norm for worldly life. Faith is a sovereign and universal blueprint for the world, an appropriate guide for making any important decision, social as much as individual, material as much as spiritual. As one Catholic put it, Christians need "to make the environment more Christian." Faith requires him to work for "the Kingdom of justice, love and peace, and that Kingdom is political, social, and economic." Less radically, several respondents are in favor of welfare state policies and extensive public regulation of business, on explicitly Christian grounds. In their view, Christians should work together and through the government toward a closer approximation of the kind of society—one with more solidarity and community—that they believe would better accord with Christian values. Such people are ready to take the risks inherent in trying to implement their goals concretely and collectively, in trying to make the Word flesh.

Many of the principles we have just been examining come up when people talk about the social role of the church. Quite a few respondents, representing many different views, speak in favor of church social action on the grounds just described. Michael Butros wants individual Christians and also the church to work for increased social welfare spending. A young African-American Baptist wants the church not to be "separated" from the "community" but to meet community economic needs, in part by advocating liberal public policies at the local level. The tradition of thisworldliness helps many Christians decide that they should link faith to material as well as spiritual concerns, and that the church should also address such concerns.

Voluntarism and the Relationship between Faith and Politics

The strand of voluntarism within Christian tradition can have varied implications for connecting faith and politics. The idea that faith should be wholistic, governing every aspect of life, is in part based on the view that Christians should be integrated persons with a single set of values and commitments informing all their actions. David Jenkins and Victor Santiago clearly hold this view, and the Quaker William Westfield is an even more articulate advocate. "All of the basic testimony" of the Quakers, he says, is based on "a centeredness that is the single standard of truth, of clothing, of speech—getting away as much as possible from playing a whole lot of different roles." This is "a kind of authenticity," and is based on "the assumption that there is that potential that we think of as God in every person, and the possibility of touching that or finding communion with that in any other person we ever encounter." This, for him, is the core of what he and other Quakers call "simplicity," and underlies his pacifism; historically, it is why Quakers refused to use different forms of address (polite and intimate) with different people and defied in many other ways the social conventions that differentiate among kinds of people. Clearly, this idea of a "single standard" can easily be seen as implying that one's political views ought to come out of the same framework of values and beliefs that one hopes will inform all one's life. And in fact William, David, and Victor all forge strong connections between faith and their political views. However, Victor makes these connections irrelevant to practical action, and David, because he is so voluntaristic and anti-materialistic, applies faith only to the procedural issue of freedom and to one-to-one relationships.

In fact, voluntaristic thinking mostly serves to ground compartmentalization for the respondents in this study. Many of them give religious meaning and apply religious standards to their private encounters with God and their one-to-one relationships with people they meet in their daily lives but not to any broader sphere. Ethics is an essentially personal matter; the idea of putting faith into practice may be accepted, (as the tradition of thisworldliness suggests) but the practice in question is confined to the spheres that touch directly on our individual lives. David Jenkins is a prototype of this use of the voluntaristic strand of Christian tradition: he explicitly equates externality and materiality with the unimportant, secular side of life. For him, otherworldliness and voluntarism work together to make economic issues unimportant.

For others, however, objections to applying faith to *social* concerns are more important than objections to applying faith to *material* concerns. Christian love, for instance, may be taken as a principle with ramifications for economic life—but only for our activities as individuals, in our one-to-one dealings with people we meet in private spheres of life. Political issues, with the possible exception of those having to do with regulating individual "moral" conduct, are then of little importance to Christians *as Christians* (whatever other importance they may have). This separates faith from economic issues just as strongly as do views based on otherworldliness; the difference is that here what makes these issues religiously unimportant is their *public* and external quality rather than their *material* and external quality. (The atomistic view of society and blindness to social structure that, as David Jenkins shows, can easily accompany ethical voluntarism, make such separation all the more likely.) If only individuals really exist and all social phenomena are sums of individual choices and behavior, then trying to raise the quality of human life by working to affect public policy or institutional arrangements is an unpromising strategy.

A great many respondents think of faith as an inward and private concern; several conclude that for that reason it should be separate from political and social issues. Here is the Baptist quoted earlier as favoring complete separation of faith and politics on dualistic grounds, defining religion: "It's you and God and your soul, and that's a personal relationship; it's not politics, church, government, or anything else." Or in the view of a middle-aged

Catholic housewife: "Faith is in your own self, and the government, that's for everybody, the whole country."

Another way in which a voluntaristic perspective can separate faith from political issues becomes apparent when people talk about electoral politics. Some of the respondents evaluate officeholders and candidates not by the ethical content of their *policies* but by their "character," their adherence to standards of behavior such as honesty, hard work, and efficiency. As one young member of a non-denominational church sees it, corrupt and sexually immoral politicians are our major problem; in Congress, "there's just pay-offs and playing around with other people's wives." People making this kind of evaluation do not perceive policy questions as issues of ethics but only of practicality or "politics," and restrict ethics to the kinds of standards one could equally apply to individuals in private settings. Others say that it *is* important that officeholders and citizens use good ethical judgment in their political decisions, but that Christian faith speaks only to building a foundation—a set of good basic values and a strong character—on the basis of which people will make better decisions. Public statements by churches and leaders, such as the pastoral letters on nuclear weapons and on the economy issued by the Catholic bishops, usually speak to broad issues of principle that it is hoped will inform policy rather than to the specifics of how to implement these principles. Given the views just described, even this is illegitimate, since faith does not define even the general principles that should inform policy but only the moral character of a good officeholder.

The tendency we noted in chapter 2 to think of ethical decision making as an essentially subjective process also helps separate religion and politics. If religious values can provide legitimate guidance only for a particular person's choices, and have no applicability to others or objective validity, how can we make ethically grounded decisions to govern our collective life? Public policy, then, can have only very limited and pragmatic objectives, to which faith has little to say.

On the whole, the kind of compartmentalization I have just described is a Protestant phenomenon; few of the Catholics among my respondents speak in these terms. Perhaps this is because Catholic tradition, compared with Protestantism, puts a little less stress on the relationship of each individual to God, and takes the church—a form of social structure—more seriously. Furthermore, most Catholics are born into the church and remain in it (even if inactive or disaffected) their whole lives rather than choosing and switching the way many Protestants do. Dissidents, to the horror of some Catholic conservatives, tend to try to change the church rather than join another. The church is a given reality, whatever one's disagreements or grievances, not a means chosen by the individual. The experience of living in such a church affects how one thinks about the nature of churches and the meaning of membership: probably few Catholics would compare the church to the Kiwanis the way David Jenkins does. Correspondingly, the Catholic re-

spondents tend to think about our society in more structural and less atomistic ways, to see more need for applying faith beyond one-to-one
relationships, and to look more favorably on church social action.

It also helps that the Catholic church itself, much more than most Protestant churches, articulates a rationale for being socially active as an organization, and uses its teaching powers to suggest to members that they
should link their own faith to their visions of a just society. Joseph Krieger
shows these influences; although he is conservative in many ways, he is clear
that government policy is an important part of having a good society, and
that Christians should push for the changes in public policy they see as
appropriate. And that applies not only to public policy issues concerning
how and whether we regulate individual behavior—gay rights, abortion, and
the like—but also to issues about the role of government in furthering
economic justice and well-being. "Christians," he says, "should take a
greater part in government"; as we have seen, he approves of the fact that
the church has not just provided direct service to those in need but also
worked to influence public policy, as in the assistance his parish gave to
people working for open housing laws. Catherine Kennedy and several other
Catholics express similar views.

Protestants, too, sometimes explicitly reject the use of voluntaristic
thinking to restrict the application of faith to the private sphere. Many
Christians decide that Christian principles apply not just to individuals
but to the social order. It is a move in this direction when Michael Butros says that corporations should be socially responsible, and yet another
when he says that government should put an ethical stance (which for
him is grounded in faith) into practice by ensuring that there are jobs for
everyone. For him, the quality of economic, material life is important,
but also he wants our social order, and not just individuals, to act out
Christian principles. Victor Santiago refuses to be involved in any kind of
political action, but that does not prevent him from analyzing our society
in terms of a Christian social ethics applied to the whole community, not
just individual behavior. For example, he condemns killing carried out by
the state in wartime just as much as murders committed by individuals—
both, he says, fall under the same commandment. He criticizes the arms
race between the United States and the Soviet Union as the kind of com-
petitiveness that goes contrary to Christian love, just as he criticizes competitive individuals who try to get ahead at the expense of others. Both
of these respondents apply faith to our social structure as well as to our
individual lives and person-to-person dealings. In the view of such respondents (with the exception of Victor), Christians should endeavor to
make the economic life of the whole community better embody God's
will, reconstructing the social order as necessary to bring this about. Our
concern for the well-being of others (grounded in the value of love) requires concern for social structures as well as individual behavior.

Data from Church Surveys about
Compartmentalization and Integration

Two surveys, one carried out by the Lutheran Church in America, and one by the larger body into which it has now merged, the Evangelical Lutheran Church in America—theologically "modernist" bodies, as opposed to the somewhat fundamentalist Lutheran Church–Missouri Synod—provide opportunities to explore some of the issues we have been discussing in the context of a broader group of church members. The results are probably not far from those one would get in most mainline denominations.[5] The responses give a sense of how prevalent the views we have been discussing are. Both surveys were conducted by mail, and went to large samples chosen in a way designed to give every adult member of the denomination an equal chance of being a respondent. Marginal members tend not to respond to such surveys, and so the results are most representative of the views of the people who actually show up in Lutheran churches on Sundays.[6]

The first survey was administered in 1982, and dealt with the subjects of how to put faith into action and what "ministry" consists of. The results suggest that almost all modernist Lutherans think that, in theory, faith should apply to every area of life, and conceive of ministry as an activity undertaken by laity as well as clergy, outside as well as inside church. However, when more specific questions are raised, the respondents indicate that they apply faith much more readily to some spheres of life—traditionally "religious" ones—than to others. Thus, they express an implicit dualism between religious and secular spheres. For example, a majority of respondents feel that being an usher in church, teaching Sunday School, giving advice to someone with a personal problem, and visiting a sick person are forms of "ministry," but only a minority say the same with regard to working, serving on a jury, or contributing money to a non-church organization. Their responses seem to reflect three sets of distinctions: church-related activities are more religiously significant than ones in other settings; activities with a spiritual or psychological effect are more significant than ones with a "material" effect; and activities in private or elective spheres (in the family, with friends, or in the church) are more significant than ones in the public, non-elective settings of work and politics. The first and second of these distinctions invoke themes based in otherworldliness; implicitly, these people are saying that their faith tells them to be concerned with "spiritual," religious issues but not with "material," secular ones. The third distinction relates to voluntarism: the respondents seem to be better able to see their activities within private spheres as ministry than their activities in the public spheres of work or politics.

The second survey, which took place in 1988, was about the social role of the church and the connections between faith and politics. One part of this survey presented respondents with a series of dilemmas bearing on personal connections; each dilemma consists of a pair of statements, each of which was expected to have some appeal. Three of these dilemmas raise issues of dualism and otherworldliness: (1) "Faith has to do primarily with our spiritual lives, not our material lives" versus "Faith concerns our material lives just as much as our spiritual lives"; (2) "Christian ethics have many implications for economic policy" versus "Christian ethics don't have many implications for economic policy"; and (3) "Christian principles are applicable to almost every social and political issue" versus "It often isn't practical to apply Christian principles to social and political issues." In each case, four-fifths of the Lutheran respondents *rejected* the dualistic answer. In theory, then, most seem open to connecting faith to economic issues, and reject compartmentalization based on otherworldliness.

Another set of dilemmas presented in the questionnaire brought up issues connected to voluntarism: (1) "As individual Christians, we are mainly responsible for living ethically in our one-to-one relationships" versus "As individual Christians, we should each put a lot of time into trying to improve our society"; (2) "To have a better society people just have to learn to act better toward each other" versus "To have a better society requires changes in public policy and how our society is organized"; and (3) "The church should deal with poverty mainly by helping people in need" versus "The church should work to change society so that there will be fewer poor people." Just over half of the respondents gave the voluntaristic answer to the first question, five-eighths to the second, and three-sevenths to the third. In short, approximately half show signs of separating faith from politics for voluntaristic reasons.

In another part of the questionnaire, the respondents were queried about possible ways a congregation could play a role in the community, ranging from promoting prayers for peace and justice to trying to affect local government policy on housing. None of the possible actions listed are regarded as inappropriate by a majority, but some generate high enthusiasm and almost no opposition, while others are viewed as very important by only a few and as inappropriate by almost half. The patterning is clear: activities that endeavor to improve community life by "spiritual" means, or by transforming or serving individuals, tend to be seen favorably; those that in any way seem to involve the congregation in politics—even where it plays an essentially neutral role, as in hosting candidates' nights open to all contenders or promoting discussion of local government policy within the congregation—tend to be seen less favorably.

There is a paradox here parallel to that found in the 1982 survey: in theory, Lutherans reject dualistic understandings of faith—strong majorities say that faith applies to many or all areas of life—and yet they make distinctions that seem like the ones that would flow from dualistic thinking. In addition, it is clear that separations between faith and social issues grounded in voluntaristic thinking are alive and well.[7]

* * *

The issues dealt with in this chapter are fundamental for the churches and for those who wish to see Christians link faith to social issues more frequently and to a broader range of substantive issues than they do now. The themes within Christian faith and the ways of appropriating them that support compartmentalization are genuine and deeply rooted in Christian tradition. They are not just rationalizations invented by conservatives; in fact, they are found among liberals as well. They probably affect the relationship of faith to economic issues the most, but they can be applied to a broad range of issues. For instance, during the 1960s and 1970s many of these arguments were used to oppose church-based anti-war activism. When opposition to particular church social actions or teachings arises, meta-issues are as likely as substantive issues to be involved.

Some commentators on the American religious scene argue that the faith of American Christians is headed toward privatization and irrelevance to public discourse.[8] What the respondents tell us, however, suggests that such a conclusion is premature. Some, to be sure, express ideas that separate faith from any but private concerns and spheres of activity. But this is not an uncontested view, and probably not even the dominant one. Whether and when to connect faith to politics, just as much as what substantive connections to make, is an issue where different perspectives compete, sometimes even within the thinking of a particular person such as Susan Wainwright. It is the outcome of this competition and debate, as much as broad historical trends, that will determine how relevant or marginal to public life Christian faith is in the future.

Some Christians advocate an almost complete integration or compartmentalization, but many are in the middle. For them, the kind of issue makes a difference: it is easier for many Christians to see that their faith has implications for non-economic issues and ones concerned with individual behavior than for economic or more structural issues. For instance, for some it is easier to see why faith should speak to whether a pornographic movie house should be allowed to move into town than to what kinds of economic inequality are unjust. One can, if one wishes, bring specific moral attitudes about sexuality to bear on the former. The latter is indubitably highly complex and can plausibly be addressed only by using ideas taken from many sources in addition to the traditions of Christianity. Faith can speak to it only with the assistance of a descriptive social analysis about the roots and consequences of inequality, and a religious community of any size is likely to be able to reach consensus, at best, only on broad principles to govern economic life. In addition to these reasons that Christians are more open to integration on some fronts than others, however, there are the influences we have been describing: the tendency of many Christians to see material and social questions as less religiously relevant than "spiritual" and individual ones.

Meta-issues, while important, are often hard to explore head-on in conversations such as those I had with the respondents. Sometimes people's ideas about integration and compartmentalization seem like intuition or common sense rather than a position one would argue about, and so it is hard for them to articulate these ideas. Also, these issues are abstract when stated explicitly and dealt with in isolation from any specific social concern; they are more removed than substantive issues from specific events, and are therefore less likely to be discussed in the mass media.[9]

Still, ideas that support integration or compartmentalization are clearly present in the thinking of many American Christians, and have a great effect on the capacity of Christians to use their faith to make a contribution to public discourse in this country. When people connect their faith to social and political issues, important things happen: passion, energy, commitment, and a burning desire to make "what is" correspond better to "what ought to be" are released into political life, creating new risks—of intolerance and conflict, for instance—as well as new possibilities for bringing life-affirming resources within Christian traditions to bear on the problems facing our country. The outcome is unpredictable, and can benefit either the Right or the Left, but probably serves least well those who prefer stability and only gradual change in the current situation. Given the appeal as well as the real human values served by stability, it is not surprising that many people fear connections between faith and politics. There are also reasons internal to Christian tradition, as we have seen, why people might favor compartmentalization. Evidently Christians are not in agreement on this issue, and the debate is likely to continue.

4

Values of Community and Sharing for Economic Life

Property,
the more common it is,
the more holy it is.

attributed to St. Gertrude

Suppose a Christian believes that it is reasonable and appropriate to link faith to economic issues. What views on these issues will he or she ground in faith?

Before answering this question, we need to say what we mean by "economic issues." There are, of course, many economic issues that Americans debate, and these change all the time: tax reform or budget deficits one year, welfare cutbacks or national health insurance another, and in the foggy past of the 1960s, even attempts to eradicate poverty. These issues are important, of course, but it is difficult to study people's views on them for two reasons. First, they are so complex and change so rapidly that it is hard for most citizens to respond to them intelligently. Often, for instance, people have only a vague sense of the particular proposals being considered by Congress, and lack the information they would need to relate their values to these proposals. Second, because these issues are so changeable, and people's responses to them are so affected by the circumstances of the moment (whether inflation or unemployment is high, for instance), one cannot easily assume from what they think about one issue at one time what they will think about another issue a few years later. Therefore we will examine, instead, the thinking people manifest when they talk about basic questions of principle about economic life. These are questions that any person can think about intelligently, without unusual access to information. They are also more enduring, having divided the political Left and Right for many decades, in some respects for centuries. Two such questions are especially important.

The first is the debate over equality and inequality, the distribution of income and wealth. What kinds and degree of economic inequality are justifiable? To what extent should we make sure that every person has access to decent food, housing, education, and other important resources for life versus relying on self-help, possibly supplemented by private charity?

The second basic question is about private enterprise, and the degree to which it should be constrained (or abolished). To what extent do private owners have the right to make unimpeded decisions about how to use productive resources? To what extent should these be constrained by workers, communities, or the government? In the course of our conversations, the respondents usually spoke directly to these basic questions. When they spoke to more narrow or fleeting issues, furthermore, they often reasoned in ways expressing positions on underlying questions. There are, of course, economic issues that cannot be subsumed under either of these questions, such as environmental protection versus short-term economic growth or the interests of humans versus those of other species, but we will focus on the two major questions just described.

On both questions, one can place people's views roughly on a spectrum from left to right or extremely liberal to extremely conservative. Economic liberals tend to favor movement in the direction of greater equality, and to be open to restrictions on the powers of private enterprise; socialists take an even stronger position. Economic conservatives tend to believe that most inequalities are justified and that it is important to maximize freedom of choice for both individuals and corporations; some are unapologetic proponents of capitalism. These positions should not be confused with being liberal or conservative on other political issues, or with identifying oneself using the terms *liberal* or *conservative,* since Americans tend to pick and choose, adopting liberal views on one issue and conservative ones on another, and mean widely varying things by these terms.

The liberal/conservative dimension is not the only way in which views on economic issues vary. Another key distinction is between what could be called *communal* and *individualistic* ways of thinking and speaking about economic life: ways that focus on the life of the whole community versus ones that focus on our individuality and self-determination. To some extent, this distinction is connected with the liberal/conservative dimension. Individualistic values, as exemplified by Richard Schenk's thinking, often support conservative views on economic issues, and values of community often support liberal politics, as Linda Watson shows. However, these are not the only possibilities. Joseph Krieger, for instance, shows how communal values can support conservative as well as liberal economic views, and we will be examining some important contributions individualistic values can make to liberal perspectives. One implication of the fact that examples of all these combinations can be found is that the values undergirding liberal or conservative economic views are not constant; even if people are at the same place on the liberal/conservative dimension, they may not have the same reasons for being there, and may have values that differ in fundamental ways. Any particular person, in fact, may use varying languages, and not just out of intellectual confusion, for one could easily argue that both individualistic and communal concerns are valid and important.

A third way in which linkages between faith and economic issues vary is in the tools from Christian faith deployed to ground economic opinions. The most frequently used themes are love, voluntarism, and universalism. The ethic of Christian love grounds communal approaches to economic life, while voluntaristic thinking encourages individualistic approaches. Universalistic ideas, as we will see, have both potentials.

With all these (and other) dimensions to vary on, ways of connecting faith to economic issues exhibit great variety. However, there are four ways of thinking and speaking, four forms of language, each with a good degree of coherence, that emerge repeatedly among the respondents. We will examine each of these, with briefer attention to some related ideas. The first is the language of corporatism, a consistently and strongly communal approach to economic life, grounded in the value of love, with both liberal and conservative components. The second, which could be termed the language of caring, is a consistently and moderately liberal perspective, also grounded in the value of love. These two frameworks, both of which are entirely based on communal values, will occupy the current chapter. In chapter 5, we will look at the other two key languages (and briefly mention some rarer ones). The first of these, and the most "left-wing" of the four languages we are considering, focuses on economic rights and equality. It includes the ideas found in the language of caring, and adds universalistic themes of equality and an individualistic component expressed by references to economic "rights." Thus, it is a mixture of communal and individualistic themes. The other framework considered in chapter 5 is the only language that is more or less purely individualistic, relying primarily on voluntaristic strands of Christian thought. This, the language of economic freedom, is the most economically conservative of the four perspectives.

Corporatism and Allied Languages

We have already discussed corporatism briefly in the course of examining Joseph Krieger's views. Now let us look at another respondent, James O'Connell, who is equally corporatistic despite a quite different theological and ethical stance. James is a somewhat non-traditional and disaffected

Catholic of Irish extraction, a fire fighter in his thirties who has been divorced and remarried (his second marriage to an immigrant from India). He does not currently attend mass or show much outward allegiance to Catholic doctrine. In striking contrast to Joseph Krieger, he is liberal on issues concerning sexuality and abortion, believing strongly in individual self-determination in religious and ethical matters. He works in one of the poorest African-American neighborhoods in the San Francisco Bay Area, under trying conditions: the equipment is in poor condition, and neighborhood residents are sometimes hostile to the fire fighters, who on their side frequently express racist attitudes. As the person who interviewed him put it, he may be short on theology but he is certainly long on witness: he does a large amount of volunteer social service work in the neighborhood he works in, regularly makes loans at no interest, and does tax preparation (at which he has become quite expert, as a sideline to fire fighting) on an ability-to-pay basis. He clearly feels a sense of calling in his work, despises the focus on getting ahead he sees around him, and expresses no racism or hostility toward African-American people.

James's perspective on economic life is a mixture of liberal and conservative views. He is strongly in favor of socialized medicine, and wants social security and other social welfare programs upgraded. He favors busing to achieve school integration, wants city neighborhoods to become less segregated, thinks we need more public control over economic life, does not believe in "business freedom," and at one point even said that he favors socialism. On the more conservative side, he sees a danger in social welfare programs, which could undermine work motivation, given how weak human nature is, and is concerned about welfare abuse. He is quite anti-union although he is a union member, and does not like African-Americans (or anyone else) "demanding things as their rights."

Even though James is theologically nontraditionalist and ethically liberal, and partakes of the cosmopolitan and tolerant spirit of the Bay Area, his statements about economic issues are motivated by a perspective so parallel to that of Catholic social teachings that it seems almost certain that it comes from his traditional Irish Catholic background. His statements also have an old-fashioned tone, and clearly manifest allegiance to a moral economy. This is evident from the reasoning and language with which he expresses the economic views just described.

For instance, when talking about socialism, James says, "The whole idea in a socialist country is to do things for the good of the whole country, and not be geared to individuals per se. It would involve such things as socialized medicine where everything would be available in equal lots to everybody. This would be a restricted society in that you have stronger controls placed upon you. But everything is geared for the betterment of the whole country, the whole family." Asked whether he thinks this is the right direction for our country to move in, even with the controls, he says yes. This is about as communal and anti-individualistic a statement as one can imagine. The good of the whole is explicitly preferred to that of individuals, and controls are accepted. The country is portrayed as a "family"—an image that has emotional overtones of mutual love and distribution of resources according to need within a social unit where people have very different characteristics and functions (old and young; female and male; wage earner, homemaker, and student), and the inequality of power between parents and children is usually felt to be "natural" and legitimate, and to serve everyone's interests.

James belongs to a union that has a reputation for militantly pursuing its own interests, but he thinks it should moderate its demands. He talks favorably about a contractor he heard about who prohibited his employees from belonging to a union and paid below union scale, but guaranteed year-round, full-time employment at good wages and provided paid vacations and fringe benefits; "all his employees are extremely happy." His objection to unions is not the one most anti-union respondents express, that unions restrict freedom and are a form of collective rather than individual action. Rather, to James, unions appear too self-interested; in a way, they are too private and free. "I think possibly control over wages might be a definite, positive good. I don't believe in the strike concept especially. I think that salaries should be arbitrated or set by somebody, an impartial party who'd step in and determine fair wages."

With regard to race relations, the reason James favors busing and more integration in housing is that these would bring African-Americans and Whites into contact more, thus improving race relations. Juxtaposing this to his opposition to demands for "rights," we can see that his first concern is with solidarity, not justice or equality. When he speaks of socialized medicine, he does favor equality, saying that this is only an example of how "everything would be available in equal lots to everybody; this would be basically my concept of socialism." However, equality here refers to consumption, not production; it is implemented by a unilateral act of the government that makes things available, not by conflict, demands for rights, or the empowerment of groups that have been kept down. The equality he desires is an expression of our solidarity, our sense of community, our status as one "family." It comes about, like the benevolence of the contractor he describes or the fair wages determined by an arbitrator, through the action of an authority armed with power and acting on behalf of the interests of the whole community, taking care of the needs of those lower in the social hierarchy.

His thinking on welfare abuse is also instructive. He blames welfare cheating more on institutions than individuals: "I don't hold with people doing this, but when you make something so readily available, it's inevitable." The purpose of curbing abuse is not to enhance individual responsibility but to make sure that people are a benefit rather than a drain on the community. James talks in a similar way—about the need for institutional structures to control the weaknesses in human nature—in several other contexts, such as looting in chaotic situations and how businesses cheat consumers. "Business," he says, "should be more responsive to the community," and although he would prefer that it be so voluntarily, he is not afraid of mandatory measures. Our whole economic system, in short, should be designed to maximize solidarity, to put love into action, and to diminish the power of self-interested, individual-centered motivations.

Communal values, grounded in the ethic of love, are central to how James speaks about economic life; the voluntaristic side of his thinking is applied only to ethical and "lifestyle" issues. These communal values ground both liberal (even radical) and conservative views. To the extent that James is conservative, in other words, it is for communal rather than individualistic reasons. He is interested in reforming our actions, not our intentions. He wants to increase our contribution to the community, not our economic freedom or opportunities to pursue self-interest. Both when he espouses liberal views and when he espouses conservative ones, his central concern is with social harmony and human solidarity. In all these ways (except for using voluntaristic ideas to understand non-economic issues) he shares opinions with Joseph Krieger.

James O'Connell and Joseph Krieger are the best examples, among the respondents, of "corporatism." (We are using the term *corporatism* in a broad, generic sense here. It can also be used in narrower senses, to describe particular political philosophies such as Italian Fascism.) This term stems from the Latin *corpus,* meaning "body," and is based on the image of society as a body. As St. Paul—a strong advocate of this point of view—put it, "We, who are many, are one body in Christ, and individually we are members one of another" (Romans 12:4). We may fulfill different functions (as do the head, the feet, and the stomach) with unequal status, but each part of the social body needs every other part, and all the parts have to work together in harmony. Our common purposes are much more important than our divisions. Clearly, corporatism is a way of using the value of Christian love to think about economic life, and it has both liberal and conservative components.

A conservative component of corporatistic thinking is its view of hierarchy and inequality. In this perspective, those in superior positions should, and can, act in the interest of their inferiors. Inequality is natural and willed by God. People who have been born with gifts for leadership are in superior positions to use their gifts for everyone's benefit. Those in authority are trusted to run things, and this applies to business leaders just as much as to government. Several respondents express views of this ilk, seeing economic inequality as natural and possibly God-ordained.

Eunice Waldfogel, a Presbyterian in her mid-fifties who works at a clerical job, learned from a former minister that people are not created equal; she expounds this point at some length. Unlike voluntaristic respondents, who assert either that big business does not have much power or else that it should have less, she says, "I think the big businesses are what make our country great. I'm worried about the power the unions have, but I'm not worried about the power of the management part of the companies." She is proud of our government and says everyone has a "Christian responsibility" to support it during a war, such as Vietnam. Speaking of the controversy over a Presbyterian contribution to the defense fund for Angela Davis, an African-American activist of the 1960s and 1970s, she says that "the church shouldn't support anyone who is against the government of the United States." Large corporations, similarly, are major national institutions, and worthy of support. Authority, more than freedom, is her central concern. Several other respondents speak of inequality as natural and even God-ordained, although few make such a strong defense of corporate and governmental authority.

Conveying another element of corporatistic thinking, many respondents express a distaste for conflict. For example, they see our society as too full of "special interest groups" working for their own good but ignoring our common purposes, or lament our inability to pull together as a team. The term *special interest groups,* in contemporary political parlance, is used for a wide range of organizations, from groups struggling for equality for African-Americans to lobbying associations formed by oil companies. When people are thinking corporatistically, they are often suspicious of all such groups indiscriminately.

Corporatistic views differ in important ways from either a perspective supporting a free market, as expressed by Richard Schenk or David Jenkins, or a more radical position of the kind articulated by Catherine Kennedy or Linda Watson. As compared with the free market perspective, corporatistic thinking puts very little emphasis on freedom in economic life and is much more interested in the practical, material outcomes of the workings of our economic system. In this way, corporatists are much more utilitarian and pragmatic than a person like David Jenkins. They also think of the economy as an arena of public morality. For the corporatistic respondents, the economy should be governed by ethical principles, not technical concerns or the working of market forces. These ethical principles are regarded as objectively valid; there is little relativism in this perspective. Politics is seen as the pursuit of the common good, not brokering differences among competing interests. Furthermore, the ethical principles of interest to corporatists concern ideas about what is just and unjust—what kinds and degree of inequality are legitimate, for instance, rather than the more abstract principle of maximizing freedom. We will make comparisons between corporatism and more radical perspectives later, after examining the ways in which Christian faith grounds such perspectives.

A Related Secular Language: Comparable Worth

Unfortunately, the interviews did not include any discussion of the idea of "comparable worth," but the debate about this idea can be illuminated by noting the similarities between the ethical language in which it is often framed and the corporatistic perspectives we have been examining.

The idea of comparable worth has been advanced primarily by feminists, in an effort to overcome gender discrimination. Equal pay for equal work is a principle that can be used against blatant discrimination, but it does not deal with the tendency for jobs held mostly by women to be paid less than those held mostly by men. To deal with this more subtle problem, some feminists propose a system of measurement that allows different jobs to be put on the same scale of worth; two jobs at the same point on the scale have comparable worth, and should be paid the same. Such proposals do not imply that inequality in pay for different jobs should be eliminated or even necessarily reduced, but only that inequality should reflect an objective standard of the "worth" of a job.

As conservative critics have pointed out, the idea of comparable worth in some ways harks back to medieval concepts of "just price" and "just wage," which were not compatible with a full-blown market economy and have retreated into the background, although never entirely abandoned. Of course, such critics are exaggerating; there are major differences between comparable worth and the idea of just wages. But there are indeed some parallels. One is reliance on images of a "moral economy." Another is that like the Christian, corporatist ideas articulated by Joseph Krieger and James O'Connell, comparable worth legitimates some inequalities on what is taken to be an objective but not market-determined base. Nonetheless, proposals for comparable worth are radical, within a market economy, not only because they work against inequalities based on old patterns of gender roles but also because they propose a self-conscious and potentially public process by which the community establishes principles determining which inequalities are just and which unjust. Such proposals combat the idea that the marketplace objectively determines values, and assert instead that if there are to be inequalities in income, these should be determined according to a set of social and ethical principles based on human values and human needs.

A Related Theme among the Respondents: Work

In practice, work can mean many things to us: a source of income and prestige, of self-worth and satisfaction, of inequality and frustration; a place where we may experience creativity, power, solidarity, lack of freedom and control, hierarchy, or oppression. In work, we sometimes create bonds with co-workers and the customers or users of the goods and services we help to produce; at other times, work involves competing or even conflicting with others. Christian traditions do not create such experiences, but they some-times provide templates by which they are understood.

There are many biblical and theological resources for understanding work. Already in the first three chapters of Genesis, we have three images. In the first chapter, God tells the first humans to be rulers and stewards of the earth, thereby giving them their first work-like task. In the second chapter, we read that on the seventh day God "rested from all the work" of creation accomplished previously (Genesis 2:2); thus, God also "works," and human work partakes of some of the honor of God's creative activity. In the third chapter, however, Adam is told that in consequence of his disobedience, "cursed is the ground because of you; in toil you shall eat of it all the days of your life.... By the sweat of your face you shall eat bread" (Genesis 3:17,19). Here, work is punishment and pain, a sign of separation from God and from other humans.

When the respondents talk about work, they use several of the building blocks described in chapter 2. Michael Butros and others speak of work in thisworldly terms as a place to do God's will, and several (such as Joseph Krieger, Victor Santiago, and James O'Connell) speak in otherworldly terms of the need to keep concerns such as getting ahead materially under control in our approach to work. Richard Schenk speaks voluntaristically, of the importance that people learn to work out of their own internal discipline rather than out of coercion. Another key theme informing the ethical ideas the respondents express about work, however, is Christian love. Work is our service to God and the community, and should be performed faithfully in order to benefit others. To work faithfully, beyond what is expected or what results in material rewards, is an act of love, improving the lives of others and expressing an orientation toward the good of the community rather than toward maximizing one's own interests.

Most of what the respondents say about work is not directly about public policy or even about the fundamental issues described at the start of this chapter (equality and private economic freedom) but, rather, about the ethical perspectives that they think should inform our everyday economic lives. Still, there are political overtones to some of what they say, and these are both liberal and conservative.

On the liberal side, several respondents express a desire for work to be more related to public service, and less to private advancement, than now; some prefer to work in the public or non-profit sector. Generally, these respondents are in the liberal half of the spectrum of economic views. This is not surprising; there is a rough correspondence between their views of work and the idea that our economy ought to be organized to give more priority to the public realm, and less to profit seeking in the private sector. Michael Butros speaks of this, as does Lucy Sandillo—a Chicana college student—who says that in a good society "every job would be a human service job, a public service job." Catherine Kennedy, as we saw, regards her choice of a career as a social worker as coming out of her faith. Others see work as central to human dignity, and draw the liberal conclusion that our society should, by government action, guarantee everyone a job.

On the conservative side, we have seen how James O'Connell and Joseph Krieger, like several other respondents, want restrictive policies about social welfare programs to make sure that work motivation is not undermined. Making this connection explicitly, a young Catholic woman says, "I believe in a work ethic, and I don't like people sitting back and accepting aid from social welfare." More broadly, many respondents speak of work as a social duty or of the importance in a Christian life of working faithfully, as a value in itself. They take this stance even with regard to menial jobs and even when the pay is low. Victor Santiago puts it in very strong terms: "The scriptures say, do all things as if you're doing them unto God. So when I go to work I relate that to my work; I give my boss 100 percent of me. I don't loaf; I do what I'm there for."

This view of work has some of the same implications as the corporatistic views just described: it tends to support existing patterns of inequality and hierarchy, whatever they are. Therefore, in a society that had actually in-stitutionalized a thoroughgoing equality, an ethical emphasis on the value of work would not necessarily have conservative implications. When St. Paul counseled slaves to work for their masters "with enthusiasm" (Ephesians 6:7), he was not endorsing slavery, but he was supporting motivations that in practice would help a slave system continue to function effectively. Mikhail Gorbachev expresses hope that revived Russian churches will help give a moral meaning to work; in other words, he desires religious support for values that will help an existing economic order maintain itself. In capitalist societies, as E. P. Thompson shows in his analysis of Methodism in the early period of English industrialism, Christian views of work can oil the "moral machinery" of factories and offices, assisting business firms in keeping their costs low and their work forces under control.[1] However, unlike corporatistic thinking, the ethical idea that one should take satisfaction in one's work and work hard does not in itself support the idea of hierarchy, and therefore serves less frequently to ground conservative views of economic life.[2]

Sharing and Caring

As we have seen, David Jenkins tries to live in a way that manifests love toward others. However, he is so committed to the primacy of free choice, so opposed to all forms of collective and public action, so unconcerned with material life, and so focused on grace experienced internally as opposed to externally visible ethical behavior, that he grounds no economic perspective, and certainly no views about public policy in the economic arena or about what kind of economic structure our society needs, in the ethic of love. Many of the respondents, however, do apply the value of love to economic life. We have just seen one way of doing so: the language of corporatism, which has a mixture of liberal and conservative implications. There is a second way that has more consistently liberal implications, although not, by itself, radical ones.

Let us start with an example: Philomena Jackson, an African-American respondent whom we have encountered several times already. She believes that our society should *institutionally* manifest adherence to the love ethic, and grounds some liberal views about economic issues in this ethic, but talks at greater length and more specifically about the standards she wishes to see Americans follow in their daily economic lives. Her comments have a critical quality with politically liberal overtones, even though she only occasionally expresses explicitly political views. (This is parallel to the way in which complaints that people do not work hard enough have conservative overtones, and often go along with somewhat conservative views about social welfare programs.)

Philomena is a religiously and morally traditional member of a congregation belonging to one (it is not clear which) of the major African-American Baptist denominations in the United States. About a decade before the interview, she was a passenger in a terrible automobile accident in which her two children, her sister, and her brother-in-law were killed; she was unconscious for two months. During her recovery, she had an intense conversion experience and became reinvolved in church. This transformed her life in many ways; a highly visible if not critical instance is that "after we came to know Jesus and accepted him as our personal Savior, we didn't drink or smoke any more." She speaks frequently and strongly of her relationship with Jesus, and of how upset she is about contemporary sexual standards (this comes up especially with her deceased sister's children, whom she has raised as her own since the accident). She watches religious television, and refers approvingly to figures such as Pat Robertson and Oral Roberts, as well as Billy Graham.

She does volunteer work, helping elderly and infirm people with shopping, medical appointments, and other tasks they find difficult. This is not entirely different from David Jenkins, but she goes further. After her accident she refused to file lawsuits to get compensation for pain and suffering, and she turned down a brother in real estate who tried to get her to invest in low-rent income properties and second mortgages. "I just feel it'd be taking advantage of the poor to do this," she says, "and my Bible tells me that loaning out your money for interest, for usury is wrong." To be a Christian, she thinks, one has to act in a way that shows by deeds, not just words, that "I am a child of God, a Christian. . . . If I know of a family that is in need, I go, and take food, clothing, whatever, lend money, my time, my talent; all this is God's, everything that I have is his."

Her rejection of lending money at interest is especially striking, since this has historically been a fundamental issue for Christian economic ethics; only in the past few centuries have the churches decided that they can live with this practice, and yet it is obviously fundamental to the operation of a capitalist economy. (James O'Connell, like Philomena, makes loans at no interest, but does not condemn the taking of interest.) Since she is not working to change America into a kind of economic order in which interest would no longer be necessary, one might say that her view is impractical; in essence, it functions not as a policy proposal but as a reference to a moral economy, expressing criticism of the American economic order for its failure to fulfill the ethic of love.[3] Usury, for her, symbolizes the fact that we do *not* live in a moral economy, that people use one another as means. Her view expresses a moral dissatisfaction with contemporary economic behavior. It is hard to express this dissatisfaction using concepts that reflect the ethos of a market society, and she is not in touch with Marxist or socialist thinking that provides one way to describe what is wrong with American capitalism. What she *can* draw on is a tradition of ethical thinking within Christianity that originated many centuries ago, and does not fit our current reality very well. This gives her a tool for articulating what she senses is wrong around her, and for asserting an "otherworldly" or transcendent viewpoint that refuses to accommodate itself to what is "practical"—that is, workable without major social change—here and now. She uses the idea that interest is bad—a pre-capitalist idea, just like many that Joseph Krieger expresses—as a way of evaluating American capitalism from outside its own cultural framework; that is, as a cultural resource for making an independent, Christian critique of economic conduct in our society.

Unlike David Jenkins, who so stresses freedom of choice and individual relationships that he opposes government action to meet human needs, she wants to see our society actually carry out the mandate of the love ethic, and draws policy conclusions from her ethical stance. "Christianity," she says, "tells us specifically the type of society we should have; that we are our brother's keeper, and we're responsible for each other, and should be able to turn to and rely upon each other for help, no matter what that help is, whether it's spiritual, financial, physical or moral." She applies this directly to social welfare programs, saying that we should have public programs to help anyone who is genuinely in need. (She combines this, like James O'Connell, with a concern to curb abuse.)

She is strongly supportive of the social service programs her congregation runs, in part for evangelistic reasons—"the only way we're going to share Christ with others is to go where they are and meet them at the point of their need"—but also because in her view (as for Victor Santiago, but with many more practical implications) faith is a sovereign guide to every aspect of life. In effect, she almost never takes her Christian hat off. "I try to seek God's will in everything that I do. And I mean everything. I guess I call on him more in the kitchen than any other place—cooking, shopping, driving. Everything that I do, I depend upon the Lord, because I know that I can't even draw a breath unless he wills it. I know that he is the source of everything that I am, that I have or hope to be." Individually, it is our "duty" to make the world better; institutionally, "the Church should not be separated from the world."

These statements by Philomena illustrate a more general point: theologically traditionalist Christians tend to talk more fluently and frequently in explicitly Christian terms than modernists. This is one reason that they often appear to be more "religious." The idea that traditionalist people are inherently more "religious," or more authentic Christians, should be rejected (this will be discussed in detail in chapter 7). It is even doubtful whether using language about God more frequently than others should be taken as a sign of being a better representative of what Christianity is all about. Nonetheless, looking at Philomena it is clear that this kind of fluency can help Christians connect faith to life, and help them use Christian values rather than (or in addition to) other cultural frameworks to think and talk about economic life. Furthermore, her uncompromising, totally nonrelativistic approach to ethical issues helps her counter the logic of market thinking, as when she rejects the taking of interest. When either of these things happens, the results are often politically liberal. Philomena, like Susan Wainwright, is more liberal when using Christian ideas to talk about politics than when talking about economic life in secular terms. The difference is that Philomena uses Christian language a lot more, and so these potentials are realized far more fully.

Philomena's language has an old-fashioned tone in another way: it expresses an aspiration for a moral economy, in part by utterances that sound as if they advocated pre-capitalist social relations. She does, in fact, believe that the United States has gone astray, and that if we could "get back" to our old religious faith life would be better. She seems to be saying that we had a moral unity and attachment to God, at some time in the past, that made us a more caring society. Historically such a claim has its problems, of course.[4] But perhaps her statements can be interpreted not as an attempt to do the same things professional historians do but, rather, as expressing an aspiration for a more communal society than we have, with more unity of purpose guiding its common life.

Many of the respondents echo the themes we hear from Philomena. Victor Santiago has a very similar perspective, in his focus on caring and his desire that this inform public policy. He is in some ways even more radical, for instance in his rather absolute denunciation of all forms of competition: the arms race among nations, economic competition among Americans trying to get ahead, and even competitive sports. Several other respondents make strongly critical statements about competition, without taking as radical a position as Victor's. As we have seen, for instance, Linda Watson feels that aggressive efforts to get ahead are opposed to the spirit of the Sermon on the Mount.

Phyllis MacIntyre, a Presbyterian engineer we have heard from several times before, also speaks several times about competition. In business, she says, "I really don't think that stepping on someone or knifing someone in the back to get to a higher position is ethical. It may be practical, but it isn't ethical." This is, in part, a statement of social criticism; as she sees it, "people are so money-hungry right now," they will "do a lot of things that two hundred years ago were totally unacceptable." Again, we see the image of a national decline from a more morally unified, more communal society—one that carried out the mandate of the love ethic better—that she thinks existed in the past. Phyllis speaks more concretely of her experience as a student in a course where students were graded on a curve. To help another student, in this situation, was to hurt herself directly, but she felt she still had an obligation to help others in their work in the course—not just to refrain from hurting them. Here she is taking a more radical position than when she condemns knifing people in the back. Her ethical stance is clearly connected to her positions on public policy issues (as seen in her comments, quoted in chapter 3, about food assistance legislation). She uses not only the same principle—the ethic of Christian love—but the same concept and terminology—a duality between the "practical" and the "ethical"—when talking about private business ethics and food-assistance legislation.

Another theme reflecting a desire to build a more communal society through both ethical and public action came up repeatedly: the principle that we have an obligation, based in the ethic of love, to help the needy. About half the respondents explicitly and spontaneously enunciate this as an implication of their understanding of faith. In a few cases, this is stated as a purely private obligation—one's own personal obligation to provide help on a one-to-one basis—but usually the respondents describe a mixture of private and public implications. That is, they feel called personally to provide help, and also feel that our society should provide help collectively, usually through a mixture of initiatives from non-governmental organizations, such as Catholic Charities or United Way, and from public agencies. Among the respondents profiled in chapter 1, Catherine Kennedy, Susan Wainwright, Joseph Krieger, Linda Watson, and Victor Santiago all express this position; Linda, for instance, says that providing social welfare programs is one measure of "whether we are a caring-type nation." Many other respondents say much the same. As one put it, "I've got every responsibility to take care of those less fortunate that I am. These are my moral responsibilities." Or in the words of another, "Morally we should want to help people in need"; this person is pleased that the church carries out this responsibility. Phyllis MacIntyre, putting the basis for her views in Christian ethics very clearly, says that "if you're a loving community, you will support those people who cannot make it on their own."

The views of many respondents are vague, remaining at the level of defining principles that a combination of private and public action should fulfill. (It could be argued that this is appropriate, given that many people do not have the information or analytical tools to devise specific strategies for dealing with need, and would require a variety of tools from non-Christian sources, such as social science, in order to do so effectively.) But in general, they express a widely held view that the value of love implies that as a whole society we should try to relieve material suffering, using government policies and programs as one part of our approach. Of course, a person could in theory accept this general principle and still adopt George Bush's approach of seeking a "kinder, gentler society" through the efforts of private "points of light." And indeed, Phyllis MacIntyre and several other respondents who express the themes we have just been examining are Republicans. Nonetheless, the respondents we have been quoting usually find themselves on the liberal side of debates about doing more or less about poverty and hunger, especially when they have their Christian hat on.

The love ethic, in short, tells many Christians that we are set on earth to serve each other, not to look out for ourselves; that we should put the needs of others ahead of maximizing our own economic interests; that we should not use others as means but only as ends; that we have an obligation to others that is independent of their deserts (since God loves us unconditionally); that competition, profit seeking, and economic self-seeking are suspect (in the views of a few, always wrong; for most, wrong if carried to excess); that we depend on one another and ought to find solidarity in that; and that there should be some degree of sharing of wealth, rather than a distribution of resources for living based solely on the workings of the market, to manifest our concern for one another. All these principles can be given a variety of political spins, but when the respondents apply them to economic issues, they usually use them to support at least a moderate liberalism. People expressing these views do not necessarily condemn a market-based, capitalist economy, but they do generally seem to feel that there are important values that such an economy, left to itself, will not achieve. They want non-market and communally motivated forms of economic action (the public and non-profit sectors, volunteer work, and so forth) to supplement the workings of the market; these forms of action are often seen as essential to a just society, and by some as better expressing the spirit of Christian ethics than market-oriented action. For that reason, even when the respondents are not expressing explicitly liberal policy positions, when they are talking in the ways described here, their statements have liberal overtones and are often accompanied by liberal opinions.[5]

A Cross-National Comparison: Attitudes toward the Market in the United States and the Soviet Union

Many observers—including critics of American culture—believe that Americans are more oriented toward the values of the market than people in other countries. Not surprisingly, those who favor converting the economy of the Soviet Union into a market-based one have a parallel concern: that Soviet citizens may have little understanding of the market or ethical acceptance of its workings. Recently a binational group of researchers conducted an opinion poll in Moscow and New York to gather data on what differences in attitudes actually exist. The same questions were asked in both cities; the topics included, among others, issues about the fairness of price increases based solely on unearned market advantages (for instance, increases in land values because a new rail line is built) and income inequality. The researchers were surprised to find out that on most issues there are no major differences in attitudes. For instance, about three-fifths of respondents in both New York and Moscow feel that it is fair to raise rents for summer homes when a new rail line is built. Only one-third in both cities, however, feel that it is fair for a factory to raise prices for kitchen tables when there is no change in the cost of production but an increase in demand. (Perhaps the difference in response is because tables are regarded as necessities and summer homes as luxuries.) The rate of inheritance tax on the estates of the wealthy favored by New Yorkers and Muscovites—about 38 percent, on the average—is almost identical.

The researchers, whose primary focus is on the Soviet Union, conclude that "in this study, Soviets appear to be no more concerned with fairness of prices than are United States citizens. They appear to be no more concerned with income inequality." Therefore, the main obstacles to a transition to a market economy in the Soviet Union (which the researchers clearly favor) do not appear to be attitudinal.[6] If we look at the findings with a focus on the United States, one might say something analogous about the possibilities for a transition *away* from primary reliance on market mechanisms. New Yorkers do not seem remarkably more attached then Muscovites to the market. It is hard to know with certainty the reasoning behind answers to questions such as those posed on the survey, but it looks as if there may be significant attachment in both countries to "moral economies." As economist Robert Shiller, one of the researchers, summed it up in a radio interview, "I don't think that Americans are particularly supportive of free markets. We have institutions that people accept but the people in this country don't seem to know what I thought was basic capitalist theory any more than the Soviets do."[7]

The uses of love to ground aspirations for a society with more sharing and caring are straightforward, consistent, and widespread. These uses vary in several ways, to be sure. Some deal with public policy in specific ways, some more vaguely, and some only with private action such as corporate social responsibility and the behavior of employers and employees toward each other. Some call for a radical rejection of self-interest, others only for limitations on self-interested action. Whatever political implications they have, nonetheless, favor liberal economic perspectives. About one-third of the respondents explicitly ground some liberal positions in the value of love, using one or another of the types of thinking just described, and another quarter draw conclusions for how private economic actors should behave— with liberal overtones, as we have seen—but do not explicitly address public policy questions on this basis.

The language of sharing and that of corporatism both express "moral economies," and both have a somewhat old-fashioned tone. The ideas about sharing we have been reviewing, however, do not focus on harmony or work as much, and certainly do not legitimate inequality in the same way as corporatism. They are less concerned with the nature of our society as a total social structure, although they are concerned with policy issues. Their focus, instead, is primarily on how we take care of one another, by public and private means. People like Philomena Jackson are less concerned than corporatists with elaborating an idea of the common good; their focus, instead, is on meeting the needs of individuals who might otherwise suffer. For a radical, the weaknesses of corporatism would be its top-down approach and its legitimation of inequality; the weakness of the language of caring and sharing would be its insufficient attention to the collective dimension of life.

There is nothing in the ways of thinking just described that is uniquely grounded in any particular theological tradition; the religious ideas used here are the common property of Christians of all kinds. Catholics and Protestants, evangelicals and members of mainline denominations, manifest essentially the same ways of speaking and thinking. If anything, it is the more religiously traditionalist respondents (both Catholics and Protestants) who are more likely to find a clear contradiction between the economic demands they see coming from Christian ethics and the way they see people behaving economically in today's America. This does not mean that religious traditionalism "makes" people more liberal. Traditionalists use Christian language more fluently than modernists, and tend to keep their Christian hat on more, and so they are more likely to relate their views in *any* sphere of life to principles grounded in faith. Furthermore, among those who make links between the value of love and views on economic issues of the kind we have been discussing, the traditionalists are more likely to make only quite vague statements (perhaps in part because they are somewhat less schooled, on the average). Nonetheless, the views of the theological traditionalists belie the claims of religious right leaders, and the fears of secularist radicals, that evangelicals and fundamentalists have a natural affinity for conservative politics on economic issues. The Christian ethic of love, after all, is based on a relationship with God in which the actual merits and failings of human beings have been systematically ignored, and in which God is felt to behave passionately—and certainly not in any way that could model a utilitarian ethical stance. It is precisely the non-rational and old-fashioned features of the love ethic that give it power and significance. These can be as available to modernist Christians as to traditionalists—they do not depend on any of the tenets of traditionalist faith—but they are certainly no more available. Therefore it is not surprising that traditionalists are as able as modernists to use the value of love to ground liberal views on economic issues.

5

Equality and Individualism
in Economic Life

In chapter 4, we mentioned four languages that Christians frequently use for relating faith to economic justice issues, and described two of them in detail. These two employ the value of love as a resource for thinking and talking about economic life. In the remaining two languages, to be dealt with in this chapter, we see what happens when Christians use other resources from Christian tradition, in addition to or instead of the ethic of love.

Equality and Economic Rights

Philomena Jackson, the African-American Baptist whose views we considered in the previous chapter, shows us a language of compassion and human concern, used to ground moderately liberal views. Considerably more radical potentials also exist in Christian faith, however, and not just in academic liberation theology or the Third World.

Two Examples

Michael Butros, whom we have heard from a few times already, expresses some of these. A fifty-year-old school administrator, he is of Middle Eastern ancestry and his parents were originally Orthodox, but he grew up a Presbyterian, and except for a period as a Congregationalist, has remained one. His religious life is a little like Susan Wainwright's, with a high level of church involvement but an uneventful spiritual life and not very much interest in theological issues. Politically, however, he is well to the left of center, speaking favorably of socialism. He regards U.S. Representative Ronald Dellums—perhaps the most radical member of Congress over the past two decades, and an explicit democratic socialist—as the public figure he most agrees with, even though he does not live in Dellums's district.

When he talks about economic life, his remarks can be summarized as a concatenation of the language of economic rights with the language of caring. The "caring" side has the same tone as the statements reviewed in chapter 4. A good society in Christian terms is one that helps those who need help. Corporations should be socially responsible (and also—a more radical view— their profits should be lower and their power less). The programs of the Democratic party, when it works for the interests of the less privileged, manifest "a humanistic concern." The basic principles of Christian love are not only, diffusely, to "love our neighbors" and follow the Golden Rule but to "clothe the poor and feed the hungry." He follows this statement by saying that a person's work life should be a place to carry out the ethic of love, "helping one another" rather than competing.

What sets Michael apart from Philomena Jackson is the addition of talk about equality and rights. Philomena talks about equality only when she says that "in front of the cross we're all equal, and I'm glad about that." But she draws no particular *economic* conclusions from this classical state-ment of universalism. Michael, on the contrary, uses it for political pur-poses. He says that "everyone should be entitled to" higher education and favors a guaranteed annual income. "There ought," he thinks, "to be a certain standard that we all should be able to live by," and then he lists the components: decent housing, ample food, medical care, and jobs to give us the dignity of earning our living. Our welfare state programs, in his view, need major expansion. He speaks strongly against discrimi-nation and of the need for public policies to overcome it. (He has suffered a little because of his ethnic background and dark skin, but concentrates on what African-Americans and Chicanos have suffered.) Expressing a more radical view, he says that in a good society not only are "people helping one another" but they are also "sharing some of the common goods. It sounds like Christianity would imply a socialistic kind of society, and in a sense it would." In any case, government programs ought to have an egalitarian intention, to benefit "the common man, the blue collar worker, the laborer."

There are two key elements of this way of thinking. One is an aspiration to equality; the issue is not just help for the needy but what he sees as a more equitable distribution of "the common goods." To be more precise, he favors increased equality of actual outcomes rather than just equality before the law or equality of opportunity—although he does think that our society has a long way to go before it will provide equality of opportunity.[1] Another key element is that he uses a tone and terminology that refer to what could be called economic rights. Rights are claims an individual can make against others or the community: the right to vote, the right to worship (or not) as one wills, and the right (asserted by Michael) to receive certain basic economic resources simply by virtue of being a member of the community and a child of God, without having to earn them.

Another way in which his language is different from Philomena Jackson's is that he gives a more directly political spin to his ideas. At the point where he speaks favorably of socialism, he is answering the same question that Philomena answered in terms of being "our brother's keeper." The views she expresses in reply are linked to her support for liberal public policies, but he is the one who directly attaches a political label: "socialistic." For her, faith guides all of life and the church shouldn't be separate from the community, while for Michael, "you're not a political figure and a religious figure, you're one person and they just have to intermingle and bear upon one another," and the church ought to "exercise some political clout" to get more and better government programs. The basic positions are similar, but again Michael is the one who draws direct conclusions for political action, while Philomena is more concerned with the church's own attempts to serve the community.

The "extreme-type" respondent chosen to represent a left-wing Catholic perspective, Thomas Gaffney, is even more radical. He is a Franciscan, ordained but not working in a parish, who has served the church in the Philippines. His perspective is not very typical, but it shows some of the radical possibilities in Christian faith quite clearly. Thomas, a forty-seven-year-old man of Irish background, has always been attracted to the contemplative life, and continues to conduct retreats as his major source of income. However, from early in his ministry he has also been deeply involved in social movements, first in an impoverished city neighborhood, and then for several years in the Philippines, until the government of Ferdinand Marcos expelled him. In the Philippines, he ran a radio station whose main offense seems to have been to educate tenant farmers about the rights they had under existing but unenforced land reform laws, rights that when asserted frequently led to armed assaults from large landowners whose control was threatened.

Thomas was promoting use of these laws as part of a larger hope for radical social change (perhaps the Philippine government was partly reacting to this underlying intention in expelling him). He is an explicit socialist, and favors "a society which is based on common ownership of the means of production, built with the social consciousness of cooperative work instead of competition. An economy which is definitely non-capitalistic, non-profit-oriented, and politically democratic. Kind of a communist form, and I guess my own penchant is toward the smaller forms of the community, a kind of political and economic life which pretty much gives control of things to ordinary people."

Like the respondents we heard from in chapter 4, he rejects competition and profits, albeit rather more completely than most of the people we quoted, and affirms the centrality of the value of community, based on the love ethic. Over and over again, Thomas speaks of community as a basic condition for a good human life. His ideas, he says, develop only in dialogue and shared action with others. He thinks it is vital for strong, and usually small, community structures, such as the Latin American *communidades de base* (base communities) promoted by practitioners of liberation theology, to develop within Catholic parishes. The aspect of his early years with the Franciscans that he remembers most clearly and talks about the most is the sense of "fraternity" within his class; how, for instance, there were no grades in seminary and the students devoted all their efforts to helping one another make it through the program rather than competing for honors and recognition. "God is community," he says, "and if we're to image forth God we'd better be in community, or else we're damned." To Thomas, this leads directly to rejecting capitalism and affirming an alternative—some kind of socialism or communism, although clearly not the kind of communism practiced until recently in Eastern Europe.

Another key component of his thinking is the idea of rights and equality, based on universalistic thinking. When talking about social welfare programs, he repeatedly uses the language of "rights," saying that people at the bottom have "a right to more than they're getting," as well as to employment. Here he is thinking like Michael Butros. The main difference is that Thomas feels an enormous urgency about asserting what we all deserve as children of God; he has seen the situation in the Philippines, and therefore seen market outcomes more extreme—deeper poverty, greater inequality, fewer opportunities for social mobility—than Michael has ever witnessed.

A third component, however, goes beyond Michael. This is a commitment to empowerment for people at the grass roots, to democracy—which he, like most other Christian radicals, is convinced is not provided very fully by U.S. political institutions. This is grounded in the way he interprets the voluntaristic strand of Christian tradition (a way quite similar to William Westfield's): that we need to live by conscience, not allowing our environment to restrain our impulses to follow a radical version of the gospel. The externals of churchly life—edifices, rigid rules, hierarchy, authority, organizational structures—are to him either inessential or an obstacle to discipleship. There is a "need to strip away an awful lot of the external entrapments of faith that are religion, and get back down to the essentials," as he puts it. Social change, as he sees it, needs to be created by its beneficiaries, not handed to them; it needs to be achieved, therefore, by struggle. He is against capitalism, not just because in his view it glorifies self-seeking and impoverishes community, not just because we are all children of God and deserve something better than what the market provides to those at the bottom, but because capitalism as he sees it is undemocratic, depriving most people of any real chance to participate in the economic decisions that strongly affect their lives.

Economic Rights and Equality as Seen by Other Respondents

We have similar statements from Catherine Kennedy and Linda Watson. Linda uses both the language of caring and that of economic rights with great fluency, while Catherine is more monolingual, talking predominantly in terms of rights. Catherine, for instance, says that in America "there isn't equality of opportunity," but, more radically, that she "would like to see equality for everybody." Furthermore, to her, equal opportunity means much more than providing a fixed starting point for the race of life. It involves making it possible for every person to live a "fulfilling and contented life," free from want, and with cultural and educational resources available to all. Linda says that "something needs to be done to make life more equal." Speaking out of the value of Christian love, she says we need to be a "caring-type nation" by providing generous social welfare programs. In addition, however, she uses the language of rights, grounded squarely in universalistic thinking, when she says that everyone has a right to help, "regardless of physical or mental capacities—we are still human."

Catherine and Linda are not alone; these languages are widely available and parts of them are used by several of the respondents. The value of universalism tells us that every person is a child of God, possessing a sacred status, and in some fundamental sense equal to every other person. This can mean many things, but for some it grounds ideas of equality and of economic rights based in our sacred status. As we have seen, Christians can use the value of love to support the idea that we should take care of one another. The idea, among the respondents, of publicly guaranteeing minimum living standards usually results from combining this idea with universalistic thinking. That is, they favor such guarantees out of compassion, but also out of a conviction that we are fundamentally equal; part of the motivation for such guarantees is to make us economically more equal—in living standards, not just in opportunities—than we are now.

For instance, consider this statement from Catherine Kennedy, talking about what "Christianity" entails: "If we're all brothers, then everybody should have the same kind of opportunity [for a fulfilling life] as you have." The term *brothers* evokes the feelings of love and solidarity that are supposed to exist in a family, and draws on the value of love. But the idea that we are "all" brothers, and that "everybody" has the same rights, is a universalistic idea. Another example is a woman who speaks favorably of socialism and says that in a good society "everyone's equal; everyone has the same rights." Linda Watson, similarly, thinks that simply being "human" is a basis for economic rights, in the statement quoted a moment ago. Susan Wainwright is yet another example; she says all the people of the world are "children of God," and therefore have a claim on her. Phyllis MacIntyre, though a Republican, believes that "everyone has a right to not being hungry."

More radically, some respondents conclude, on the basis of the love ethic and the principle of universalism, that their faith is more congruent with socialism than with capitalism. Thomas Gaffney is a clear socialist, and several other respondents express sympathy with socialism at one point or another in the interview. We have already seen this in Michael Butros, the fire fighter James O'Connell, and Catherine Kennedy. Linda Watson makes similar statements, as does another evangelical woman with a very low income: "The principles that communism is built on are much the same type of beliefs Christianity is built on: everyone's equal; everyone has the same rights; no one should be above someone else."

Obviously people differ about what they mean by equality, and how far it can or should be achieved. Still, in statements that support equality on Christian grounds we can usually find universalistic thinking. Such statements come out of a clear sense that our responsibilities to one another concern every person, without limit. They also bespeak the assumption that we are all equal in the sight of God, that we ought to treat one another the same way, and that a good society will put this principle into practice.

The language of equality and equal rights does not always take as radical, or especially as unified, a form as it does in the thinking of Michael Butros, Thomas Gaffney, Catherine Kennedy, and Linda Watson. Many of the respondents occasionally make statements drawing on this language, while using other languages most of the time. Such people are most likely to draw on ideas of equality, grounded in Christian universalism, when they talk about race relations rather than when discussing other kinds of economic inequality.

The Christian Witness for Racial Equality

In one form or another, the principle of racial equality is widely affirmed. Even some quite conservative respondents think that all employers have a clear duty to avoid discrimination, and we have seen how hard Joseph Krieger has worked to put this into practice, as a personal ethical principle. Usually this is combined with support for laws against discrimination. (David Jenkins is the exception because he is so voluntaristic. Recall how he spoke about fair housing: discrimination in renting is wrong, but should be corrected by individual acts of conscience.) Victor Santiago speaks strongly about the importance of racial equality. He says proudly that people of all races are treated equally among the Jehovah's Witnesses, but also thinks a just society would not permit discrimination. Victor wants practical equality, here on earth, although of course he thinks this is impossible outside the community of the saved, until the present world ends.

Over and over, the respondents repeat this theme: "If you're a Christian, and you say you believe in God, you cannot be prejudiced," as one put it. "I was brought up [in church] thinking everyone's created equal," says a

Catholic, but "I don't think people are treated as equals." She criticizes the church for being racially insensitive, and for having oppressed Native Americans in the past. Another Catholic speaks of the issue of racial equality in a directly political context. Talking about Martin Luther King, she says it's incredible and terrible "when you think of people feeling that because a person's skin is a different color that they aren't as good as the next guy. We're all God's people, no matter what color we are."

Altogether, twelve respondents explicitly and spontaneously link their faith to condemning racial inequality. This is a very high number to bring up a single theme spontaneously; quite likely all or almost all the rest would have endorsed this theme if asked.

Visions of an Undivided Community

Another element of universalistic thinking sometimes found when respondents talk about economic life has to do with social divisions. One way of appropriating the value of universalism is to assert that over and against the existing structures of social differentiation, with all the inequalities they imply, and the individualistic and competitive patterns of life they are often associated with, we should set a vision of humanity as an undifferentiated community. The anthropologist Victor Turner characterizes this vision in terms of a concept he calls *communitas*. He says that at certain "liminal" points in human life, when we are between or outside normal social statuses, we can experience a sense of solidarity in which we feel keenly the ways in which we are first and foremost equal and the same (brothers or sisters, members of the same community, depending on each other) rather than having different roles that are unequal and often in tension with one another (chief and subordinate, rich person and poor person, and so forth). As a paradigm, he examines the life that groups of African boys live together when undergoing initiation, but he generalizes what he finds there to many other kinds of liminal situations.[2]

Many Christians aspire to have more of our lives resemble the liminal situations Turner describes. Pentecost—the occasion on which the Holy Spirit, overcoming the legacy of Babel, speaks to people of many nations, each in their own tongue—is a beautifully condensed image of how Christians can aspire to overcome all the lines that keep humans apart: language, culture, nationality, gender, race, class, and even religion. We are to do this out of the value of love but also for universalistic reasons—because human divisions are of no account in God's eyes. War and social conflict have to be overcome. But whereas the value of love asserts this as an implication of caring for one another, universalistic thinking sees human divisions as a denial of our equal and identical status as children of God. In one sense, then, human divisions are based on cognitive error, an irrational perception of which human characteristics are important. (Nonetheless, universalistic thinking, as we saw in chapter 2, is also non-rational in important ways.) In addition, though, human divisions are based on something ethically wrong or sinful: valuing our own characteristics too much, and other people (who are equally children of God) too little. That is, universalism reminds us of our common humanity, of the ways in which we are equal and alike.

Joseph Krieger puts this implication of universalism clearly: "If we love our neighbor, then we are honoring God, because we are God's children. And if people could only learn to follow that concept, why I guess there'd be very little antagonism and wars." He specifically condemns divisions between Catholics and Protestants in Ireland. James O'Connell, similarly, condemns hostility between Whites and African-Americans, and between Jews and Italians. Several respondents speak, as does Catherine Kennedy, of how we should show love and provide care for people "whether we know them or not," whether we have ever met them, and whether we like or approve of them or not; all are children of God. The Quaker William Westfield sums up this perspective elegantly in a statement we have already seen, where he says that pacifism, like the other Quaker testimonies, is based on "the assumption that there is that potential that we think of as God in every person, and the possibility of touching that or finding communion with that in any other person we ever encounter." Here universalism, which in William's thought grounds radically egalitarian views, is stated in terms of God's presence inside us—a relationship to God more abstract, but if anything even closer, than being God's child.

Universalism and Love

In many ways, the uses the respondents make of the themes of universalism and love are similar or complementary. Both can be used to stress the importance of human solidarity; both can support communal values for economic life and be used to oppose individualistic ones. Both are frequently used as a basis for supporting welfare state programs or even public guarantees of a minimum living standard for all. Furthermore, universalism helps define the scope of love. Love says we are to care for our brothers, sisters, and neighbors. Universalism tells us that this includes every person—the Samaritan just as much as our biological siblings and our physical neighbors.

Yet it can make a big difference when Christians use these two themes together rather than basing a communal approach to economic life only on the value of love. This is one way of describing the difference between the egalitarian and sometimes radical language just described, and the two languages—especially the corporatistic one—described in chapter 4. In a radical vision, the way in which we get a society where there can be more solidarity and community is to break down the structures of inequality that divide us. Some of the respondents have aspirations that go in this direction. Thomas

Gaffney, for example, sees a thoroughgoing equalization of human living standards and power as a basic precondition for the sense of community he desires so strongly. Catherine Kennedy, expressing a more typical stance, is deeply committed, on the basis of Christian universalism, to the "rights" that each person should be able to claim as a child of God. To her, Whites and African-Americans are "brothers" in an abstract community that does not yet exist. She is not very interested in promoting solidarity within our currently existing social structure, except for the solidarity that arises among people working together for racial justice, crossing racial lines and thereby prefiguring the society she hopes for.

Most people would like to see a more loving society, a situation where conflict and especially violence could be reduced. But this aspiration can have varying political meanings. It can ground views with a significant conservative component when people do not regard actual differences of interest among social groups as major factors contributing to violence and conflict, think that these differences are almost always amenable to a compromise that will seem fair to all parties, or put the goal of harmony above that of deciding which inequalities are unjust and then remedying them. For corporatists, the main problem is our disharmony; they give less attention to the sources of disharmony. That source, of course, is largely our differences—cultural and economic, rational and non-rational. Humans have diverse values, beliefs, and cultures, and many Christians see this as a gift from God, even though it sometimes makes life more difficult. But we also have diverse interests, and sometimes find that our particular interests, or those of a group we belong to, seem much more important or ethically valid than "pulling together" with everyone else on behalf of the interests we share with other people and groups in our society. Corporatists want to remedy this situation by a combination of more justice imposed by those at the top and a greater spirit of solidarity on everyone's part. Christian radicals, at the extreme, tend to say that this is falling into the trap of pretending that we are not fallen, or that the Kingdom has already come, and can lend too much legitimacy to the current state of affairs. Radicals tend to focus on our solidarity within a new, abstract, non-empirical community. When people think corporatistically, on the contrary, they often hope for more solidarity within existing communities (the neighborhood or parish, for instance), which can sometimes be unified largely by race or ethnicity and have shared values radicals would despise (authoritarian, nationalistic, sexist, or racist ones). Or, when people think corporatistically, they may hope for solidarity in imagined communities of traditional kinds: a nation that has some of the feelings of a "family," for instance, or families as they are thought to have existed in the past.

When people think universalistically without making much use of the value of Christian love, at the other extreme, one possibility—not much seen among the respondents, but visible in parallel secular languages—is that they may devalue all traditional and non-rational forms of solidarity. In Marx's view, this was an important historical function of the capitalist market: to destroy all nationalistic, ethnic, and religious bonds, putting each person alone in the market, while creating the potential for new bonds based on the modern, universalistic criterion of class. In his words:

> The bourgeoisie has played a most revolutionary part in history. . . . Wherever it has got the upper hand, [it] has put an end to all feudal, patriarchal, idyllic relations. . . . It has drowned the most heavenly ecstasies of religious fervor, of chivalrous enthusiasm, of philistine sentimentalism, in the icy water of egotistical calculation. . . . The bourgeoisie has torn away from the family its sentimental veil. . . . National one-sidedness and narrow-mindedness become more and more impossible.[3]

The same historical trajectory can be promoted by Marxists. The sociologist Yudit Jung, describing conflicts within the revolutionary movement in the period before the Russian Revolution, shows how Lenin embraced a strict universalism that allowed no place for a politically significant Jewish identity within a socialist movement or nation, since this would be a religious or ethnic identity, cutting across class lines and undermining the single-minded unity of purpose required for the revolutionary struggle. (Clearly Lenin's position was based not just on a thoroughgoing universalism but also on his belief that only a highly centralized party could make a successful revolution.) In the view of Lenin and his allies, a socialist revolution would abolish anti-Semitism and the need for any separate ethnic identity. Jung, believing that ethnicity is a constitutive part of human identity and that ethnic/national self-determination is a key form of human liberation, recalls to memory the proposals of the Jewish Bund—proposals that expressed a vision of a democratic, socialist, multi-cultural society. In the 1990s, with *glasnost,* she hopes that the debate terminated by Lenin can begin anew, in ways that allow both the claims of our common humanity and of our cultural particularity to be respected.[4] Recent developments in the Soviet Union and formerly communist countries of Eastern Europe suggest the difficulties involved in finding ways to reconcile these claims.

Taking a somewhat parallel position, critics of American assimilationism and conformism argue that there has been little toleration of genuine cultural differences in the United States. In this view, American culture, like the bourgeoisie as Marx saw it and the Leninists described by Jung, and despite our quiltlike ethnic, religious and cultural diversity, often tends toward devaluation of differences.[5]

The kind of strict universalism just described, which opposes non-rational bases for solidarity, has individualistic overtones; as we saw in chapter 2, this is quite "logical," given the theological kinship between universalism and voluntarism. The language of economic rights also manifests the individualistic side of universalism, and this kind of individualism can help support radical visions. Universalistic thinking supports people when they assert "rights," helping them say, "This situation is unjust; we have a right to be treated equally and with dignity." Non-Whites can use Christian universalism to support their claims on our whole society. This goes against the corporatistic idea that people should not press their claims through social conflict, or "demand" things. Universalistic thinking reinforces not only economic but cultural and political egalitarianism, helping people to question authority and to value their own opinions and capacity for affecting the world.

Universalism and Individualism in Welfare State Politics

In chapter 2, we pointed out that voluntarism and universalism reflect much the same theological premises. That the social distinctions dividing us—race, gender, and so on—are religiously irrelevant means that we are all (as the religious phrase goes) "one in the Lord," but it also means that our Christian identity is established for each individual separately, and that traditional community structures may seem less important. The common parentage of universalism and voluntarism is apparent whenever people talk about the rights of humans or citizens: these rights concern individual freedom but are universal. Ideas of economic rights—the "entitlements" of the welfare state—are an extension of this way of thinking to economic life. In a secular context, legal theorist Charles Reich expresses this possibility in a particularly strong form when he argues for the civil liberties of welfare recipients by asserting that welfare benefits are "the new property."[6] Property, he says, is a sphere of freedom from arbitrary government action, and so he tries to protect welfare recipients by conceptualizing their benefits as a form of property. Note in Reich's perspective how an individualistic approach to economic life can actually serve *liberal* political purposes.

Reich's position may sound extreme, but in practice welfare state programs can have individualistic outcomes—which can be seen as liberating or privatizing, depending on one's point of view. When disability befalls people, for instance, if they can depend on benefits they receive on an impersonal basis from the government, as a matter of "right," they can feel a certain sense of dignity, are not beholden to their relatives or private charities, and can continue an independent existence. When people retire, if they have social security they need not depend on or live with their children. One could evaluate the consequences as gains for individual dignity and freedom, or as attenuation of social bonds, but in any case individuation is the result. Liberals tend to favor this kind of individuation, even though they may attack what they see as excesses of individual freedom in other aspects of economic life. At the same time, as we have seen, the reasons Christians cite for supporting social welfare programs usually have a strongly communal component; such programs are an institutional means of expressing our solidarity with one another, and of fulfilling the universalistic mandate to respect the dignity of every child of God.

The English social theorist T. H. Marshall takes a position that, compared with Reich's, has more of the balance of individualistic and communal elements found in Christian universalism. He articulates a set of rights that he says have evolved as part of our sense of citizenship. One component of these is economic: rights to education, housing, medical care, and the like. These basic resources are due to individuals as members of the community, and he points out explicitly that they are based on status or ascription, not achievement—on the simple fact of having been born or living in a country, without having to merit anything. The playwright W. S. Gilbert makes the same case by *reductio ad absurdum,* satirically describing citizenship as something one achieves in the well-known song "He is an Englishman!" from *H.M.S. Pinafore.*[7] Because the rights of citizenship are rooted in community membership, not individual deserts, they should not be asserted in a way that contradicts the needs of others or the community. According to Marshall's logic, for instance, in a time of severe recession it would not make sense to hold to one's absolute right to receive cost-of-living increases in government benefits, as if this were a contractual right like cost-of-living increases for earned income negotiated by one's union. At the same time, the rights of citizenship are appropriately claimed by individuals. Thus Marshall's language, like that of economic rights when rooted in Christian universalism, has both communal and individualistic components.

Economic Democracy and the Voluntaristic Component in the Language of Economic Rights

Although the dominant Christian themes supporting the language of economic rights are love and universalism (with the latter grounding both communal and individualistic but still liberal perspectives), this language can also have voluntaristic overtones. Among the respondents, this comes out most clearly in Thomas Gaffney's thinking, when he speaks about empowerment of quiescent day laborers, sharecroppers, and tenant and small farmers in the Philippines. (Michael Butros, Catherine Kennedy, and Linda Watson make occasional remarks with a similar tone.) Here, Thomas is close to the perspective of United States movements that are working for "economic democracy." The idea of economic rights, when linked with social welfare programs and the idea of equality, means a goal of maintaining the dignity of every child of God by equalizing economic outcomes or providing resources for consumption—food, housing, medical care, and so forth. Thomas Gaffney goes further; like economic democracy activists, he wants to work for broader participation in the making of economic decisions that affect our lives. This way of thinking is heir to the New Left of the 1960s, and of course to the long tradition of radical democracy and populism in the United States.[8]

The perspective of economic democracy has both communal and individualistic components. It is communal in that it envisages an economic order in which we would make many decisions *together*—in workplaces, communities, and the nation—and so decisions would be less private and more social than they are now. Allocation of productive resources among competing purposes would be driven not just by the individual consumer decisions about what to buy that govern allocations in a market system but by self-conscious social decisions based on our values as a community. Furthermore, economic democracy advocates envisage *discussions*—an interactive, public process, much less private than voting—as a prime way for citizens to be involved in making decisions.

This perspective also contains significant individualistic components, however. Economic democracy activists argue that what we have in the United States is a despotic economic system in which a small elite makes the important decisions and dictates to everyone else. One of their prime goals is to recover the power of ordinary, individual Americans to affect their fate, to be self-determining. Some critics, such as Robert Bellah and his co-authors of *Habits of the Heart,* argue that "economic democracy" lacks a substantive vision of social justice and of a good economic order. According to this critique, economic democracy essentially says that we should have whatever economic arrangements emerge from democratic discussions among us: whatever arrangements, therefore, most individuals want, assessing their own priorities (for themselves and for the whole community) as individuals (in the context of discussions with others, however). In other words, because it is first of all concerned with democracy rather than justice, economic democracy remains an individualistic perspective in important respects. A similar analysis could be made of contemporary versions of "populism" articulated by some left-of-center thinkers. In fact, on the left there has been extensive debate over the past fifteen years or so of the relative importance of talking about democracy and equality.[9]

Conclusion: Variety in the Uses of Universalism

As we have seen, universalism can be used in quite radical ways: to favor sharing of wealth or even the kind of communism practiced by the apostles; to advocate greater equality than we have now, as a way of overcoming the divisions of wealth and status that always threaten to alienate us from one another; and to say that we have strong obligations to the weak, untalented, and even the "unworthy," for all are children of God.

Such potentials, however, are not always realized. For fire fighter James O'Connell, as we saw, racial discrimination is to be opposed more because it manifests lack of love and creates hostility than because it violates a God-given equality. Therefore he is uncomfortable with assertions of "rights" by

African-Americans. Joseph Krieger, on the other hand, does apply universalistic thinking strongly to race relations but not to economic inequality more generally. The equality we possess as children of God, he makes clear, is a spiritual equality. In Philomena Jackson's classical understanding of universalism, similarly, there are no economic implications drawn. The equality she and Joseph favor might be described as our equal opportunity to be saved, regardless of our economic situation. That is, one can take universalism to apply only or primarily to spiritual life; that in Christ there is no slave or free, male or female, and so on, means that our religious status does not depend on our earthly, "material" one. People in all stations of life are equally children of God and valuable in God's eyes. Whatever inequalities may exist in other spheres of life, they fall away in our religious life; we do not need to deal with material inequality in order to be religiously equal. Such a view is certainly less conservative (and probably more true to the spirit of Jesus' teaching) than thinking, as some Christians do, that the rich are especially favored by God, but it has few implications—political or ethical—for economic life.

We saw in chapter 2 that universalism is modern and "rational," but not in every way. As Christians understand it, we all have equal value because of a supernatural fact: our shared relationship to God. That relationship gives us a "holy" and noble status, by birth, not by achievement, just as if we were the child of a powerful monarch. Our value and self-esteem are based on our standing with our heavenly parent. Thus, the imagery of the principle of universalism is partly familial and partly that of the system of inherited status of the feudal world. Furthermore, it rests on our relationship with God, a non-empirical reality.

As we have seen before with other strands of Christian faith, the traditional, not so modern, not so rational characteristics of the principle of universalism are not necessarily obstacles to liberal or radical politics. They help Linda Watson face down the cues of the marketplace—which tell her she is of little value—as she asserts rights to economic assistance and actively participates in political life. On the other hand, the "modern" elements in universalism can serve to support liberal politics. They help people transcend "traditional" forms of social solidarity—those based on ethnicity, race, or gender exclusion; neighborhood, region, or nation—and form new bonds on new bases. This is what the early Christians did in the church, and it is what universalistic Christians do today when they try to build interracial organizations to work for justice.

Economic Freedom

A fourth major way in which the Christians in this study relate their faith to economic issues remains to be examined: the language of economic freedom, which we have already seen in the thinking of David Jenkins and Richard Schenk. In this perspective, most of the communal themes we have discussed hitherto are missing; the individualistic side of universalism and the economic implications of voluntarism are emphasized.

George Hoffman, the economically conservative mainline Protestant among the "extreme-type" respondents, expresses this perspective in a rich and sophisticated way. George is a good contrast to the Franciscan Thomas Gaffney, since he and Thomas are the only respondents who have had theological education, and he can articulate the "logical" implications of his faith perspective in a clear and persuasive way. At the time he was interviewed, he was in his early forties and working as an accountant for a non-profit organization. Thus, unlike some who speak strongly for the superiority of capitalist economic organization, he does not maximize his income but puts other concerns first. Thereby he presents a good example of exactly the principle that is fundamental to his thinking: the value of choice. This does not apply only to economic life. Asked to describe what a good society in Christian terms would be like, he says that it would be one "where lifestyles are as varied as anyone wants them to be."

George speaks of the primacy of free choice, and how this is rooted in his faith, over and over. One of the most arresting examples is his exegesis of the biblical story of Jesus' temptation in the wilderness—a story he returns to several times in the interview. In Luke's version, Jesus, after his baptism, spent forty days fasting in the wilderness; refused the devil's suggestion to turn stone into bread; and then resisted an even greater temptation:

> Then the devil led him up, and showed him in an instant all the kingdoms of the world. And the devil said to him, "To you I will give their glory and all this authority; for it has been given over to me, and I give it to anyone I please. If you, then, will worship me, it will all be yours." Jesus answered him, "It is written, 'Worship the Lord your God, and serve only him.' " (Luke 4:5–8)

One could concentrate on many different strands of this story: Jesus' refusal to do miracles to establish his status or satisfy his hunger, his rejection of earthly goals and glory, and so on. But for George, the key point is that "Jesus specifically rejected the worldly controls over other people in the wilderness, where he rejected the political power to make people do the right thing." A minute later, he says, "My whole political, economical, ethical response comes out of letting people be free to be themselves, using all your powers of persuasion for them to do the right thing, but rejecting the control over their lives. And that flows straight out of Jesus' experience in the wilderness." In the story, Jesus says he refuses the devil because the conditions under which he will give Jesus power contradict the first two commandments: the rule against idolatry, against worshiping what is not God, or things of this world. For George, the refusal is equally because of what the devil offered: political power. Rejecting political power is one of the most basic ways in which we stay clear of idolatry, of being seduced by the things of this world. The idolatry Jesus avoided, the worldly path he rejected, was the approach to solving human problems that relies on political power as a coercive instrument. Thus, George says that "the tyrannous power of the modern state is the greatest threat to Christian society there is."

Expressing this religiously grounded view in terms much like John Stuart Mill's, George says: "Only when it impinges on other people's freedom have we a right to restrict somebody else's." This principle governs every aspect of his thinking. Applied to economic life, it yields a perspective that he explicitly sums up as the principle of "economic freedom." Thus, "political power is far more demonic than economic power, because it's more concentrated; . . . socialism is very anti-Christian, in the sense that it's an attempt to substitute political power for economic power." Private enterprises deserve maximum autonomy; economic freedom is a right (in this way he differs from David Jenkins, who is more concerned with economic freedom as a condition for people's spiritual and ethical growth).

George is strongly opposed to attempts to create greater equality: "I do not believe that equality of opportunity means equality of result, and I don't believe it should." There should be "equal opportunity under the law," but not any compensation for the different life chances of those born poor and rich, and no compensation for historic discrimination: "I'm very much opposed to affirmative action; I think it's demonic and racist and sexist." The term *demonic* is theological and uncompromising, showing how strongly felt and grounded in faith his views are.

The Conservative Side of Universalism

George Hoffman's views on equality show how the principle of universalism can be used to support a conservative, meritocratic position, in which the idea of equal opportunity is understood quite narrowly. George's hostility toward all affirmative action, for instance, is grounded in the idea that the law should be strictly color-blind. It is, he says, a matter of "theological fact that all Black people are full human beings with all rights and privileges of society." This does not mean "equal result, but equal opportunity and equal humanity." He favors anti-discrimination laws in employment, but regards affirmative action programs as demonic and racist because they are race-conscious.

George's way of understanding universalism is quite congruent with the spirit of capitalism, and quite opposed to the value of love. The love ethic, after all, tells us to reward one another *regardless* of deserts, in response to need, not ability. George takes the principle of universalism to one logical conclusion, where it entails a social ethic of strict distributive justice in which each person—dealt with as a solitary individual, independent of all social categories and groups—gets exactly what he or she deserves by virtue of merit. Whereas the values of love and universalism complement and support each other in the thinking of people like Thomas Gaffney and Catherine Kennedy, for George they have opposite implications.

George's position here is quite logical (although hardly the only logical appropriation of universalism) and is parallel to arguments that are often heard in secular contexts using terms such as *reverse discrimination*. However, none of the other respondents expressed this understanding of universalism. Where they related faith to conservative economic views, they drew on other strands of Christian tradition. The respondents who did talk in universalistic terms either did not relate this theme to economic life (Philomena Jackson would be an example) or, more frequently, related it to egalitarian views.

Voluntarism: Freedom as the Central Value for Economic Life

The most frequent way in which conservative views on economic life are grounded in faith is through the value of freedom. A great many respondents take freedom to be the central value for social life in general, grounding this conviction in faith and applying it to economic affairs as one aspect of life. Faith, for such people, supports the language of economic freedom in an indirect but nonetheless important way, by grounding a generalized allegiance to freedom.

Most of the respondents speak of freedom spontaneously, without ever being asked. Many also express voluntaristic religious or ethical views, and there is usually a link between these views and the respondents' preference for freedom. Obviously there are many sources for the commitment most Americans have to individual freedom; still, Christian tradition is an important source for many.

The form of freedom with the most obvious link to faith is freedom of religion. Of course, religious perspectives can be opposed to religious freedom. The Roman Catholic church until fairly recently opposed the kind of separation of church and state Americans tend to favor, and some Christians today want prayer in public schools, which could well be argued to be an infringement on religious liberty. Nonetheless, voluntaristic understandings of faith are a great support for religious freedom in the United States today—one might even argue, a more politically potent source of support than secular ideas about separating church and state.

Many respondents mention this freedom, but the striking fact is that most understand it quite narrowly: in almost every case, they speak only of one's right to attend the church of one's choice. It becomes a right parallel to the right to buy the products of one's choice, or understood within analogies between religious freedom and other freedoms of private choice. Hardly anyone speaks of broader, more public-oriented forms of religious freedom, such as the right of people of all religious persuasions (including humanists and atheists) to be recognized as conscientious objectors to military service, or of churches to speak and organize against public policies they oppose, without governmental retribution. As one put it, "I appreciate the freedom that we have, and especially freedom to worship," or in the view of another, "We in this country are really fortunate to have a government which lets us be a church."

Sometimes, respondents speak of more than one kind of freedom in the same breath, include them together in a list, or even make analogies between them. When they do this, they make an implicit comparison, which provides clues as to how they understand each kind of freedom. For instance, Susan Wainwright says, "I feel proud of the fact that there really is freedom of choice in this country in many areas, including religion." A Catholic describes how thankful she is for our "freedom of speech, freedom of religion, freedom of opportunity." Susan's statement conceptualizes religious freedom in terms of "choice," which has overtones of private, individual decision making. The second statement does make an analogy between religious freedom and freedom of speech—a public form of freedom—but also between religious freedom and what she here calls "freedom of opportunity," by which (it turns out as the interview continues) she means private enterprise. About one-quarter of the respondents compare freedom of religion to other freedoms, and the comparisons indicate that they tend to think of religious freedom in essentially private terms. Of the comparisons they make, only one-third are to even the most basic kinds of public freedom, such as the right to vote. Another third are to economic freedoms (such as the right to choose one's line of work), and the final third to freedoms of private action (to follow different lifestyles, do "whatever you want," and so forth).

Obviously freedom of religion is only one aspect of a free society. For David Jenkins, Richard Schenk, and George Hoffman, voluntaristic religious and ethical beliefs have much broader implications: they are the guiding criteria for many or all aspects of social life. In this these three respondents are not alone. Phyllis MacIntyre, the Presbyterian engineer, puts this view in classical form: "According to Christianity, an ideal society would be a state where you don't need policemen, because no one would step on somebody else's rights." Similarly, she believes, "There would be no need for law because once you love your neighbor as yourself you would not need that as a determining factor." In short, if people act out of a well-formed Christian conscience, we will not need coercion; in fact, we will not need much government or any enduring institutions with the power to constrain individuals. Almost all of life can become private and spontaneous. Thus, in her way of thinking, as for many Christians influenced by the voluntaristic strand of Christian tradition, freedom is equated with minimizing restraints on private choices.

If individual freedom is one's central social value, it is easy to conclude that our economic arrangements should be guided by this principle. Government interference in the economy should be kept to a minimum; businesses and consumers should be free to do more or less whatever they want. Free enterprise is a good thing, in the view of one evangelical, "because part of what makes up a person is the freedom to be able to get into whatever kind of business they want to, to make a go of it or not." Or on the consumer end, "Having your own home is wonderful, because then you can do what you want."

Notice that in these statements—and many others not quoted—the key point is not that a free market is efficient; these people may think that it is, but that is not the argument they make. Rather, their concern is to maximize individual freedom, as an end in itself. This concern, typically, does not just apply to economic issues. Asked what the disadvantages of socialism were, one respondent replied, "To me it's more like a dictatorship, where I don't think we'd have the advantages we have in our democracy, and there would be a few people who are making the rules and benefiting by them." Unions are sometimes opposed by respondents, usually because they are too coercive and powerful; for instance, one says that "unions are almost telling us how to live."

The statement quoted a moment ago about the importance of our freedom of speech, religion, and opportunity, along with many others, shows how economic freedom fits into a general adherence to freedom as a central social value. Similarly, the statement about socialism as "dictatorship" makes a connection between economic and political freedom. Picking up more directly on ethical voluntarism, a somewhat disaffected evangelical complains in parallel terms (although at different points in the interview) about the moral regulations—no dancing and so forth—her church placed on her, and the government regulations she and her husband are facing in the course of trying to start a small business. In all these connections, we see how ethical voluntarism, a focus on individual freedom, and economic individualism can be tied together in a common concern that individuals be able to make autonomous decisions.

Not every way of understanding and valuing economic freedom is conservative, as we saw in the case of ideas of "economic democracy." But if one concentrates on freedom to make private, separate decisions with no restraints, and thinks of business enterprises as being essentially like individuals, one is apt to draw conservative conclusions from applying the value of freedom to economic life. The connections between faith and such views take varying forms. Some respondents, like David Jenkins, Richard Schenk, and George Hoffman, make the link quite plain. Others, like Phyllis MacIntyre, explicitly link a general social value of freedom to faith, and then apply that value to economic affairs; here the connection to faith is indirect. For still others the connections are not made in such a logical, deductive manner but are visible more in analogies and overtones by which free enterprise comes to share in the honor and approbation given to other kinds of social freedom, and to the fundamental freedom a Christian needs: to follow conscience in matters of faith.

Self-reliance

A voluntaristic perspective emphasizes individual freedom but also individual responsibility. If we are ethically autonomous, we are free from external constraints, but at the same time we are directly accountable to God for following the right path. We cannot take refuge in saying, "I was only following orders," unless the orders are from God. People like David Jenkins focus on our responsibility to take care of others. Many more respondents, however, speak of our responsibility to take care of ourselves, to be self-reliant and independent in our economic lives.

A middle-aged Catholic woman shows the link between ethical voluntarism and self-reliance clearly. She struggled for years with the issue of birth control, and the struggle was especially acute because she had been advised that a pregnancy would be dangerous for her. Eventually she concluded that the church would not take responsibility for her family if she should die, and decided, "You've got to take care of your own self. There's nobody else." This statement, in context, is one aspect of how she decided, in good voluntaristic fashion, that she could put God above the church and make a morally correct decision against church law. This has nothing to do with the glorification of self-interest that is often associated with talking about self-reliance, but it does lead her to feel that she has to take care of herself and her family's material needs without outside help.

Sometimes there is an explicit link between religious and economic self-reliance. We have seen that in Joseph Krieger and Richard Schenk, and it comes out in other respondents, as well. For instance, early in the interview a Methodist said that "no man can help you into heaven; you've got to do that on your own," and then, a few minutes later, "I believe anybody can work if they will get out and apply themselves." Or as another Methodist said, "Doors open, and it's up to us either to go through them or not. God opens doors; that's a figure of speech, of course. But opportunities come, and it's our responsibility to either take advantage of them or ignore them." Later, making the connection between religious and economic self-reliance explicit, he says that when he hit bottom economically, "it was up to me to figure out a way to start crawling back up"; others, he thinks, can do the same. "God helps those who help themselves," says a Baptist, and she goes on at length about what this means (the phrase is from Benjamin Franklin's *Poor Richard's Almanac*); apparently God expects us to make our own way in the world, pushing ahead competitively and individualistically, on our own. Nothing can intervene between us and God in our spiritual lives, and similarly, nothing can intervene between us and the market in our economic lives. In both arenas, self-help is the order of the day. In all these respondents' statements, voluntaristic thinking serves to support the idea of economic self-reliance.

The theological perspective implicit in some of these statements comes out of a strand of Christian thought, often called "Arminianism," that emphasizes (as against Lutheran and Calvinist ideas of grace) our own role in determining whether we will be saved or not. Some historians of American religion have argued that the development of American capitalism produced a lack of fit between people's experiences and the older Calvinist theologies. The Arminian tendencies in American evangelicalism were persuasive in part because they matched the experiences and needs of people in their new situations better than the old orthodoxy did. In particular, they paralleled the assumption of individual self-determination and responsibility for one's own economic fate that characterized the new, more mobile and capitalistic economic order, in which one's fate was not predestined and could change rapidly. This kind of historical argument implies that one could expect to find Arminian religious themes alongside statements of economic self-reliance. This is certainly true among the respondents in this study; repeatedly, we find parallel statements about self-help in the economic and religious realms.[10]

Social Life as the Sum of Individual Choices

Americans pay little attention to the ways in which social and cultural forces affect our lives, and this has a major impact on how we think and talk about economic questions. Geoffrey Hawthorne, a historian of social thought, writes that "the only social institutions" we are aware of are

> property and the state. . . . Americans [have] no firm grasp of what from England to China has always been taken for granted, . . . that there are if not immutable then certainly enduring complexes of institutions that do not merely . . . serve to constrain individuals, but by virtue of the individual's membership in them from birth to death serve in good part to constitute and define him as a person.[11]

This tendency undoubtedly has many sources, but voluntaristic religious thinking is one, in that it emphasizes our direct relationship to God as over against any social connections that might help define our personality and identity. Thinking of social life as the sum of individual choices is consonant with the central role the self-determining individual plays in the religious drama as scripted by Christians thinking voluntaristically. Our religious identity, for instance, is established by our personal experience with God. We try to be autonomous individuals, capable of making decisions that are influenced only by God, not our social environment. In addition, biblical literalism is logical only on the premise that humans do, or at least can, receive God's word in a way not significantly affected by their historical and cultural settings.

Hitherto we have mostly seen the ethical implications of voluntarism. Here we are dealing with a more "cognitive" or "descriptive" perspective. Applied to economic life, this perspective implies that individual efforts and decisions can control most of what happens—so that if people are poor, for example, it is their own doing—which supports ideas of self-reliance. We have seen an instance of such thinking in Joseph Krieger's rather Arminian view of how salvation comes about, which he links to his conviction (quoted in chapter 1) that in America "you can really lift yourself up by the bootstraps if you're willing to work." The other side of this cognitive framework is a considerable degree of blindness to the importance of the institutions and social structures within which we live, in determining our fate and personality and defining our identity.[12] The only structural force given much attention is racism; the respondents often speak of racial discrimination as a reality. Yet they still often hold African-Americans responsible for their poverty. And very few speak of other ways in which the fate of individuals is, in fact, strongly affected by structural phenomena such as unemployment rates or the mechanisms permitting the relatively affluent to transmit their status with reasonable predictability to their children.

Views in which the only significant forces are individual decisions are found among most of the respondents—even liberal and radical ones. For instance, the Quaker William Westfield, who wants major changes in our society, says that first each of us has to decide to change his or her lifestyle in the direction of simpler living. David Jenkins, as we have seen, thinks the way to bring about change is to lead an exemplary life. If we would "turn to God" and get "our hearts fixed on the right things," another evangelical thinks, everything would be put right. A woman who experiences sexual discrimination at work says there isn't anything the government can or should do about it, because "that's just people; it's all individuals and they have a right to think the way they want to."

Similarly, for many respondents, a good society means simply one where people treat each other well in their one-to-one relationships. A good society, says one, is where we "get back to just love and family. Love of your husband, your home, your neighbors, just pure love. If we ever got back to that, we'd have no problems." Or in the view of a fairly liberal Catholic, "If you really care about your fellow man, that would solve everything." Such views are found among people with varying amounts of schooling, and among evangelicals, mainline Protestants, and Catholics alike.

When people hold such views, any criticism they may make of patterns of economic life is likely to be at the level of personal morality. The use of government is not just a violation of individual freedom but also useless, since it does not get at the root of the problem: individual sinfulness and bad choices. In chapter 6, we will see how these views affect beliefs about the means we should use to seek social change, and in chapter 3 we saw how they could be used to separate faith from politics. Here, the main point is that they provide another set of reasons to oppose public intervention in economic life, and to favor leaving all economic decisions in the hands of individuals.

Ethical Voluntarism and the Relativism of the Market

In chapter 2, we explored in some detail the relativistic ways in which many of the respondents interpret their voluntaristic approach to ethical issues. For George Hoffman, this is directly linked to favoring the market. "The basic power in a market economy is the right of the person doing the buying to reject" a product. Recall that George also hopes for a society "where lifestyles are as varied as anyone wants them to be." The market is a key place where personal and private decisions about lifestyles or priorities can wield their power. George is right in seeing the market as a place where personal or at least private decisions are instrumental; as a social mechanism, what it does best is to respond flexibly and efficiently to the desires of those who put dollars into purchasing goods and services. The market is neutral and relativistic; it does not inquire as to the origin or validity of the desires it responds to. It is a perfect democracy, if one dollar (not one *person*) is one vote and we do not think we require discussions about our use of resources but are willing simply to sum up dollar-backed private desires. There is a rather good correspondence between these characteristics of the market and the relativistic, subjectivistic ways of thinking about ethical issues we saw in chapter 2. Ethical decisions, in the view of many respondents, are not subject to discussion and cannot be judged by others; they are a private, unaccountable act of each separate individual. We should not be judgmental or moralize about the choices others make. The market fulfills these mandates nicely. The operational relativism of the market, then, is religiously and ethically more acceptable when people's ethical thinking is fairly relativistic. Among the respondents, the ones who voice explicit complaints about how the market works or about people's behaving in market-oriented ways tend to be persons with traditional ethical and religious ideas, such as Philomena Jackson. Their traditional ideas give them a basis for condemning the outcomes of the market and rejecting the relativism with which it operates.

Rarer Perspectives: Pessimism and Economic Conservatism

Three other ways of thinking about economic life occurred less often than the ones discussed so far, but often enough to deserve mention. These all come out of one or another form of pessimism—sometimes explicitly grounded in faith, sometimes only consonant with it—about the human condition. These views tend to ground conservative economic opinions.

The first is a focus on economic self-reliance *not* based on a concern for freedom. Usually, when people speak in favor of self-reliance they do so because they favor individual freedom and responsibility. But occasionally they speak of self-reliance because they are pessimistic about the world, and especially about the capacity of humans to solve problems. For instance, Victor Santiago works to support himself and his family, and not for any wider purpose, because (he believes) there is no wider purpose humans can fulfill in their work lives, given how disordered the world is. Furthermore, he believes that the present world order is falling apart, and therefore self-reliance is essential for survival. To give another example: a mainline Protestant who feels intensely how much God controls our lives says that "God takes care of the world; I can't. We're dependent upon God, and we're dependent upon ourselves"—but apparently not upon one another—"which are the guidelines I try to live by." So each person has to look out for her or himself, simply because the world cannot be expected to do any better; for now, we have to survive on our own.

A second, related theme is the necessity for restrictive policies about social welfare programs—in essence, for not getting carried away by the implications of the love ethic—based on pessimism about human nature. We have already seen this in Joseph Krieger and the fire fighter James O'Connell, and it crops up in several other respondents. Usually such statements occur without any reference to the Fall or other religious imagery about human nature, and so it is not clear to what extent they are grounded in faith.

The last of these themes is pessimism about improving the human condition—specifically, the economic order—through any kind of efforts, public or private. Such views make a few respondents feel that what we have is as good as we are likely to get, thereby legitimating our present economic arrangements.

Varying Implications of Faith

We have heard from four principal languages that relate faith to economic issues. One (economic freedom) is clearly conservative, one (corporatism) mixed, one (sharing) moderately liberal, and one (equality/rights) liberal to radical. Of these perspectives, only economic freedom is primarily individualistic, although the language of equality and economic rights has some individualistic components. Table 5-1 displays some of the characteristics of these four languages.

The two more conservative languages—corporatism and economic freedom—are almost diametrically opposed; their conservatism is based on different values, and their tone is quite different. Voluntaristic ideas are so basic, especially in Protestantism, that they appear axiomatic until one en-

Table 5-1. Key Languages Linking Faith to Economic Issues

Language	Political stand	Basic values	Main building blocks used
Corporatism	Mixed	Communal	Christian love
Sharing and caring	Moderately liberal	Communal	Christian love
Equality and rights	Strongly liberal	Mixed	Love, universalism, voluntarism
Economic freedom	Conservative	Individualistic	Universalism, voluntarism

counters a different view. They do not require any suspension of disbelief, commitment to Jesus, or acceptance of the authority of the church or the Bible. They are propositions that are easy to accept and seem quite modern. For example, the idea that religion and ethical decision making are very private matters seems completely non-controversial—just common sense— to most Americans. Those who make private choice their key value for social life and apply that perspective to economic issues may encounter opposition to their conclusions but usually not to their premises. Joseph Krieger's point of view, on the other hand, would sound old-fashioned and restrictive to many Americans, and it relies heavily on direct and explicit references to the specific religious premises of his Roman Catholic tradition.

On the liberal side there is no such opposition of basic values. The different themes and values grounding liberal economic views—love, universalism, and occasionally voluntarism; communal values and occasionally individualistic ones—shade into and mostly complement each other (with some exceptions that we have seen).

Both conservative and liberal views on economic issues are regularly and strongly grounded in faith; far from being irrelevant to these issues, faith serves both sides of public debate in significant ways. By bringing fundamental ethical values into how people think and talk about economic life, the resources of faith enrich public discourse. But they have no single meaning; Christian faith is ineradicably multi-implicational. Debate among Christians about the social implications of faith sometimes stalls, from fear of conflict or views favoring compartmentalization, but not because there is consensus among Christians; debate among Christians is potentially at least as intense as debates in the political arena about economic justice issues.

Furthermore, the ways in which *both* liberal and conservative views are grounded in faith are "logical" and "authentic": most of the time, they are reasonable and legitimate uses of ideas that any Christian—Catholic or Protestant, modernist or traditionalist—would find acceptable if expressed in the appropriate dialect. There would not be the same consensus about the *uses* of these shared ideas, but the principal uses have many historical precedents in the thinking of important figures in Christian history. Even though few of the respondents have read Augustine, Aquinas, or Luther, they are able to express ideas reminiscent of such thinkers, drawing on the accumulated traditions of Christianity.

What, then, of the balance between liberal and conservative uses of faith? The respondents for this study are relatively few, and were chosen in a way designed to maximize variety of perspectives; they cannot be used to determine whether the net impact of Christian faith is liberal or conservative. In chapter 7, we will examine data from public opinion polls, and see that they, too, provide no ready answer to the question of the overall political impact of Christian faith with regard to economic issues. In fact, we will discover that the question itself is of dubious relevance and meaningfulness. And as we have seen, Christian faith is multi-vocal.

According to the analysis of Robert Bellah and his colleagues in *Habits of the Heart,* however, the values available in American secular culture for thinking about economic life are predominantly individualistic. Other strands of secular culture are present, and are promoted at times by the labor movement and political movements of the Left. However, even these movements rely on individualistic values much of the time, and when Americans are liberal, it can easily be for somewhat individualistic reasons, as in the secular languages of rights parallel to the Christian perspectives reviewed in this chapter. Communal values are present in America, but they tend to be most apparent either in religious contexts, or when people talk about non-economic concerns such as patriotism and maintaining what are thought to be traditional patterns of family life (patterns that are felt to give priority to self-sacrifice rather than self-interest).

Christian faith, as we have seen, provides strong support for both individualistic and communal values, and properly so even from a radical perspective, since the dignity, freedom of conscience, and self-determination of ordinary individuals is a key goal of the Left. In the uses of Christian faith we have been examining, individualistic and communal strands seem in some balance, with perhaps a slight edge for the communal side. In secular culture, by contrast, the balance appears to be weighted heavily on the individualistic side. When people put on their Christian hat, therefore, they have more chance of bringing communal values to bear on economic life than they do without that hat; Christianity makes a more distinctive contribution to communal thinking about economic life than it does to individualistic thinking. This does not, however, translate directly into political stances, resulting in a favorable balance for liberals; as we have seen, there can be individualistic grounds for liberal views and communal grounds for conservative ones. Still, the tension between Christian values and the way things work in the United States appears greater than for secular values, and even the more conservative perspectives we have encountered in the foregoing two chapters stand in some tension with the dominant forms of individualism found in secular culture.

Both the liberal and conservative uses of faith crosscut theological and denominational lines, drawing on ideas accessible to all kinds of Christians. There are, however, some differences worth noting. The denominational differences have to do more with *why* than with *whether* Christians are conservative. Some Catholics are quite voluntaristic about the church and ethical issues such as birth control, but few apply this to economic life. Consider for a moment just the one-third most economically conservative of the respondents. The few evangelical Protestants in this group are all conservative for voluntaristic reasons, out of an allegiance to freedom of ethical choice. For most but not all of the conservative mainline Protestants, voluntaristic thinking is central. Not one of the economically conservative Catholics, on the other hand, grounds economic views in voluntarism to any significant extent; their conservatism is grounded in corporatism or in the pessimistic ideas described a little while ago. It is also true (as confirmed by public opinion polls) that Catholics are somewhat more liberal economically than Protestants; they appear to be partly immune from the more extreme forms of economic conservatism, which rest on a degree of individualism most Catholics find uncongenial.

Differences between modernists and traditionalists are less evident in the different ways respondents relate faith to economic issues. The theological traditionalists (both Protestant and Catholic) are a little less prone to relativistic thinking and its economically conservative potentials. They are, however, more likely to focus exclusively on the ethic of love in their economic thinking, adopting one of the two languages described in chapter 4 rather than the more radical language of equality and economic rights. And they are a little more likely to adopt a compartmentalized perspective that denies the possibility or validity of grounding any economic views, liberal or conservative, in faith.

If denomination and theological traditionalism/modernism do not matter enormously, what does? The sense in which anything "matters" will require further examination, but if anything does, it is the individual's interpretation and application of the values of voluntarism, love, and universalism. One basic condition affecting the use of any of these values is fluency: Christians who have less capacity to put on their Christian hat, to talk about a variety of questions using the resources of Christian tradition, are less likely to use any of the kinds of languages identified here. With regard to conservative uses of faith, another key condition is whether people use the theme of voluntarism as a template applicable to every issue or—like liberals or Catholics among the respondents—regard economic life as a sphere in which other concerns take precedence. On the liberal side, there are variations in how radical an interpretation people give to the ethic of love. At one extreme, it calls us to a life of self-sacrifice in which we emulate as closely as our nature allows the model of Jesus on the cross; at the other extreme, it is a kind of non-aggression pact, telling us only not to do anything violent or illegal in our economic lives. Furthermore, as we have seen, there are immense variations in Christians' willingness to connect love, as an ethic based in faith, to either public or material questions. Universalism is understood by the respondents in a more uniform way, but George Hoffman is able to give the idea a meritocratic interpretation, and some give it a predominantly spiritual meaning.

The contributions of Christian cultural frameworks to public discourse in the United States rest partly on values specific to the Christian tradition—otherworldliness and Christian love, for instance. Especially in regard to communal values, which are weak in the secular frameworks most readily available to Americans, this is indeed a major contribution. Most of the values for economic life we have examined, however, could be articulated on a secular basis, or on the basis of a religion other than Christianity. Faith adds accessibility to these values and reinforces them, but the values themselves (community, freedom, equality, and so forth) are not uniquely Christian. A partial exception is the ethic of love, which in its classical formulation rejects the pursuit of self-interest far more radically than is easily justified in a naturalistic ethical theory; this is partly why the love ethic has such an old-fashioned tone.

It is a mistake, however, to underrate the importance of what might be called the "religious" character of Christian perspectives on life. It is not just the ethical guidance given by the values held by Christians but also the *ways* in which they are held that provide potentials for how Christians talk and think about economic life. When people think and speak in Christian terms, they look at life in the context of the relationship between humankind and God, and are heirs to a tradition that still possesses a significant component of otherworldliness. Because of their relationship with God, they usually regard certain ethical principles as sacred: principles to be followed not primarily because they are conducive to either the common or individual good but because they are an appropriate response to God. (This can be because certain rules are divinely ordained, but not necessarily; a principle can be seen as a way of presenting God's image to the world, or as a response of gratitude for God's gifts to us.)

These "religious" characteristics of Christian thinking make the impact of love, universalism, and voluntarism different from what they might be if these values were grounded in a purely humanistic tradition. Even voluntaristic thinking, which looks most like the individualistic utilitarianism described in *Habits of the Heart* as rampant in America, has characteristics that set it apart from utilitarianism. The value of freedom, as understood by the voluntaristic respondents, is an absolute principle, not advice on how to organize things most efficiently, or primarily a means to enhance our material well-being. As interpreted by David Jenkins or George Hoffman, voluntaristic organization of the economy is supposed to provide the space for people to make individual choices. However, David and George hope that these choices will be based on values exalting not affluence but spiritual growth, human relationships, and a life rich in meaning. The persuasive power of their viewpoint is probably increased by its otherworldly quality and the fact that it does not glorify self-interest.

A similar quality is found in the other values and languages we have been examining. Joseph Krieger takes work and service to the community to be forms of service to God. Philomena Jackson (talking about usury) and Phyllis MacIntyre (talking about food assistance) are willing to speak in impractical terms—in a language very different from that used among public officials in Washington when discussing the costs and benefits of policy alternatives—about how economic life should be organized. Philomena posits a non-empirical "better" kind of reality than what we see around us when she says that "in front of the cross we're all equal," implicitly contrasting "in front of the cross" to "in the world." When Linda Watson refers to the idea that the lowly will be exalted and the mighty brought down, she is saying that God's realm—a model Christians should work toward here on earth—will operate on entirely different principles from those dominant in the world today. She is also emphasizing the disparity between status in a true scale of value and the inequalities found in the world, and finds in her faith resources to resist the valuation the labor market puts on her. When Victor Santiago speaks of his co-religionists as "brothers," he uses the term so naturally that at one point the interviewer became confused and had to ask him whether he meant his biological brother or a fellow Witness. A non-empirical sense of "brotherhood" dominates his thinking, here expressing solidarity formed on ideological lines and cutting across kinship. Elsewhere this meaning of "brotherhood" applies more widely—beyond his religious group—contributing to the strength of his universalistic and egalitarian values (even though he does not act on them in the political arena).

The otherworldliness of Christian tradition, in sum, can help people understand their values radically rather than moderately. As in the case of Phyllis MacIntyre, otherworldliness can help Christians apply their values in ways that they would have difficulty doing if they were using a purely naturalistic framework of values and beliefs. Just as in order to use a lever one needs a fulcrum placed at a distance from the object to be moved, Christian faith has the most impact on how people think and speak when it can refer to realities and values that have some distance from the empirical world. An otherworldly faith, also, can be a source of vision and persistence, as we see in this passage from Paul's letter to the Hebrews (11:1, 8, 13–16):

> Now faith is the assurance of things hoped for, the conviction of things not seen. . . . By faith Abraham obeyed when he was called to go out to a place which he was to receive as an inheritance, not knowing where he was to go. . . . [Abraham, Sarah, and many others] all died in faith, not having received what was promised, but having seen it and greeted it from afar, and having acknowledged that they were strangers and exiles on the earth. For people who speak thus make it clear that they are seeking a homeland. If they had been

thinking of that land from which they had gone out, they would have had opportunity to return. But as it is, they desire a better country, that is, a heavenly one. Therefore God is not ashamed to be called their God, for he has prepared for them a city.[13]

This is the stance of otherworldly Christians, and also of those seeking social change who are in the struggle for the long haul. Such persons desire a better country, and reject opportunities to return, out of faith in something that they have seen and greeted only from afar.

6

Public Involvement and Means for Change

Social and political change do not happen just because people desire a better country; we have to go in search of our new homeland. Shall we do this, and if so, how?

We have seen how Christian faith can provide support for both liberal and conservative perspectives on economic life. This means that Christians—when their faith is not compartmentalized—can be a constituency for political movements, organizations, or parties. But a passive constituency is not the same thing as a group of active supporters, and supporting a goal is not the same as supporting the means that may be required to get there. We have examined the question of whether and how faith should have implications for economic life, and explored the ways in which faith helps Christians articulate their values and visions for a good economic order. Now we will see how faith is linked to views on questions related to the *implementation* of these values and visions. The answers to these questions will be shown to bear on the odds that a person will make an impact on the world.

Some of the questions have to do with *goals:*

- Is change in economic arrangements possible?
- Is quality of economic life an important concern, or does it pale by comparison with spiritual concerns or other political issues?
- Should we use ultimate, transcendent, perhaps even utopian goals to guide our activities, or should we concern ourselves only with goals that are practically achievable fairly soon and without major social change?
- Are our goals *structural*—that is, do they involve changing public policies or institutional arrangements—or are they concerned only with patterns of individual, person-to-person behavior?

- To what degree are each of us, as individuals, responsible for trying to improve economic life beyond the spheres we are personally involved in, as opposed to tending our own gardens and dealing well with people we meet in the course of our daily lives?

Other questions concern *means:* how we work toward achieving our goals. These questions involve two types of considerations. First is the *technical* issue: what means are likely to be successful in achieving our ends? Second is the *ethical* issue: what means are ethically permissible, or in accord with our fundamental values? Questions about means include:

- What is the appropriate balance between earthly, practical means and spiritual ones such as reliance on God and prayer?
- Are one's actions seen as morally neutral means for achieving one's values, or are they to be judged intrinsically, independent of their effects, as expressing one's values?
- Should we use laws and other coercive means or restrict ourselves to persuasion?
- Should we rely on collective means, working through organizations or movements or getting involved in politics, or act only as individuals?
- What degree of social conflict, what disruption of harmony and solidarity within existing groups and communities, is acceptable in pursuit of our values for economic life?

These questions about goals and means could be said to concern "implementation" issues. Like meta-issues, implementation issues arise across the spectrum of political and social life: we have to decide whether and how to work toward implementing our values in foreign policy, race relations, abortion, and civil liberties, just as in the economic arena. However, issues about implementation in economic life have a special quality because of the obviously "material" character of the substantive issues.

Also like meta-issues, implementation issues are independent, in theory, of what image of a good economic order people hold. Liberals sometimes think of themselves as people who are open to action and change, and there is some truth to this self-conception. But in the 1980s Ronald Reagan, who considered himself a conservative, probably did more to change the direction of American economic policy than any president since Franklin D. Roosevelt, while liberals found themselves defending existing programs and policies. Conservatives and liberals alike face the question of how their word might become flesh. Among the respondents, correspondingly, views on implementation issues can vary independently of substantive views. For instance, Victor Santiago has quite radical views on substantive economic issues, but by choice and conviction he is totally inert politically. At the opposite extreme, George Hoffman—one of the most economically conservative respondents—is very concerned about public policy questions, hoping to change our laws and institutions in ways he believes will improve our economic lives.

Christian faith has important implications for implementation issues, just as for meta-issues and substantive ones. The key to these implications is in how Christians negotiate the potentially competing demands of otherworldliness and thisworldliness—what might be called the spiritual–material polarity—and of the other three building blocks, constituting the individual–social polarity. We will examine each of these polarities in turn.

The Spiritual–Material Polarity

Otherworldliness and Viewing Economic Goals as Unimportant

In a radically otherworldly vein, one can hold that a Christian ought positively to avoid concern with material issues. This is the position taken by Victor Santiago, and in some ways by David Jenkins, though by few other respondents. More frequently, when Christians compartmentalize faith and economic issues, they hold that economic issues are religiously insignificant. As we saw, this does not necessarily mean that economic issues are unimportant, only that they do not matter *in one's identity as a Christian.* Economic issues could still be important on non-religious grounds.

In practice, however, many Christians invest more energy and concern in their faith and churches than in anything else outside their families and jobs, and non-Christian bases for public involvement are strong for only a small proportion of Americans. Other things being equal, therefore, those who separate Christian concern from "material" issues are less likely to put passion or thought into economic issues than those who take a more wholistic view. Furthermore, many respondents think of "spiritual" concerns as competing with rather than complementing material ones. In general, therefore, within a dualistic perspective the most "material" spheres of life—economic affairs and sexuality—are devalued or at least unvalued. Both of the positions just described imply that putting one's values for economic life into practice is not a very important goal; those values may be conservative or liberal, but one will not do much about them. The Baptist who says that religion concerns "your soul, not all these mundane things," is indeed totally uninvolved and uninterested in politics. This kind of dualism, in short, not only compartmentalizes faith and politics but also tends to be demobilizing.

A second way in which otherworldly views can make goals for economic life seem irrelevant is when Christians hold a pessimistic religious perspective, believing that the chances for improving economic life are low. The eschatologically oriented respondents (such as Victor Santiago) expect change, but not within history as we know it; Joseph Krieger thinks that inequality is inevitable and that people will always need a lot of coercion to keep them working; and the pessimistic respondents described in the last chapter believe that what we have is as good as can be achieved. The respondents who believe that earthly and heavenly life are organized on very different principles say that one therefore cannot use religious values to guide material life but must rely instead on more "practical" considerations; these people also tend to see only quite limited improvements in economic life as possible. Given any of these perspectives, changing the economic order to fulfill one's values is not a logical goal.

Otherworldliness and Choosing Pure Means

Respondents such as Victor Santiago, relying on the tradition of otherworldliness, espouse purely spiritual means; they rely solely on prayer and on God's power rather than human efforts to bring about change. Other people stress what might be called purity about means to achieve social aims, desiring that such means be loving, non-violent and Christ-like. Among the respondents, the Quaker William Westfield expresses views of this kind most clearly, but others, including Joseph Krieger and Linda Watson, speak in ways that hint at the same position. This perspective comes in part from the value of Christian love, and relates to the individual-social polarity. But partly it reflects a desire to be otherworldly in one's manner of action as well as one's purposes. The focus is on action as a way of expressing our values rather than as a technical instrument for achieving our ends. Note that this position, while certainly orthodox, is not more so than the alternate view—that one should define goals on the basis of religious views and then use whatever means will best achieve them.

These ideas about means—that they should be "pure," and in full accord with one's goals—are clear in William Westfield's thinking. He has been strongly influenced by Gandhi, in the direction of non-violence (he is an absolute pacifist) and also of a certain kind of asceticism. He is deeply involved in the "simple living" movement, and regards it as crucial that Americans free themselves from what he terms our "addiction" to a high material standard of living. He sees this addiction as an obstacle to worldwide economic justice and a menace to the world's ecology; however, fundamental issues about faith and ethics are also involved.

Christian asceticism can easily be caricatured as a tradition of self-hatred, and especially hatred of the body. St. Paul and many other Christians, to be sure, have felt their bodies to be the channel by which temptations to sin reached them, and have spoken of the body as inferior to the spirit. As Paul puts it, "While we are at home in the body we are away from the Lord" (1 Corinthians 5:6), or "Those who are in the flesh cannot please God" (Romans 8:8). But even for him the primary concern is to find the right way to accept God's offer of and call to new life, to be free from bondage to sin; hatred for the body is secondary, coming from the idea that our carnal nature is a key source of bondage to sin. In what I consider the best traditions of Christian asceticism, this same concern is not linked to any general distrust of the body; material concerns are relativized but not devalued. Rather, there are two main strategies involved in asceticism.

The first is to free ourselves from the constraining power of values that might keep us from responding to whatever call we hear from God. These include material security and affluence, but also less material concerns, such as popularity, honor, power, or being in harmony with the people around us. In this way we hope to follow true values rather than idols, and to live a more genuinely human existence, rich in freedom, meaning, and joy. This may involve sacrificing lower priorities if necessary, but not as an end in itself or in a spirit of self-punishment.

The second strategy is to have a system of self-discipline in order to be able more consistently to follow the desires and intentions at the center of our being, striving to be what God intended us to be. Thus we avoid being distracted by what are traditionally called "temptations" or "sinful propensities": those motives and drives within us (not necessarily primarily in our bodies) that pull us in other directions. Both of these strategies are ways to keep our priorities straight; in Christian terms, to avoid idolatry.

William Westfield is clearly in this tradition, even though he is very untraditional theologically. Simple living is a way to resist an enslaving, death-dealing addiction. Non-violence comes partly from his Quaker conviction that the spirit, and therefore possibilities for redemption and religious or political conversion, are in some way found in every person. It also comes partly from wanting to use, in the service of new life, only means that are intrinsically life-affirming. William does not divide politics into goals and means chosen to reach them but sees it as part of a seamless web of life in which means and ends, personal and political spheres are almost identical; one's actions are a representation of the values one holds more than a means for achieving them. We should work for a new world, he thinks, using modes of action of the kind we hope will prevail in the new world we seek. We speak to others through example (here he is a classical voluntarist, just like David Jenkins) and we change the world by "speaking truth to power" (to use the Quaker phrase).

William and Victor Santiago are in many respects particularly otherworldly respondents. They are almost completely unalike in every other aspect of religious faith, and thereby show that being otherworldly does not depend on taking any particular theological stance. Otherworldliness is deeply orthodox within Christianity, but William shows that theological traditionalists, who tend to think that they are more orthodox than others—and are so categorized by many social scientists and journalists—have no special claim to otherworldliness.

Otherworldliness and Concern with Economic Issues

The kinds of views we have just been considering can delegitimate concern for economic issues, but they can also legitimate such concern. The other-worldly strand of Christian tradition asserts the importance of a transcendent framework of values, and this can be a basis for criticism of the existing social order. For instance, in Linda Watson's thinking, we have seen how the otherworldly themes of the *Magnificat*—that earthly scales of value will be reversed—help make her feel that we should work for something dramatically different from what we have now. The other world is not just a separate place but also a source of legitimation and hope in demanding change here and now. God's will is to have a very different kind of world, and so Christians should work toward this goal.

The tradition of asceticism, furthermore, implies that one should be ready to sacrifice material well-being and even social acceptance—which are taken to be peripheral to one's core religious identity—if necessary to answer God's call. This can be a source of courage and commitment in pursuit of a better world, helping Christians overcome the sense that it is not in their personal interest to try to make the economic order correspond better to their values.

This is why effective revolutionaries are often in a certain sense ascetic. They, like people following the strategies of Christian asceticism, try to maintain a discipline that helps them keep priorities straight, and are willing to subordinate concerns of personal gain and popularity to their fundamental goals. Self-interest, after all, has limits as a motive for revolutionary action. Someone from a background or group ranking low in the social class hierarchy, who has developed the capacities required of an effective revolutionary, is clearly a very capable individual, and could probably succeed materially more easily and surely by seeking personal advancement within an unchanged social structure than by trying to change that structure. This is especially true in a society like ours, which provides some possibilities for individual mobility. People from higher-class backgrounds who decide that fundamental change is needed are also working against their material interests, presumably in the interest of what in traditional Christian language would be called saving their souls. In both cases, personal material concerns are subordinated to more ultimate goals. However much some revolutionaries may believe that material forces are the engine of history and that their appeals to others must be based on material interests rather than moralizing, their own actions are motivated, in the fashion of ascetics, in good part by ethical considerations.

This side of asceticism is evident in William's life. Simple living means, among other things, that he does not need much to live on, and he has been free to work at low-paying but meaningful jobs—which often include working for social change—and to resign well-paying ones if they start to seem socially harmful rather than beneficial. The freedom he speaks of here is essentially the same as that David Jenkins wishes for, despite their theological differences, and similarly requires preventing money from controlling one's life. When Joseph Krieger speaks of how one has to save one's soul rather than seek profit, and draws the conclusion that one should therefore be involved in the world and care about social and political issues, he is drawing on the same tradition to support a sense of personal responsibility for improving the economic order. Here the anti-materialism of Christian tradition reinforces rather than counteracts the principle of thisworldliness.

In theory, also, Christian faith, understood in an otherworldly way, can be a source of hope: God will not abandon us to evil and death. The idea of "providence" can be a source of activism, not just of passive waiting for God to take care of us. However, this possibility is not much in evidence among the respondents. That God desires more equality, community, and social justice in America is apparent to many respondents, but that God will actually work through and alongside us to bring this about is not. Still, there are some hints of such a perspective in Linda Watson and another evangelical woman with strongly left-of-center economic views—both of whom experience God as a nurturant, protective presence—and also in the Presbyterian engineer Phyllis MacIntyre's views.

Furthermore, as Phyllis shows us, an otherworldly perspective can provide a basis for maintaining social concerns despite lack of immediate success, for being utopian in the best sense and rejecting views that would put hardheaded, practical concerns ahead of Christian values. Since people with left-of-center economic views have not been very successful in the United States since the 1960s, this capacity may be especially important for them at present, helping them continue working for change when success seems distant and uncertain, to seek their new homeland rather than return even after many years in the wilderness.

Anti-materialism can even be a reason to seek a particular kind of economic change, change aimed at creating an economic order that is less "materialistic" than our present one. Pope John Paul II's encyclical on work, *Laborem Exercens* [On Human Work], puts this perspective forward with great clarity, vigor, and persuasiveness.[1] He criticizes both Marxism and capitalism for their materialism, for thinking that economic prosperity is the most important goal of economic life, and for treating humans as means. Capitalism puts profits above people, using human beings as tools or means when they should be ends. Soviet-style communist societies, on the other side, are so obsessed with economic growth and prosperity that they, too, are inhumane. Both put quantity of goods above the human and ethical quality of economic life. His vision of a good economic order is one with which many socialists, especially those influenced by the culture and politics of the 1960s, would find much to agree. In such an economic order, human relations and community will be the primary concerns; people will be the subjects of work as a creative activity, having a sense of satisfaction in their work and of participation in organizing it; and technology and capital will be used only as means, to enhance our lives and dignity as human beings made in the image of God rather than controlling our lives as an alien force. John Paul grounds this vision squarely in the anti-materialistic strand of Christian tradition.

Many of the respondents, too, use anti-materialistic themes to articulate a vision that is "anti-economistic," and at variance both with what they see around them in America and with some versions of socialism. William Westfield is one example, but there are many more. Susan Wainwright criticizes Americans for attachment to consumption; instead, she says, we should "live a simpler kind of life." Phyllis MacIntyre says, "It's time the United States sits down and looks at its priorities, and dethrones monetary value as the be-all and end-all." The "extreme-type" respondent chosen to represent a left-wing evangelical stance is very critical of what he takes to be a "materialistic, bourgeois society," and says we have to get out of our "individual consumerist" pattern of life. As in many such statements, two critiques are going on at once: we are too individualistic, and too materialistic.

This combination is not accidental. One can be selfish in one's spiritual pursuits, or selflessly focused on material concerns, but selfishness in pursuing material goals is what the respondents tend to criticize. Therefore anti-materialistic sentiments serve to support communal images of a good economic order, and liberal to radical views on economic issues, in the respondents' thinking. The tradition of otherworldliness is in this way linked to values of community. Both our excessive attachment to material things and our tendency to pursue our own interests rather than those of the community are aspects of our moral disorder, in traditional language our state of fallenness or original sin. This is clear, for instance, when a young, left-liberal Catholic says that "people are undisciplined in this country, and they will not deprive themselves of any comforts for the sake of mankind." Her statement combines the themes of criticizing moral disorder ("undisciplined"), using communal standards ("the sake of mankind"), and advocating a less materialistic way of life (as opposed to focusing on "comforts"). Thus we see again how ambiguous the social implications can be of even such a theme as the Christian stress on otherworldliness—a theme that might, at first glance, seem likely to promote only a quiescent tolerance of the current state of social life.

Appropriations of Thisworldliness

In chapter 3, we saw how the principle of thisworldliness helps some Christians feel that economic life is religiously important. Whereas compartmentalization reduces the passion and energy people feel about economic issues, giving religious value to economic issues puts energy into the economic world and makes people more likely to feel that economic change is an important goal. It can also help counter pessimism and give people a sense of personal responsibility to be authors of social change, as part of their relationship with God. Such ideas are clear in the thinking of the school administrator Michael Butros, some strands of Susan Wainwright's thinking, statement after statement from Joseph Krieger and Catherine Kennedy, Philomena Jackson, and many other respondents. As Susan puts it, "Christians should, whenever they can, try to work for the welfare of the society as a whole"; we should "try to get people interested in government." A liberal, affluent Catholic housewife, expressing the same sentiment, says people had "darn well better step in and start taking a little bit of interest in their government."

In addition, thisworldliness has implications for means. It tells some Christians that we should plunge into the world, using the most effective means available—in the view of many respondents, collective action, conflict, or laws—to put values into practice. In the context of quite conservative values, an evangelical speaks in this way, saying, "I feel that Christians should take a stand where they feel that things are [wrong]; I don't think they should sit back and do nothing, saying this is an evil world and things are going to happen anyway." The use of law is an important case: laws have a coercive component, and are (as David Jenkins points out) a material, external force. At the extreme, a position like the one just quoted becomes an ideological crusade in which one tries systematically to order a whole society to carry out God's will. Such a crusade appeared in what is often called the Puritan Revolution in England, and appears today in movements ranging from the Moral Majority to liberation theology. Sometimes critics argue that there is a potential for authoritarianism and violence in movements of this character, but to their proponents the critical point is that they have the power to overcome obstacles to change that other means have failed to dislodge. Here we are confronted with contradictory evaluations of what happens when people mix religion and politics. More moderately, the principle of thisworldliness indicates that it is one's duty not just to witness to true values but to try to make them "flesh"—to give them practical form within an imperfect world. That may lead to feeling that one needs to tolerate some amount of moral ambiguity in political practice. Such a view can help Christians find it acceptable to become involved in practical political work to implement their values.

However, thisworldly themes can also be appropriated in ways that delegitimate the kind of utopianism Phyllis MacIntyre expresses. In chapter 3, we saw that some respondents want Christians to be very idealistic when they have their Christian hat on but to enter into politics bareheaded, making political decisions on a very different basis. In a parallel secular formulation, this is what the sociologist Max Weber called an "ethic of responsibility," as opposed to an ethic of ultimate ends.[2] By ethic of responsibility, he means an entirely instrumental view of means, and determination of policy based on the choice of the best that can be realistically obtained (which may well be a lesser evil). That is, one should emphasize the actual likely consequences of an action rather than its motives or intrinsic ethical qualities. Weber believes that this is the only appropriate ethos for those who want to practice politics. The similarities to the views we examined in chapter 3, and contrast to the perspectives expressed by William Westfield and Phyllis MacIntyre, are clear. Both the Christian stance separating idealistic faith from practical politics, and Weber's position are based in part on a kind of thisworldliness: a desire to be practically effective for good in the world as it is. (In the Christian version, there is a strand of otherworldliness as well, in the desire to keep oneself clean and uncompromised in one's identity as a Christian, and in the dualism established between heavenly and earthly domains.) We should note the political ambiguity of such a stance: it encourages political engagement, but at the same time, by its pessimism and its implicit endorsement of the instruments of political efficacy currently available, it is vulnerable to the criticism of being too uncritical, too worldly. The theologian Reinhold Niebuhr, a proponent of views with some things in common with those we have been discussing, has been criticized on the grounds that his perspective gave too much comfort to those justifying the cold war—in other words, that it was too easily turned to the service of realpolitik and too easily legitimated the policies of those in power.[3]

Conclusion

Once again, we see that Christian faith has multiple political and social implications. Otherworldliness is a core, traditional element of Christianity, and it can either facilitate or obstruct involvement with economic issues. The more modern-seeming strand of thisworldliness can also work both ways, although it is more frequently used to legitimate being involved, as a Christian, with economic issues. People seeking to mobilize support for changes in our economic order therefore need a discriminating attitude toward Christianity. Christianity is not their enemy; otherworldliness and theological traditionalism are so only to a limited degree. However, concern for economic issues and practical activity intended to put economic values into practice are less likely on the part of Christians who hold views that devalue (not just relativize) economic life and focus energy solely on spiritual concerns, persuade people that social change of any useful kind is impossible, mandate extreme purity in the choice of means, or lead people to accommodate themselves without much tension to their environment by being perfectly "practical." Such views are found among theological modernists and traditionalists alike. They are also found in non-Christian religious perspectives and secular culture.

The Individual–Social Polarity

Three of the building blocks—voluntarism, love, and universalism—help define how a Christian understands the religious significance of the individual and the community. Voluntarism focuses on the individual, while love emphasizes social involvements. (We should emphasize that a voluntaristic focus on the individual need not be selfish. The key point is that every person is understood as a self-determining actor relating separately to God. A secular parallel would be civil libertarians who are as protective of the civil liberties of their political opponents as of their own.)[4] Universalism, as we saw in chapter 5, can help ground both individualistic and communal values. As people like Catherine Kennedy and Linda Watson use this theme, it emphasizes the sister- or brotherhood that comes from our all being children of God, laying the basis for new solidarities in new communities, but it is individualistic in that it can delegitimate many of the actual forms of solidarity found in human life.

William Westfield and David Jenkins: Voluntarism in Action on Implementation Issues

We have met the Quaker William Westfield several times, and it is probably already obvious that he thinks in extremely voluntaristic terms—logically enough, given that he is heir to the Quaker tradition of radical antinomianism. Let us hear from him at greater length, discussing the Quaker "testimonies" or principles:

> Pacifism is only one aspect of the Quaker view of man and God and man's relation with man. I think I would broaden pacifism to include all of the basic testimonies. Simplicity [one of these testimonies] is another way of describing a centeredness that is a single standard of truth, of clothing, of speech, of getting away as much as possible from playing a whole lot of different roles, a kind of authenticity or centeredness. In fact, all of the testimonies are related to the assumption that there is that potential that we think of as God in every person, and there is the possibility of touching that or finding communion with that in any other person we ever encounter.

This is truly a classical statement of the voluntaristic ideal for human personality: we are to be centered, autonomous selves, constant across all social situations and in the face of all social pressures. What makes this possible is that every person in a sense possesses God, and can be touched by true values. And this is one basis for William's commitment to persuasion and non-violence: to coerce people is to give up on the possibility of reaching their hearts, to see them as incapable of regeneration or devoid of God, and to deny them the space within which they could move in the right direction voluntarily. (The other basis for William's embrace of non-violence is the value of love, implying a duty not to harm others. The value of love is the central basis in faith for Victor Santiago's pacifism—like most Jehovah's Witnesses, he is a conscientious objector—and probably for most pacifists. For William, however, voluntaristic grounds seem more important.) Note the parallel to David Jenkins: William wants people to have moral choice, and hence favors persuasion and non-violence, while David, also to enable moral choice, objects to social welfare programs.

William's ethical position about the means for implementing his values is based on a proposition about how God is present within human lives. He also has more practical reasons, grounded in views about how social life works, for putting the individual at the center of the process of social change. He says that our country's wrongheaded policies "are not going to change as long as the basic American lifestyle requires that we have the kind of access to resources that we now have. That is rooted not just in the system, it's rooted in my lifestyle as well," and so we, as individuals, have to be ready to change our lifestyles before we can do anything about institutions. Unlike some people, he *is* interested in changing institutions and policies. But essentially he hopes for a kind of mass conversion in which large numbers of Americans would change their lifestyles voluntarily, out of a concern for justice and community. He hopes for this partly because he values individual freedom and regeneration, but also partly because he believes that mass conversion (not, of course, of the traditional religious kind) is a necessary precondition for social change. Just as with his otherworldliness, means and ends, technical and ethical considerations, come together.

David Jenkins's views are quite close in spirit to William's, despite the enormous differences between them on most religious and political issues. (This shows, once again, how unimportant theological modernism and traditionalism can be.) Like William, David endorses only those means of achieving social change that eschew coercion and rely on persuasion and conscience. For both, the reasons are at once ethical and technical: both believe that freedom of choice is a key end in itself, and both think that converting individuals is the only effective way to make society better.

Their shared perspective also indicates some of the ambiguities in the way positions on individual–social polarity relate to positions on implementation issues. Voluntarism can be connected to lack of interest in social structure and public policy, or with a perspective on implementation that eliminates many forms of political action. In other ways, however, voluntarism can also contribute to public involvement. To seek their new homeland actively, especially if their values are seriously at odds with how things work currently, people need to take personal responsibility for the public order and have values they can articulate and hold to despite pressures from their social environment. This requires not only a certain kind of otherworldliness but also a significant degree of individuation. In addition, an agent of change needs to be open to the possibility that received ideas and social arrangements are wrong.

David Jenkins shows these capacities in some ways, for instance in taking the initiative, all on his own, to start systems of helping people in need; and in holding views on sexuality that are quite different from those normative in his denomination. William incarnates the same capacities more clearly and extensively. He is willing to live in great tension with his social environment, and to think for himself on every issue. Some of this is true of Quakers in general, not just William: the Quaker emphasis on the sanctity of individual conscience supports conscientious objection to military service and skepticism about official claims for the necessity of our interventions overseas, and more generally about all official claims. That is, there is an anti-authoritarian and anti-nationalistic strain in Quakerism that comes naturally out of its antinomian religious heritage, and that makes important contributions to American public life.

On the other hand, the kind of voluntaristic views William and David hold also serve to support somewhat demobilizing views on implementation issues. William has strong aspirations for community. However, his ideal for human personality, embodied in his conception of simplicity, tends to exalt a certain kind of individualism: social life is in part an obstacle to be overcome by Westfieldian individuals, a set of pressures that the individual has to resist in order to be constant across all situations. Furthermore, all evidence indicates that humans are much more vulnerable to their social environment than William would wish; some Christians might even conclude that God made us that way, and had a reason for doing so. In the face of this reality, William's views have a somewhat purist tone: the means for change he favors are fairly limited, and could be readily practiced only by a small elite of especially dedicated and non-conforming individuals. These characteristics of his views on implementation issues are related to both the voluntarism and otherworldliness of his perspective. For both William and David, in fact, otherworldliness and voluntarism work together, grounding quite different views on implementation issues than when otherworldliness and love work together (as for Pope John Paul II and some of the respondents).

Voluntarism and Implementation Issues in Other Respondents

David and William present in an explicit and coherent form ideas found, less articulately and alongside other ideas, in the majority of the respondents. Many of the people who say that we ought to behave more lovingly toward one another in economic life do not see themselves as criticizing our economic *structure* but only our average behavior. Such respondents do not merely place great value on the individual but show little awareness of the *existence* of any social reality beyond the individual. Society is a sum of individuals and their behaviors. A social problem consists of a high rate of individual errors or misdeeds, and results from the choices of individuals, not the characteristics of our social structure. Indeed, within this framework social structure does not really exist. Persons who feel this way can care about economic life, and wish it to conform better to Christian values, but draw no implications whatsoever for public policy, or at least give their attention primarily to the issue of reforming individuals.[5]

Philomena Jackson says she "believes that a lot of the ills of our country could be solved if the people turned to God." Expanding on this, she continues, "If we could just change the little world we know, it would act just like when you throw a stone in the water and watch a wave go out." Speaking in fairly traditional language, the young Assemblies of God member Jennifer Habib, despite her moderately liberal views on substantive economic issues, says that saving souls is the most important thing, because people "that are saved are going to think the right way" and reform institutions. Similarly, we find a mainline Protestant saying that the way for Christians to improve social life is to "urge people to attend church."

Think back, for a moment, to the spiritual-material duality. The people we are speaking of here, unlike some of those described in the first part of this chapter, may believe that economic, material questions are important, but they approach these issues only as problems of personal morality, and are not concerned with their public and systemic dimensions. As we saw with regard to David and William, just as voluntarism and otherworldliness work together to separate faith from political and economic issues, they work together to make these issues seem unimportant. The result is that one's substantive goals for economic life may be radical or communal, but one's approach to getting there will be individualistic. In fact, the same basic position often has implications for both means and ends. In terms of means, respondents of this kind counsel person-to-person action; in terms of desired outcomes, they describe changes in patterns of individual behavior, not changes in policy or social structure. Furthermore, given this perspective, the responsibility of private citizens tends to be limited to the spheres they participate in directly.

David and William are unusually systematic in how they reason from their basic premises, but the core elements of their views are widely shared. Over half of the respondents *spontaneously* spoke in a way showing at least some attachment to a voluntaristic view of implementation issues or an atomistic view of how social life works. This is a very high proportion to express a single kind of opinion, except in response to a question specifically calling it forth.

Christians can even conclude, on the basis of voluntarism, that their personal responsibility is confined entirely to the private sphere. Partly, this is based in a kind of relativism: not wanting, as George Hoffman puts it, to be telling others what they should do. Partly also, it is based on an idea of the diversity of callings: some are called to be responsible for public life, but most of us are not. And partly it is based on the view that one affects social life only by person-to-person activities.

Voluntarism about Implementation Issues: Survey Evidence

We can get some sense of how prevalent such views are among mainline Protestants in general from the responses to two Lutheran surveys: a 1983 survey conducted by the Lutheran Church in America and the 1988 Lutheran survey discussed in chapter 3. In the 1988 survey, just over half the respondents preferred the statement "As individual Christians, we are mainly responsible for living ethically in our one-to-one relationships" to the alternative provided, "As individual Christians, we should each put a lot of time into trying to improve our society." In the 1983 survey, in response to a question about the "responsibility [of] individual Christians with regard to [racial] discrimination," one-quarter preferred "Our only responsibility is to treat people of different races and colors equally ourselves, as individuals," while three-quarters preferred "In addition to our responsibility to treat people of different races and colors equally, we each have a responsibility to work to reduce the amount of discrimination found in our society." The difference between these two outcomes is probably partly a matter of wording ("only" versus "mainly" in the corresponding answers, for instance), but also partly because Christians have more clarity and consensus on opposing discrimination than on other issues, and relate this issue more directly to faith. Taking the two surveys together, it appears that from one-quarter to one-half of mainline Protestants, depending on the issue, are likely to disavow individual responsibility for the public domain.

With regard to means, the 1983 survey found that a slight majority preferred "We should set a good example, and appeal to people's consciences, so that people will decide *voluntarily* not to discriminate against members of minority groups" to "We should use laws, as well as example and appeals to conscience, to *make sure* that members of minority groups will not be discriminated against." This is in spite of the fact that the less voluntaristic alternative spoke of the use of *both* persuasion and law and spoke only to discrimination (as opposed to more controversial subjects such as affirmative action), and that laws against discrimination are not unfamiliar to Americans. On the 1988 survey, three-eighths preferred "Except in extreme situations, we should use persuasion (setting a good example and appealing to people's consciences) rather than laws to make society better" to the alternative, "It's often necessary to use laws to make society better." Five-eighths preferred "To have a better society people just have to learn to act better toward each other" over "To have a better society requires changes in public policy and how our society is organized." These results, suggesting that about half of Lutherans (and probably other mainstream Protestants) take a clearly voluntaristic position about means, and perhaps an anti-structural view of goals, point to serious obstacles for activists, in and outside the churches.

Here, as with otherworldliness, we encounter bases on which Christians judge means intrinsically or expressively, rather than judging them just as ways of attaining one's goals. Many voluntaristic respondents want those who seek social justice to eschew all means with any coercive element. This often includes boycotts, picketing, and strikes, and for many it includes laws. At the extreme, anything beyond acting right in one's own immediate spheres of life is excluded, and voluntaristic restrictions on means become hard to distinguish from rejecting responsibility for anything beyond private life.

The Prophetic Spirit and Universalism

In the language and thinking of radicals of both left and right there is a spirit that harks back to the prophetic writings of the Jewish scriptures. Over and over, the prophets say that God hates religious observances in the absence of doing justice and repenting in one's heart. Here are characteristic statements from Isaiah:

> What to me is the multitude of your sacrifices? says the Lord. . . . Trample my courts no more; bringing offerings is futile; incense is an abomination to me. . . . Wash yourselves; make yourselves clean; remove the evil of your doings from before my eyes; cease to do evil, learn to do good; seek justice, rescue the oppressed. . . . Zion shall be redeemed by justice, and those in her who repent, by righteousness. (Isaiah 1:11–13,16–17,27)

The language of the prophets is both public and private; it is addressed to the community that does not institutionalize social justice and to individuals who do wrong. It is concerned with both the inward and the outward, demanding change in outward behavior and also an inner change of heart.

When radicals of either the left or the right speak today, they—like Isaiah—often use strong language; they are confrontational, and have little fear of conflict. They are often impolite and moralistic, speaking (they believe) for a God who judges, or (if they are secular) for ethical standards they believe have universal validity. They have little interest in preserving traditional arrangements; rather, they put everything "that is" under judgment of abstract standards of "what ought to be," and stand ready to uproot any rule, way of life, or institution that is not of God. They are concerned with the public arena, desiring concrete changes in our life together so that it will be more pleasing to God. Those on the left have a passion for social justice combined with an egalitarian idea of what that means.

The prophetic spirit can be grounded in various strands of Christian tradition. Clearly, one is thisworldliness, which emphasizes a practical response to God's love rather than just spirituality or religious observance. Another is the otherworldliness implicit in a conception of God as external and superior to the world, and God's values as conflicting with those of the world. A third basis for such a perspective is the theme of universalism. Jesus described the universalism of his message in the famous passage where he says he will bring not peace but a sword; "I have come to set a man against his father, and a daughter against her mother.... Whoever loves father or mother more than me is not worthy of me" (Matthew 10:34–37).[6] In this passage, kinship is devalued; our relationship to Jesus takes preference over all traditional bonds. Jesus is clear that this implies upset, even conflict. The early apostles made the same decision, with equal clarity about the conflict involved, when they decided to baptize gentiles as well as Jews, on the basis, as articulated by Peter, that "in cleansing [the gentiles'] hearts by faith [God] has made no distinction between them and us" (Acts 15:9). Here, ethnicity and the concrete, particularistic community formed by the history and religious life of the people of Israel are secondary to forming a wider Christian community, and to the demands of seeking the Kingdom.

Universalism is a way for humans to overcome their divisions and become more unified, but it may require painfully breaking down existing group loyalties, and therefore lead to conflict within existing social units such as families and ethnic groups. A Christian is willing to be in conflict in pursuit of abstract, otherworldly goals; Christians form an ideological "camp," at odds with others. The strife may be non-violent, but it is far from painless, and is sure to create bitterness and hostility, to turn people against one another. This kind of universalism has implications for the means to be used in implementing social values: in pursuit of justice and a better, broader community, it is legitimate to create conflict, even to attack the solidarities of existing communities. The egalitarianism implicit in thinking of people as children of God can also legitimate disregarding or attacking traditional authorities, who usually do not want major social change. If traditional bonds are weakened, it is easier to maintain unconventional ideas because one can elect to live primarily among those who will accept them.

Nowadays, religious conservatives often provide the best examples of this potential. The religious right in the United States is not afraid of speaking up for what it believes to be true values. In Cincinnati, an organization called Citizens for Community Values is working to eradicate pornography. This is an effective organization: there are no adult bookstores and no X-rated videos or movies available for view or rent anywhere in Hamilton County (Cincinnati and the near suburbs), and few in the surrounding counties. The members are mainly traditionalist Protestants, with a few modernists and Catholics. Attending meetings of this group, I heard of two cases in which families were divided by its struggles; in one, an active member was working with the local prosecutor to bring her mother-in-law to court on criminal charges for renting X-rated videos. Thus this organization disrupts bonds among family members on behalf of a higher loyalty.

Some of the respondents show signs of this appropriation of universalism, although overall it is not greatly in evidence. Catherine Kennedy was interested in participating in civil rights demonstrations—a confrontational act, especially in the early 1960s—for the reason, which she specifically describes as a religious principle, that African-Americans are her "brothers." Linda Watson has also been willing to be confrontational, and speaks of how that relates to her understanding that she is a child of God, fundamentally equal to others in spite of her low income and status. James O'Connell, a committed anti-racist, knew he was getting himself into trouble when at a meeting he raised questions about some tactics being used by people working for racial justice in housing, but felt he needed to in response to principles transcending racial differences. Despite his corporatism, Joseph Krieger shows some potential for a prophetic approach; for example, he backed the priest who invited a speaker to present the case against an anti-fair-housing ballot initiative, even though this created upset and discord within the parish.

The implications of universalism, however, are not unambiguous. It can be argued that by devaluing all concrete, historically derived, particularistic communities, universalistic thinking can deracinate people; this is Yudit Jung's argument with regard to the Jewish Bund before the Russian Revolution, and the view of some left historians. Few of the respondents, however, seem to use the universalistic strand of Christian tradition in this way.

Love and Means

Many Christians are far from the prophetic spirit. For most, conflict is quite unacceptable; here we see how the value of love can be demobilizing. In the view of many Christians, one should use only loving means to bring about change. One should eschew violence, certainly, but also anything that would foment hatred, bitterness, or division, or turn people against one another.

This attitude can reflect a radical commitment to non-violence and love as kinds of purity of action. This is William Westfield's view, as we have seen. He is committed to non-violence but is willing to be quite confrontational; this, however, is a relatively rare combination.

The rejection of conflict can also stem from ideas best expressed by Joseph Krieger: what unites us is more important than what divides us. It is critical not to threaten the unity of the community, even for the sake of pursuing justice. Such views make it hard to articulate claims for justice if one believes they can be fulfilled only at a cost to others, or to legitimate conflictual, confrontational means such as strikes and boycotts. In a way, Joseph's perspective is the exact opposite of the deracinating universalism mentioned a moment ago: it focuses commitment on actual, existing communities, as opposed to the abstract, not yet existent ones into which universalistic thinking invites us. (This may be part of why he is more sensitive to the violence of those demanding change than to violence used by "legitimate" authorities.) Here Joseph has something in common with critics of radical politics who have maintained at least since the French Revolution that people who tinker with an actual, functioning society and its web of bonds in the name of an abstract, ideologically defined community are dangerous. A corporatistic perspective also provides a ready-made legitimation for inequalities of power and authority, and can encourage citizens to wait for justice to be achieved top-down by the actions of those in authority rather than becoming activists themselves.

The 1988 Lutheran survey shows significant worry about conflict. A little over one-third of the respondents preferred the statement "It is almost never acceptable to try to change our society by means which cause conflict or set people against each other" to the alternative, "It is often necessary to work for change by means which *do* cause conflict." A slightly larger proportion (39 percent) agreed that "the church should avoid issues which are likely to be divisive within the congregation." In both cases, a substantial proportion—though clearly a minority—of Lutherans seem to give a strong priority to harmony.

Love and Concern for Public Life

On the other hand, love mandates concern for the whole community, and gives value to community life as something real and important in itself. This, especially combined with a voluntaristic sense of one's responsibility to take independent action, can help make public involvement seem desirable.

Among the respondents, the value of love leads many to the conclusion that public issues are important, and that we have a *personal* responsibility to be involved in *public* life. In the eyes of Joseph Krieger, Catherine Kennedy, and Linda Watson, love implies concern for the world, a sense that the life of the whole community is important, and as part of that, concern for how people are faring economically.

The theme of love helps counteract the atomistic perspectives we have described earlier by giving value to our involvement with one another, and also by communicating cognitive frameworks, such as the image of being one Body in Christ, that make collective levels of reality easier to experience. This is clear, for instance, in listening to Joseph Krieger or James O'Connell. (Experiences of love, in addition to ideologies of love, may be important. The experience of Christian community and worship, and especially of the Eucharist, helps many Christians be aware of the collective dimension of life.)

Another example of avoiding atomism is Michael Butros, who says that "salvation will come from the kinds of things I will be doing every day, in business" and his other practical dealings with people. He thinks that corporations should be socially responsible and that government should take an active role in making sure there are jobs for everyone, out of a "humanistic concern"—that is, for ethical reasons. In other words, the ethical imperative of thisworldliness is linked to concern not just about economic life but about the *public* (governmental and corporate) dimensions of economic life. Faith is connected to issues of social rather than just personal ethics. Clearly this is an important counterweight to the voluntaristic ideas reviewed earlier.

Implementation Issues and Social Change

What are the dimensions on which views on implementation issues vary? On meta-issues, we can distinguish compartmentalized and integrated perspectives; on substantive issues, conservative and liberal views, or (this is not the same) individualistic and communal values. On implementation issues, the distinctions are more complex.

With regard to goals, views on the importance of economic life and possibility of improvement, and degree of interest in structural (versus person-to-person) issues, have been termed "mobilizing" and "demobilizing." This analysis is based not just on what the respondents say but also to some degree on assumptions about social change. The assumptions need to be made explicit, although it is beyond the scope of this book to demonstrate their correctness. People who disagree with these assumptions will interpret some of the views described in this chapter differently. To them, views that are here termed demobilizing may seem to encourage a high level of social involvement, with at least as much likelihood of improving human life as the views here termed mobilizing. Many of the respondents do not share my views about social change. Therefore when their views are characterized as demobilizing, that does not mean they themselves understand them to be demobilizing but only that in my judgment the actual outcomes of these views are likely to be so.

The first assumption is that intentional human effort by significant numbers of people is one necessary condition for improving the quality of economic life—that life-affirming changes are unlikely to come about through the unconscious workings of technological change and economic forces, or through changes introduced by small elites in the absence of a mass constituency seeking them. Radicals of both the Left and the Right largely appear to agree with this assumption. People in the center, by their mistrust of social movements and citizen mobilization, indicate that they also agree, since they desire stability rather than change. Given this assumption, views that remove commitment and energy from the public sphere, or provide grounds for concentrating on intimate spheres of life, are demobilizing and favor stasis rather than change—or at any rate are unlikely to influence the direction change takes.

A second assumption is that policies, institutions, and social structures do matter, and have to be addressed if economic life is to be improved. There are social phenomena that are not just the sum or result of individual behaviors and characteristics. Thus the skills, decisions, and perseverance of individual members of the labor force may well determine who, at any moment, is employed and unemployed, but these factors do not determine the unemployment rate; if twice as many people are unemployed this year as last, that is not because individual workers have become less skilled or interested in working but because of forces beyond the control of individual workers. A good society, then, requires not only individuals who behave well but social structures that create well-being. Those respondents who want to improve our society but address their efforts entirely to one-to-one relationships—to serving or transforming individuals—may be active and admirable but are less likely to contribute to social change than those who address structural issues as well.

Turning to means: What choices make it more or less likely that one will succeed in incarnating one's values? This is a complex and controversial question. Clearly people with strongly held ultimate values—whether religious or not—will often make their choices of means based on ethical as well as technical considerations, on what seems legitimate as well as what will have the most practical impact on the world. It is ethically quite plausible to rule out certain means, no matter how valued the ends. (The "rules of war," as expressed in the Geneva conventions, are an example of limitations usually followed even when the issues at stake are deemed so important that nations resort to violence.) It is even likely that placing principled limits on the means we employ may help us to be more rather than less effective in achieving our ends. Furthermore, there is room for a variety of means— for prayer and "speaking truth to power" (to use the Quaker phrase) as well as for more "practical" means.

Nonetheless—and here is my third assumption—some restrictions on means do make the chances of incarnating one's values for economic life smaller. Those who rely entirely on prayer, witness, person-to-person activities, moral exhortation, setting a good example, and appeals to conscience are less likely to succeed than those who are also willing to use organizations, movements, and institutions; make lasting commitments to organizations in which they coordinate their work with others[7]; can accept the degree of coercion inherent in laws (not to mention strikes, demonstrations, and boycotts); are not afraid of a certain degree of conflict and confrontation; and are willing to get involved in the practical work of organizing constituencies, going to meetings, passing out flyers, talking to strangers, and the myriad other tasks that are likely to arise in work for social change.

Table 6-1. Christian Themes: Implications for Issues about Change

Theme	Change-inhibiting implications	Change-facilitating implications
Otherworld-liness	Dualism and reduced concern for economic life; pessimism about making change; use only spiritual means or think of means only expressively	Social involvement to save one's soul; transcendent standards; trust and hope (providence); work for less materialistic society
Thisworld-liness	Ethic of responsibility: anti-utopianism; means limited to ones socially defined as "practical"	Economic life religiously important; personal responsibility to make it better; use practical means
Voluntarism	No coercion; change society by re-forming individuals; goals non-structural; personally responsible only for private sphere	Take initiative; individually responsible for social order; maintain unconventional ideas against social pressures
Universalism	Delegitimate loyalties to concrete or traditional groups	Encourage prophetic spirit; conflict acceptable; aspiration for new/broader communities
Love	Choose pure/loving/non-coercive means only; avoid all conflict	Responsibility for community; value and concern for public/structural side of life

Thinking about means instrumentally as well as expressively and using a broad range of means tend to facilitate social change. This is true regardless of whether one's image of a good society is conservative, liberal, or radical.

Thus the central difference on implementation issues is between views that tend to facilitate social change and those that make no contribution or tend to obstruct change. Table 6-1 summarizes the contributions themes from Christian faith make to change-facilitating and change-inhibiting views.

On balance, the ways in which faith supports ideas that might facilitate social change seem slightly weaker, among the respondents, than the ways in which faith supports views that are likely to inhibit change. On implementation issues, in other words, the impact of faith is less favorable to the project of the Left than it is on the substantive issues we have considered. This is especially true for some (not all) of the theological traditionalists; here—there may be a connection between certain forms of theological conservatism and a certain kind of political "conservatism."[8] The views described here also show how much independence there can be between views on implementation and substantive issues. For instance, some of the same ideas that promote liberal views about economic life in Joseph Krieger's thinking have change-inhibiting implications on implementation issues. And finally, in looking at views on these issues we see again how deeply voluntaristic thinking—to a large extent rooted in Christian faith—is ingrained in the minds of Americans, and what an obstacle this is to the work of movements for social justice. This kind of thinking often serves to blunt the potential radicalism of political perspectives and activities grounded in Christian faith.

Tools for Understanding
Religion and Politics

7

Public Opinion Results and Underlying Assumptions

So far, we have been concerned with the depth-interview respondents and their relationship on one side to Christian tradition and on the other to economic issues. In this chapter we will broaden our horizon by looking at the results from public opinion research on the relationship between religion and views on economic issues. This will give us a sense of how larger and more nationally representative groups of respondents think. We will also examine the assumptions made in this research—assumptions also found in the way many journalists and religious and political figures conceive of the connections between faith and politics—and show how the findings from the depth interviews make sense of the results from public opinion research.

Results from Public Opinion Research

Extensive public opinion research on a great variety of political issues has been conducted by polling organizations such as Gallup and academically based survey research organizations such as the Survey Research Center of the University of Michigan and the National Opinion Research Center at the University of Chicago. Probably the most widely used source of data in recent years has been the General Social Survey conducted almost yearly since 1972 by the National Opinion Research Center. Many General Social Survey questions are repeated from year to year, which allows pooling of the data from several years to make comparisons among relatively small groups in the population, say, members of different religious denominations (such comparisons are usually impossible using the data from a single survey because there are too few respondents in any one group). All the surveys mentioned so far have a great variety of questions on political issues but relatively few on religion; in the General Social Survey, for instance, the only questions available for most years relate to denomination, worship attendance, frequency of prayer, and biblical literalism.

In striking contrast to these surveys are others on religious topics conducted by denominations or individual researchers. Denominational surveys (such as the Lutheran ones used in previous chapters) often are nationwide in scope but almost always restricted to particular denominations; independent surveys are usually low-budget affairs, involving members from a handful of churches of differing denominations in a particular local area, or occasionally a student population. These surveys include a wealth of religious questions, but often they are constructed *ad hoc* for the particular study, which makes comparisons of results from different surveys difficult. When they are concerned with religion and politics, they often have several questions on the political issues under study, which usually appear to tap the conservative–liberal dimension on those particular issues reasonably well.

We will supplement the results from past research (which have been well summarized by literature reviews[1]) with some new analysis of General Social Survey data, based on the pooled data from 1984 through 1989.[2]

The results from past research and this new analysis are the same and can be simply stated. *The only religious factor consistently related to economic attitudes is denominational group: Catholics and those with no religious preference are consistently but not dramatically more liberal on economic issues, and Protestants belonging to predominantly African-American denominations are much more liberal than White Protestants—particularly those in mainline denominations.* (People of other faiths—Muslims, Buddhists, adherents of new religions, and so forth—are too few and too diverse to permit meaningful analysis.) For the purpose of understanding the impact of Christian faith, the most important part of this finding is the difference between Catholics and Protestants. On this axis, the sociologist Andrew Greeley finds quite large differences, and Kenneth Wald and many others find moderate ones, but seldom does research show no clear difference; Catholics are demonstrably more liberal on economic issues.[3] This remains true when Catholics and Protestants of the same social class, race, or region are compared; thus, non-religious social factors do not account for denominational differences.

No other religious variable is consistently associated with whether people are liberal or conservative on economic issues. Occasionally a researcher finds an association (usually a weak one) with a particular religious variable, but the finding is not confirmed by other researchers using the same variable.[4] Biblical literalists and non-literalists have essentially the same economic views; members of theologically modernist and traditionalist denominations do not consistently differ; frequency of prayer and worship attendance make no difference. As with differences between Protestants and Catholics, all these patterns are the same (for all practical purposes) when the comparisons are made with class, race, and region held constant. The strongly and widely held belief that religious and political conservatism go together is simply false with regard to economic issues.

Table 7-1. Differences between the Responses of Biblical Literalists and Non-Literalists to 39 Questions on Economic Issues

Of 39 economic questions dividing liberals from conservatives,

None	(0%)	show literalists as a lot more *conservative* than non-literalists
1	(3%)	shows literalists as somewhat more *conservative*
3	(8%)	show literalists as slightly more *conservative*
11	(28%)	show literalists and non-literalists to hold essentially *the same views*
12	(31%)	show literalists as slightly more *liberal*
10	(25%)	show literalists as somewhat more *liberal*
2	(5%)	show literalists as a lot more *liberal*

Note: "A lot more" is defined as a Pearson correlation coefficient of ±.200 or more; "somewhat more" as a correlation of ±.100 to .199; and "slightly more" as a correlation of ±.050 to .099. Coefficients of smaller magnitude are interpreted as indicating that literalists and non-literalists hold essentially the same views.

Results from the General Social Survey

The results we will examine here are illustrations drawn from analysis I have done of General Social Survey data on religion and politics.[5]

In the 1984–1989 General Social Surveys, there were thirty-nine questions that clearly fall within the liberal-conservative dimension with regard to economic issues.[6] It is helpful to use this large set of questions, rather than just one or two, because the pattern of answers to one question can differ markedly from that for another question on a similar topic; such differences average out over a large set of questions, providing a more reliable sense of what relationships between religious factors and economic opinions really exist.

Table 7-1 shows the relationship between biblical literalism and this set of thirty-nine economic questions. Biblical literalism is measured in the General Social Survey by a question which has been widely used in surveys on religion:

Which of these statements comes closest to describing your feelings about the Bible?
   a. The Bible is the actual word of God and is to be taken literally, word for word.
   b. The Bible is the inspired word of God but not everything in it should be taken literally, word for word.
   c. The Bible is an ancient book of fables, legends, history, and moral precepts recorded by men.[7]

Relatively few people (less than one in six overall, and fewer among Christians) select answer c, and therefore the differences between those who see the Bible as the "actual" versus "inspired" word, and do versus do not take it literally, are the major factors in the responses we will review.

Toward the top of the Table 7-1 are counts of the questions on which the literalists are more *conservative* than the non-literalists and toward the bot-

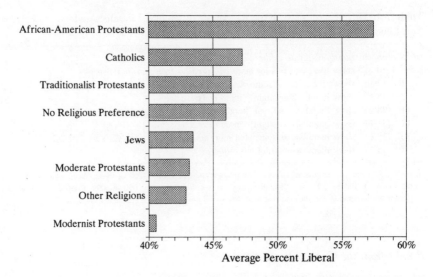

Figure 7-1. Denominational Group Differences on Economic Issues: Average Responses to 39 Questions

tom the questions where the literalists are more *liberal*. On only four of the thirty-nine questions is there even a weak connection between being a literalist and being economically conservative; on eleven questions, the literalists and non-literalists hold essentially identical views, and on the other twenty-four questions the literalists are more liberal, although usually not by a large margin. On balance, these findings suggest that literalists are if anything slightly more liberal than non-literalists—the exact opposite of the usual stereotype.

If factors such as race and income, which are also associated with economic attitudes, are taken into account, the results are still anti-stereotypical. (The "taking into account" is done through a statistical procedure called multiple regression analysis.) The slight connection between literalism and liberalism suggested by Table 7-1 is attenuated but not reversed; that is, the connection is still visible but so small as to be of no practical significance.

Another analysis of these same thirty-nine questions was done to see what differences exist among denominational groups. The pattern corresponds roughly with that described above (and found in previous research), and is shown graphically in Figure 7-1.[8]

For this analysis, Protestant denominations were divided into four groupings: theologically modernist groups such as the Episcopal Church and the United Church of Christ; theologically moderate groups such as the Evangelical Lutheran Church in America (despite the connotations of its name, the largest and most modernist Lutheran group in the United States); traditionalist groups ranging from the Lutheran Church–Missouri Synod and the Southern Baptists to fundamentalist and Pentecostal groups; and predominantly African-American denominations. The first two of these groupings—the modernist and moderate groups—together approximate what is generally called "mainline Protestantism."

Note that this is a division of denominations, defined by the answers respondents give to a question on their religious preference. The relatively few African-Americans in mainline denominations are counted as modernist or moderate Protestants, and the occasional Episcopalian with a staunchly traditionalist personal theology will still be categorized as a modernist Protestant.

In addition to Protestants, there are Catholics, Jews, people who report they have no religious preference, and adherents to "other" religions. This last grouping is extremely heterogeneous; it includes politically very liberal groups such as the Quakers and politically conservative groups such as the Mormons.

For each of these groups, the graphical display shows the average percentage who gave the liberal answer on the whole set of thirty-nine questions. (Some questions provided only liberal and conservative options, but some also provided a way to take a neutral or centrist position; therefore, of the people not shown on this figure as liberals, some are centrists and some are conservatives.)

The modernist Protestants are the most conservative group on economic issues, and therefore one can describe the other groups in terms of the degree to which they are more liberal than the modernist Protestants over the whole set of thirty-nine questions. Members of predominantly African-American denominations are the most liberal—on the average, over the thirty-nine questions, seventeen percentage points more liberal than the modernist Protestants. This difference is undoubtedly partly ethnic, partly religious, and partly cultural, reflecting the history of African-American Christianity, molded by the practical experiences of African-Americans but also constituting a distinctive and important line of religious development.

Catholics are next, seven percentage points to the left of the modernist Protestants. (The modernist and moderate Protestants are the appropriate Protestant groups to compare the Catholics to, since Catholic theology is fairly modernist by the standards of theological debate among Protestants.) The Catholics are followed closely by traditionalist Protestants, who are six percentage points more liberal than their modernist sisters and brothers, and people with no religious preference, averaging five points more liberal. The Jewish respondents are few in number on any one question, but over the set of thirty-nine their responses should fall into a reliable pattern, and they average three points more liberal than the modernist Protestants, as do the theologically moderate Protestants. The adherents of "other" religions come in as the next-to-most conservative group, about two percentage points more liberal than the modernist Protestants.

Overall, the differences among the predominantly White groups are small, largely because they are somewhat inconsistent; Catholics, for instance, are much more liberal than modernist Protestants on some economic issues, but hold the same or occasionally even more conservative views on other issues. As with biblical literalism, the results go against stereotypes—the members of traditionalist groups are actually slightly more liberal than members of more modernist groups.

One might argue that this result is just an artifact of class, and that the *religious* influence of traditionalist groups is economically conservative. The argument would be that the dispossessed tend to join traditionalist groups, that Catholics are also less privileged than Protestants, and that what we are seeing in Figure 7-1 is an expression of the class interests of such people, as opposed to the interests of the upper-middle-class people found in modernist Protestant denominations. (The assumption on which this argument is based is somewhat shaky, because the class differences between modernists and traditionalists are only modest, and between Protestants and Catholics almost non-existent. This represents a change from forty years ago, and of course it is possible that historical class patterns could still be affecting economic opinions today.)

To test this argument, personal factors—race, income, and personal religious traditionalism, as measured by biblical literalism—were held constant.[9] When this was done, the differences between modernist and traditionalist denominations became quite small, but—like differences between literalists and non-literalists—were not reversed. Thus, members of modernist and traditionalist denominations have essentially the same economic views once we factor out the influence of the personal social and religious characteristics of their members. The Catholic/Protestant difference, however, remains even when class and race are taken into account.

We also examined the relationships between the set of thirty-nine economic questions on one side, and church attendance and prayer on the other. With regard to both prayer and attendance, the relationships with economic opinions are even weaker and more inconsistent than the ones we have been reviewing so far, and this remains the case when other variables are taken into account.

To make this analysis a little more concrete, tables 7-2 and 7-3 show how people with different stances toward the Bible, and in different denominational groups, respond to a single question. This question was selected out of the thirty-nine we have been dealing with because it is shows the most "typical" pattern of response; that is, the differences between literalists and non-literalists, and among denominational groups, are close to the average for the whole set of thirty-nine questions. The question asks the respondents to agree or disagree, with an option for a neutral response, to the statement, "The government should provide a decent standard of living for the unemployed."[10] About equal numbers of people agree and disagree

Table 7-2. Differences between Biblical Literalists and Non-Literalists with Regard to Helping the Unemployed

	View of the Bible		
Position on helping the unemployed	Actual Word of God, to be taken literally	Inspired Word, but not everything to be taken literally	Ancient book of fables and moral precepts recorded by men
Liberal	47.2%	31.8%	37.4%
Neutral	23.0%	26.8%	22.3%
Conservative	29.8%	41.4%	40.3%
Total	100 %	100 %	100 %
Base (= 100%)	(359)	(463)	(112)

with this statement and about one quarter of the respondents choose the neutral answer.

Table 7-2 shows only the responses of Christians, since the literalism question would either be nonsensical or have a different meaning for a non-Christian. It shows that literalists, by a fairly large margin, are more liberal than those who think of the Bible only as inspired. Those who hold the Bible in least awe (speaking of it as a collection of fables) are in the middle, but closer to the non-literalists.

Table 7-3 shows the denominational pattern.[11] The members of predominantly African-American denominations are the most in agreement with generosity for the unemployed. At the next level of support (still above average) are the Catholics and the traditionalist Protestants. The Jews and people of no religious preference are the most likely to pick the neutral answer instead of taking either the liberal or the conservative side. The two mainline Protestant groupings have a clear conservative tilt, and to a lesser extent the same is true for the heterogeneous "other religion" grouping. The differences among White groups are not enormous but of some importance, with the Catholics and traditionalist Protestants fifteen to nineteen percentage points more likely to give a liberal answer than the mainline Protestants.

Mistaken Assumptions about Religion and Politics

These results strongly contradict prevailing stereotypes about religion and politics. Over and over again, one encounters the expectation that religion is a politically conservative force, or at least, that "conservative" religion (what we have been calling religious traditionalism) and conservative politics go together. Jerry Falwell and other fundamentalists on the right believe that the natural, authentic implications of Christian faith—or at least of the

Table 7-3. Denominational Group Differences in Regard to Helping the Unemployed

				Denominational Group				
Position on helping the unemployed	Modernist Protestants	Moderate Protestants	African-American Protestants	Traditionalist Protestants	Catholics	Jews	Other Religions	No religious preference
Liberal	26.3%	29.3%	55.5%	45.5%	44.1%	35.1%	34.5%	30.9%
Neutral	28.9%	27.4%	30.9%	23.1%	23.9%	35.2%	23.8%	35.7%
Conservative	44.8%	43.3%	13.6%	31.4%	32.0%	29.7%	41.7%	33.4%
Total	100 %	100 %	100 %	100 %	100 %	100 %	100 %	100 %
Base (= 100%)	(140)	(330)	(21)	(371)	(398)	(23)	(166)	(103)

theologically traditionalist faith that to them is the only real Christianity—are politically conservative on almost every issue, including economic ones. Political activists on the Left (many of whom are secular) often assume that the same is true. For instance, in 1982 Alan Wolfe wrote (rather optimistically) in *The Nation* that while the Right was being routed in the "secular environments" found almost everywhere in the West, it was still doing well in the "rhetorically religious" United States because of similarities between Calvinism and Reaganism; the conservative economic "agenda can work only if a strong tradition of religious concern is accepted by all."[12] Despite their political and religious differences, people such as Falwell and Wolfe agree, descriptively, on the nature of the connection between faith and politics. As one can see from the literature reviews and the data presented a moment ago, however, the proposition they agree on is badly mistaken. With regard to topics such as sexuality, to be sure, religious traditionalism and political conservatism do go together. But on economic issues (and many others) they do not.

So powerful and pervasive is the belief that religious traditionalism and conservatism go together on all political issues that many public opinion or survey researchers hold onto this assumption, despite the large body of evidence to the contrary. From this perspective, the results they have come up with—the lack of associations between religiosity, or at least religious traditionalism, and economic conservatism—represent a failure to demonstrate the relationship they are sure must be there.[13] In fact, one finds in their analyses a striking commitment to maintaining their assumptions in the face of disconfirming evidence. Author after author explains away the recurring non-relationships, arguing that special circumstances or inadequate methods of research must be masking the true relationship.

Leo Driedger says that

> ideas have consequences. . . . There must be a relationship . . . between religious beliefs and attitudes toward social issues. The inconsistencies found so far [here he is referring to Wuthnow's literature review[14]] must be due to inadequate measures of religious beliefs and to inadequate clustering of social issues. . . . A sample of clergymen might increase the associations.[15]

Jeffrey Hadden similarly dismisses his own results. After saying that "our data do support . . . [the] conclusion that theological belief is strongly associated with the way a person views the economic order," he presents data showing no relationship at all between biblical literalism and economic attitudes. He then interprets this finding as due to the laity's lack of interest in or comprehension of theology.[16]

In a more recent study, using a Muncie, Indiana, sample, Joseph Tamney, Ronald Burton, and Stephen Johnson argue that fundamentalists should be economically conservative because they "continue into the present the Puritan justification of capitalism." But they find that Protestant fundamentalists are if anything more liberal on their "economic restructuring" measure than less traditionalist Protestants. In the discussion, they reiterate their view that fundamentalism is allied to the politics of the Christian Right (apparently including its economic politics) and explain away their findings with the statement that "Protestant Fundamentalists in our study tended to support economic restructuring because of the continuing influence among them [in the Midwest] of ideas once associated with the Prohibition and Populist parties." Special historical and geographical factors, in short, are adduced to explain the disconfirmation of their expectations.[17]

None of these authors responds to data clearly showing that religious traditionalism *is not* connected to economic conservatism by questioning or revising the assumptions and frameworks they started out with. Rather, they explain away the findings and look for different methods or populations that might yield the expected results.

Why does the popular stereotype about the conservative implications of faith persist? Why does the same assumption continue to be held by researchers even when their own research contradicts it? Why has public opinion research on religion and economic attitudes failed to meet its goal of correlating religious and political variables? One possible set of reasons lies in some ways of thinking about religion and its relationship to politics that are occasionally explicit, and even when they are not, appear to influence the ways in which people frame issues.[18] Let us examine these ways of thinking.

A Unitary and Unexamined Idea of the Liberal-Conservatism Continuum

When we read about politics in newspapers or magazines, very often we find people or groups being described as "liberal" or "conservative." The problem is that these words mean very different things in different contexts. We can be conservative in our lifestyle or ethical standards, believing, for instance, that sex outside marriage is always wrong. Or we can be conservative on any one of the variety of political issues under debate in the United States today, such as civil liberties, abortion, race relations, women's rights, foreign policy, or economic issues. Results from public opinion polls repeatedly show that most of us pick and choose our political views, holding liberal views on some issues and conservative ones on others. The connections between views in different issue areas are weak.

To give an example of how unconnected views on economic and noneconomic issues can be, let us look at how views on the economic issue presented earlier—help for the unemployed—are related to views on abortion. The question on abortion was the last in a whole series on different circumstances under which a woman might seek an abortion, and asked, "Please tell me whether or not *you* think it should be possible for a pregnant

Table 7-4. Differences between Pro-Life and Pro-Choice People in Regard to Helping the Unemployed

Position on helping the unemployed	*Position on women having an unconditional right to a legal abortion*	
	Pro-Life	*Pro-Choice*
Liberal	41.2%	31.9%
Neutral	25.6%	27.2%
Conservative	33.2%	40.9%
Total	100 %	100 %
Base (= 100%)	(890)	(596)

woman to obtain a *legal* abortion if . . . the woman wants it for any reason?"[19] Table 7-4 shows the result: pro-life people, despite their conservatism on abortion, are actually more *liberal* on help for the unemployed than are pro-choice people. Of the pro-life people, 41 percent take the liberal position on helping the unemployed, compared with 32 percent among pro-choice people. If liberalism and conservatism were coherent packages, one would expect, on the contrary, that people would tend to be liberal on both issues or conservative on both. When one examines the relationship between a particular economic issue and a particular non-economic one, sometimes this expectation is fulfilled, but often (as we see in Table 7-4) it is not, and even when it is the relationship is usually quite weak.

Some observers interpret this to mean that many people are inconsistent or at least non-ideological, but it is also true, as we have seen from our respondents, that a combination of views that seems illogical to one person may seem logical to another.[20] David Jenkins, for instance, has good reason, given his basic perspective on life, to be extremely conservative on economic issues but moderately liberal on issues concerning the public regulation of sexuality. One could argue, similarly, that the unifying thread explaining answers to General Social Survey questions just described is that many people decide to what extent they want an activist government, and then apply the principle to the issues of unemployment and of abortion. The logic connecting the views considered liberal on a variety of issues into one central "liberal" perspective—a logic expressed in journalistic categorizing of people and in the arguments of many leaders and movements of both left and right— is simply not that strong. People who violate this logic are therefore not necessarily inconsistent or non-ideological. In sum, the terms *liberal* and *conservative* are useful as a shorthand for talking about views on a particular issue, but they do not describe whole philosophies of life, systematically applied to a broad range of issues, for most Americans.[21]

Views on different kinds of political issues not only are relatively uncon-nected but also seem to relate in different ways to other variables. People who have had large amounts of formal education, for instance, tend to be more liberal on abortion than people with less schooling, but more conservative on economic issues. Evangelical and fundamentalist Protestants are more conservative than modernist Protestants on abortion but essentially the same (with a possible slight tilt in the liberal direction) on economic issues. Roman Catholics tend to be liberal on economic issues compared with mainline Protestants, but conservative on abortion.[22]

For all these reasons, talking about the social implications of Christian faith in relation to politics in a global sense—as when people think of fundamentalists as politically conservative, without specifying the issue—is not likely to be very fruitful. The ways in which faith serves grass-roots Christians as a resource for thinking about political issues varies depending on the kind of issue; we can make sense of the relationships between religion and politics only by proceeding one issue at a time, understanding with care the special kind of ethical considerations that, for instance, economic issues raise.

Difficulties in Defining Religious Variables

Public opinion research normally involves "dependent" variables—the phenomena one wishes to explain—and "independent" ones—the factors, usually conceived of as causal agents, that might influence outcomes on the dependent variables. For instance, considerable research has been done on the ways in which people's social position (a set of independent variables) affects their economic opinions (the dependent variable).[23] Similarly, survey researchers on religion and politics have defined religious factors as independent variables that might affect people's attitudes on economic issues. If we wish to understand the political impact of Christian faith, we have to define what, for research purposes, that faith is, and we also need some kind of contrast or conception of what it is not; we can assess the impact of faith (as with any independent variable or causal factor) only by *comparing* people who differ. It is easy to devise concrete criteria by which to differentiate people—denomination, church attendance, biblical literalism, and the like—but the interpretation of these criteria is quite tricky. It is in the nature of definitions of orthodox faith and religious commitment, and perhaps of any religious variable, to be controversial and value-laden.

The bulk of public opinion research on religion and politics has been focused on a single dimension, loosely corresponding to the terms *traditionalist* and *modernist* we have been using. This is most naturally a theological dimension, since its origin is in the controversies and divisions—most notably about the authority of Scripture—that developed in U.S. Protestantism (different ones developed within Catholicism) in the late nineteenth and early twentieth centuries. However, this dimension becomes a template by which many kinds of religious differences are understood and bound together into a loose unity.

This dimension is more often than not interpreted or described using terms such as *commitment, religiosity,* or *orthodoxy,* which imply a judgment that to be traditionalist is to be more true to the Christian tradition, more religious, and a more committed Christian. Thus the dimension becomes quantitative rather than qualitative: it becomes a way to compare people who are religious to a different degree rather than just people who are religious in different ways.

This tendency is well illustrated in the most widely cited literature review, by Robert Wuthnow. Summarizing the criteria he found in the literature, Wuthnow states:

> The more religious people were judged to be:
>   1. Those who belonged to doctrinally conservative denominations. . . .
>   2. Those who subscribed to traditional tenets of Christian faith. . . .
>   3. Those who engaged in private prayer . . . and so forth. . . .
>   4. Those who have great knowledge of their faith. . . .
>   5. Those whose primary friendships are with coreligionists. . . .
>   6. Those whose organizational energies are primarily spent in church-related groups. . . .
>   7. Those who attend church more frequently. . . .
>   8. Those who exhibited greater religiousness on some combination of [the] above. . . . [24]

Wuthnow himself expresses doubts about the appropriateness of such definitions; the researchers whose work he is examining, however, had few doubts indeed. Note that even denomination gets subsumed under this quantitative approach to religiosity. A high proportion of the questions on religious beliefs that have been used in public opinion research also fit under this rubric because most concern issues on which theological traditionalists and modernists disagree.

One problem with this approach is immediately obvious: it accepts the traditionalist camp's view that it has the real thing, making its theological position into a social scientific definition of religiosity. Oddly enough, many of the researchers who have taken this approach are personally religious modernists, and regard fundamentalism as both religiously and socially harmful; nonetheless, they give it a kind of religious priority.

The problem is most blatant with the first two of the criteria of religiousness listed by Wuthnow. Measures of "orthodoxy" are widely used, and clearly represent a particular judgment about what the core elements of Christian faith are—a judgment that is sure to be at variance with the religious perspectives of many Christian communions. With regard to denomination, surely only a few Christians—even those with traditionalist beliefs or definite denominational preferences—would maintain that denomination in itself indicates how good a Christian a person is. Just as people can believe that marriage is good without denying that some are destructive, one can regard one's own denomination as the best choice without conflating the boundaries of its membership with those of God's people.

This is an issue of importance not just theologically but for understanding religion and politics. Jerry Falwell must know that many people who call themselves Christians are not in agreement with him politically, and yet he is not relativistic about the social implications of faith. Because he regards as secular and non-Christian the theological perspective of many who disagree with him, he can ascribe their social views to secular influences; the social implications of his brand of Christianity are then the natural and authentic implications of Christian faith. More moderately, Anthony Massimimi, writing in the *National Catholic Reporter,* characterizes at least some liberal activism among Christians as "leftist capitulation . . . to the secular world." Some left Christians take the reverse position, attributing to secular influences (the media, the hegemony of the market, and so on) the conservative social implications other Christians find in their faith, and occasionally they, too, attack the theological frameworks of those they disagree with politically as heretical or even in some sense non-Christian. (However, public opinion research on religion and politics seldom uses their point of view for measuring religiosity.) Massimimi, showing evenhandedness, approvingly summarizes how a book he is reviewing "describes in journalistic detail how the Christian Right uses religion to mask an aggressive, cynical promotion of anticommunist ideology."[25] Words like *mask* and *cynical* indicate his perception that the motivation is not genuinely religious.

From either of these perspectives, people who are highly religious or committed (for the left Christians just referred to, this might be expressed in terms such as being fully faithful) will presumably manifest more of the social implications of faith, and fend off secular influences better, than those who are lukewarm. Thus one can make comparisons between the committed and uncommitted, and use the results to disentangle the influence of Christian faith from secular influences.

Otherwise—if one is relativistic, and thinks all who call themselves Christians are equally entitled to define the social implications of Christian faith— it is hard to establish empirically the social implications of Christianity from what individual Christians think. Those who identify themselves as Christians constitute about nine out of ten Americans; therefore, it is necessarily true, for purely arithmetic reasons, that the views of Americans Christians on any political issue one examines will be almost identical to the views of all Americans. More substantively, in a situation where one religious tradition has such dominance, it is often hard to tell what is a religious and what a general cultural influence. In any case, no distinctive Christian political stance can be delineated empirically by comparing the views of Christians and non-Christians. (However, such comparisons can be of interest for what they tell us about the views of Jews and people with no religious preference.)

Thus, within a public opinion research approach there are important considerations that might motivate researchers to adopt a less subjective and relativistic and more specific conception of what a committed Christian is like—despite the dangers of bias this choice brings. Furthermore, theologically even many mainline Protestants and Catholics feel that being a Christian should surely mean *something,* however hard to define in specific or behavioral terms, about a person's faith or life. Evangelicals and fundamentalists, of course, go much further, often using the word *Christian* in a restricted sense to refer only to people who meet their definition of having been "born again."

What the depth-interview respondents tell us, however, casts grave doubt on the idea that one can disentangle the social implications of faith from other influences by including as truly rooted in faith only certain political views, only those views expressed by particularly "religious" people, or only those views expressed by people with particular kinds of theological slants. It is clear from the respondents' statements that many different economic stances can be rooted in Christian ideas with a clear descent from undeniably orthodox themes, that these connections can be made by people with an amazing variety of theological perspectives, and that they are found in the thinking of people who vary in the kind of "commitment" survey researchers typically define.

The problem of bias is less blatant but still present with regard to the other criteria Wuthnow describes. One criterion is clearly implausible and another doubtful: few Christians would maintain that having more friends among co-religionists makes one more religious (although such friendship networks might *result* from religious involvement), and many Christians have traditionally resisted giving any great importance to knowledge (in theological terms, to do so might be called a gnostic heresy). The others, taken together, make up a kind of caricature of a highly conventional idea of the religious life. Many Christians would say that prayer, worship attendance, and organizational involvement are in principle good things, but many— perhaps most—would not want to equate the package thus formed with what Christian faith is really about. Even many of those who fulfill these criteria would have trouble with this. Consider how David Jenkins conceives of the life of faith: having particular beliefs and involvement in the church are secondary. More broadly, fully 78 percent of Americans, and 70 percent even of the churched, believe that one can be a good Christian or Jew without attending a church or synagogue.[26]

Another striking characteristic of the ideas of religiosity that researchers typically use is that they apply dimensions in a non-contextual way to people who belong to very different religious traditions. Orthodoxy is best understood as a relational concept, having to do with one's stance relative to what is normative in a group one is or was attached to. There are many "orthodoxies," and most of them could provide a plausible genealogy showing the origin of their perspective as a development out of one or another strand of Christian tradition going back many centuries; any list of the "traditional tenets of Christian faith" is bound to be controversial. The same views that would make one an orthodox Presbyterian, in full agreement with the Presbyterian Confession of 1967, would make one a heterodox Southern Baptist. What sense does it make to ask Unitarians about the Bible and then class them as less religious, committed, or orthodox because they reject literalism? They would be total misfits within Unitarianism if they were literalists. Even Catholics have a clearly defined orthodoxy that gives Scripture much less authority than traditionalist Protestants give it. And yet, study after study uses literalism as a measure of orthodoxy, applying the measure to Catholics, Unitarians, and traditionalist Protestants alike.

Other criteria of "religiosity" are subject to the same criticism; for instance, a level of religious giving manifesting high commitment in one denomination might be regarded as unacceptably low in another. (To give a sense of how large these variations are, among Mormons who attend worship at least weekly, average giving is 8.5 percent of income; for Catholics with the same frequency of attendance it is 1.9 percent.)[27]

A final difficulty with ideas of religiosity is that they bring together under the same concept rather diverse issues. To be sure, there are empirical correlations among many of these variables. Members of evangelical and fundamentalist denominations, for instance, tend to give more generously to the church than modernists. Wade Clark Roof and William McKinney use General Social Survey data to show that 58 percent of members of traditionalist denominations attend worship regularly, compared with about 40 percent for members of what they call moderate or liberal denominations.[28] Yet the highest levels of giving are found among Mormons, whose theological stance is strongly at odds with that of evangelical Protestants (and also of modernists). This suggests that it is not the traditionalism per se of evangelical Protestants but something more specific about life in their churches that results in higher giving. Furthermore, variations within denominations are as striking as differences between them: Christians of all denominations can be generous or stingy givers, be involved or uninvolved, hold personal religious views that are modernists or traditionalist. The fact that a person is a member of a denomination or theological tradition in which attendance and giving tend to be high does not justify defining *that person* as more religiously committed.

In response to all these problems, some researchers, while using similar survey questions to measure religious variables, use terms with a more qualitative or relativistic cast to interpret the answers. For instance, they may speak of measuring "fundamentalism" rather than "orthodoxy" or "commitment." These measures are then seen as indicators of *different ways* of being religious, without any assumption that one way is more authentically religious or Christian than another. For instance, we can compare modernists to traditionalists, or members of mainline denominations to members of evangelical and fundamentalist denominations. This avoids the problem of religious bias while still providing groups to compare. The idea is that different kinds of Christian faith may have different social implications; hope for discovering the implications of Christian faith per se is abandoned.

This, of course, raises anew the problem a non-relativistic approach was intended to solve: how to disentangle the influences of faith and secular currents, a problem made especially severe by the fact that most Americans are Christians. That is, there is no easy way to determine whether the different stances taken by different kinds of Christians are the result of different but distinctively Christian perspectives, or of the different ways and degrees to which different kinds of Christians are influenced by secular culture. This approach also has its own exclusionary quality, in that it implicitly denies the *non*-relativistic theological position many Christians take.

In any case, this approach remains focused on dimensions differentiating between those who do and do not adhere to the characteristic beliefs and encouraged patterns of behavior found within evangelical and fundamentalist Protestantism. The problem is that these are unimportant dimensions for understanding economic issues, and probably many others as well. As we have seen from the depth-interview respondents, the key ideas used to support both liberal and conservative economic ideas—themes such as voluntarism, love, and universalism—are available and commonly appropriated by modernists and traditionalists alike (perhaps in slightly different language). These are *shared* themes. Voluntaristic thinking is essentially the same, and has essentially the same implications, in the thinking of David Jenkins and Richard Schenk; the principles of love and universalism are the same theologically, and are used in the same way to make political judgments, for Catherine Kennedy and Linda Watson. Religious issues—how much priority one gives to voluntaristic ideals, and in what ethical, social, and political contexts; how one thinks the values of love and universalism should be applied to social life; and so forth—are important, but the religious issues that matter are not how one reads the Bible, how much authority one accords the pope, or the like.

Therefore, it is quite predictable that in public opinion research religious variables that mostly separate modernists from traditionalists are unrelated to economic views. One reason for the failure of public opinion research to meet its own goals in the area of faith and economic attitudes is that this kind of research has focused excessively on such variables, which represent a theoretically inappropriate dimension. There really is no persuasive reason to think that being theologically traditionalist should make people conservative on economic issues. Suppose, for instance, that one is a biblical literalist. In the Bible one can find: indignation at economic injustice and calls to rectify it; fatalistic views; counsels to withdraw from the world; a focus, particularly in the New Testament, on the individual (which people like David Jenkins can draw on to ground conservative economic views);

and even a few passages that could be interpreted as direct affirmations of capitalism. Or suppose one has a strong sense of the presence of the supernatural in earthly life. It is clear, historically, that this only sometimes leads to passive acceptance of current social arrangements, and sometimes leads to just the opposite. Therefore, it is far from surprising that ways of categorizing people based on these divisions do not yield group differences on economic issues.

Furthermore, a focus on traditionalism ignores a host of other dimensions of variation among Christians. There is enormous political and religious diversity within the mainline denominations, and also among traditionalist ones. Pentecostals and traditional fundamentalists, for instance, are deeply at odds. Catholics and mainline Protestants are about equally non-traditionalist but are vastly different religiously in other respects; as we have seen, Catholics are more liberal on economic issues than mainline Protestants, and so these differences may be more important than the ones between modernists and traditionalists. The traditionalism-modernism dimension really concerns a debate internal to Protestantism, and the persisting focus on this dimension in discussions of religion and politics manifests a kind of ethnocentrism in the face of the reality that Protestantism is far less dominant within American religious culture than it was a century ago.

All in all, it is not surprising that public opinion research on religion and politics, when dealing with economic issues, has not accomplished what the researchers have hoped. This tradition of research has conceived of both political and religious variables in unhelpful ways. Nonetheless, the findings are illuminating, by providing good grounds for rejecting permanently the assumption that religious traditionalism has conservative implications on every issue. The depth interview respondents show us why this assumption is false and are evidence against it, but they are few,[29] and therefore it is valuable to have this complementary evidence from public opinion research.

8

Theoretical Issues

The public opinion research examined in the previous chapter points to assumptions and stereotypes that make it hard to understand religion and politics. As we saw, these assumptions are not unique to research using opinion polls and questionnaires; they are also widely influential among journalists, people in the churches, and political activists. Furthermore, they come from ideas about the social role of religion that affect not just public opinion research but also other forms of research, and even people's practical activities in political and religious realms. Our task now is to criticize these ideas and suggest alternatives.

Theoretical Obstacles to Understanding Religion and Politics

Misleading Conceptions of Secular Culture and Its Social Implications

The idea that religion is a conservative political force is partly based on an unspoken contrast to an imagined more secular situation in which religious influences were weakened or removed. This situation, it is assumed, would be more hospitable to liberal or radical values. Such a contrast, however, depends on shaky assumptions about secular culture.

Even though the United States could be argued to be a highly religious country, secular frameworks of many different kinds are pervasive and influential; even Christians mostly think in terms of ideas and values that do not come directly from Christianity. Those other ideas and values are not Jewish ones, nor are they usually "secular humanist" ones, if by that we understand a coherent worldview that explicitly defines itself as different from and better than religious ones. Rather, they are the kinds of values and beliefs actually found in this country. Some of these, such as feminism or the sense of solidarity sometimes expressed by labor movements or community organizations in the Alinsky tradition, favor liberal or radical views on economic issues. But the dominant frameworks are probably those described by Robert Bellah and his colleagues in *Habits of the Heart*.[1] These are predominantly individualistic; they have quite conservative implications for economic issues, and little capacity to motivate people to be involved in public life. If by some cataclysm or miracle American Christians all lost their faith overnight, therefore, it is not very likely that they would adopt the political values held by secularist liberals and radicals. Instead, whatever capacity they now have to relate Christian themes to either liberal or conservative political opinions would disappear, and they would either think about those issues less, or think about them using the kinds of frameworks Bellah and his co-authors describe.

In other words, secular culture, like Christianity, is an arena of struggle, in which radicals, liberals, and conservatives contend. Based on Bellah's work and the views of the respondents, it looks as though liberals have slightly better chances, and certainly not worse, in the Christian than in the secular arena.

Furthermore, the secular arena, just as much as religious contexts, is socially constructed rather than natural. Secularist liberals and radicals often imagine that if the distractions and irrationalities of religion could be removed, most people would tend to accept what they themselves see as a natural, logical, rational, and humane set of social values. It is possible that there is a core of shared values that any rational person would accept if properly presented, but it is unlikely that the values in this core would be specific enough, as applied to economic life, to favor the general philosophy of either the Left or the Right. At best, therefore, they would define some terms of debate rather than influence the outcome in any clear direction.[2] Therefore, it is doubtful, philosophically, that a sure foundation for a vision of social justice, making no reference either to religious traditions or to other disputed values, can be constructed (which by no means implies that one ought to take a relativistic position). But regardless of whether in theory such a foundation might be constructed, empirically it is clear that no consensus has been reached. Given the extremely varied economic viewpoints—from revolutionary socialism to total advocacy of free markets—that are put forward without religious backing, it is highly unlikely that the removal of religion as a cultural force would bring such consensus about. In short, secular frameworks are as culturally particular, as constructed and artificial, and as potentially varied in their political implications, as religious ones.[3]

Furthermore, it is striking how much non-religious frameworks rely on beliefs and commitments that go far beyond what one could conclude on a purely empirical, naturalistic basis. This is not to take the position—which secular people rightly find offensive—that everyone is religious without knowing it, that belief in God or some absolute is a necessary basis for morality or a good society, or that religious perspectives are ethically superior to secular ones. Rather, it is to argue that passion for justice, the conviction that all people are in some fundamental sense equal, and a burning desire for a more loving community typically come, even for people with no religious faith, out of something more than an intellectual inquiry that fits the model of science and Enlightenment social philosophy. Christianity is one source of such a "something more," but there are clearly other sources as well.

Evolutionary Thinking

The idea that there is a "natural" social philosophy to which people would tend in the absence of religion can be based on an explicit or implicit philosophical position. Sometimes, however, it is based more on a form of evolutionary thinking. By this I mean a tendency to assume that changes in different spheres of life—technology, economic organization, politics, and culture—are governed by an underlying dynamic that tends to move each sphere forward in a definite direction, corresponding to the direction of evolution in other spheres. Technology becomes more powerful, economic and political organization become more complex and differentiated, and culture becomes more individuated and in some sense secular.

When people use the term *modern* (or even *post-modern*), often they are implicitly thinking in evolutionary terms. For instance, when speaking of culture, they may be assuming that there are certain forms of culture that are more compatible with the direction in which our society is moving. Such cultural phenomena might include the value of tolerance; skepticism about claims to absolute truth and about inherited ideas and customs; respect for scientific knowledge; and openness to social and technological change. Furthermore, they may believe that this direction is not just accidental or unique but an instance of underlying forces affecting most societies. From such a point of view, there is a "natural" direction for religious or cultural change not because of universal standards of rationality but because of the necessity for cultural frameworks to be plausible and useful within their social, economic, and technological environment.

Furthermore, since political and cultural (including religious) change follow corresponding trajectories, modern religion and modern politics (which in this context is usually taken to be liberal) will fit together, as will traditional religion and traditional (that is, conservative) politics. Because the basic direction of cultural change is taken to be toward secularity and away from religion, the most modern religion is no religion. The less religious people are, or the less traditional form of religion they adopt, the more liberal they will be politically. Traditional theology and conservative politics, likewise, are natural partners. From this standpoint, mainline denominations and theological modernism represent a kind of half-way station between secularity and the religion of the past.

This point of view is widespread. To categorize religious beliefs as modernist or traditionalist (as we have in this book) can easily imply an evolutionary dimension: modernist beliefs are seen as those compatible with modern society, as opposed to beliefs that would be compatible with traditional or pre-modern society. Traditionalists, it may be inferred, are in some way resisting or reacting against modernity.

James Davison Hunter's influential *American Evangelicalism: Conservative Religion and the Quandary of Modernity* explicitly adopts this model. In his view (the emphases are his):

> *Modernity* is the inevitable period in the history of a particular society that is characterized by the institutional and cultural concomitants of a technologically induced economic growth.... The picture of the world presented in religious doctrine and symbols is not necessarily denied ... but is *disaffirmed* and therefore becomes less plausible.... [4]

The idea that there is an "inevitable period in the history of a particular society" indicates Hunter's conviction that there is a single direction of change and that the same basic pattern of change will happen in every society. By speaking of the "concomitants of a technologically induced" change, he suggests that the driving force is technology and that other spheres of life, particularly culture, will inevitably change in determinate ways in response to technological change. Modernism in overall culture appears inevitable, but religion, thus threatened, faces some choices. The religious response is some combination of resistance, accommodation, or (more rarely) withdrawal. Since modernity is much stronger than religion, their intersection results in "*cognitive contamination* of the religious world view"; this is a form of accommodation.[5] But modernity also "creates certain circumstances that evoke the bold reassertion of religious meanings that can be, and in most cases are, directly contrary to the nature of modernity."[6] Evangelicalism manifests a combination of resistance and accommodation; mainline Protestantism appears to have mostly followed the path of accommodation, becoming secularized and losing most of what might be distinctive in a Christian worldview.

This analysis states explicitly an idea that is often only implicit in the definitions of religiosity and religious commitment discussed in chapter 7: that the traditionalists have the real thing, whereas the modernists, while more modern and rational, have to a large degree lost their faith (via "cognitive contamination"). This view carries the kind of theological bias considered previously. It also shows the distorting power of some evolutionary readings of history, since the faith of modern-day traditionalists is in many respects quite "untraditional" in terms of continuity with the past of Christian doctrine. For instance, biblical literalism as we encounter it today is a modern phenomenon, invented within the last century or so, significantly influenced by popular understandings of science, and strongly at odds with the views of sixteenth- and seventeenth-century Lutherans and Calvinists and with the Catholic position of Christendom's first millennium and a half. The Puritans, like Aquinas, welcomed the "cognitive contamination" of the best available philosophical and scientific thought, regarding it as contributing to rather than competing with their enterprise.

Hunter's conception of evangelicalism as in reaction against modernity well fits the assumption of a clear link between theological traditionalism and political conservatism. As we have seen, however, some very "old-fashioned" religious and ethical ideas have the potential to support radical views on substantive issues and change-facilitating ones on implementation issues. The criticism of our present economic order that is sometimes grounded in these old-fashioned ideas does not emerge simply from lagging behind the march of modernity and therefore wanting the social order to return to what it was when one's values and worldviews were dominant.

Evolutionary thinking is also imbedded in some of the thinking and terminology of the Left, especially the term *progressive,* with its overtones of progress, of the assumption that as time goes on things are getting better. People on the left have often thought that they were on the side of the future, and of course one does hope, and want to assert, that one has the values that will be most conducive to abundant life under the actual social and economic conditions emerging in the world. The themes and images of Christianity, too, can be appropriated relatively easily in a way that is highly compatible with the idea of progress. But in addition, liberals who feel themselves to be on the side of "progress," and equally Marxists, are heirs to nineteenth-century evolutionary thinking, involving considerable faith in future movement in a desirable direction, not just in technology (where an evolutionary perspective seems most plausible) but in social structure and culture as well. This legacy clouds views of the political role of religion.[7]

Evolutionary thinking can contribute to our understanding, if formulated and used cautiously. But the statements of the depth-interview respondents indicate limits to its usefulness, and it appears to be an important source of the assumption that conservative politics and religious traditionalism are strongly linked.

Misappropriations of Max Weber's Theories about the Relationship between Protestantism and Capitalism

The sociologist Max Weber argued that there was an affinity between the ethos of ascetic Protestantism and the motivations, perspectives, and personality structure required for capitalist activities to come into being in the absence of a pre-existing capitalist structure.[8] Weber's argument is often transmogrified into the theory that there is an ideological correspondence between pro-capitalist views and traditionalist Protestantism. For instance, in an article we discussed in the last chapter, Joseph Tamney, Ronald Burton, and Stephen Johnson say that "fundamentalists, more than their liberal counterparts, are a continuation into the present of the Puritan heritage." Puritanism, they think, is an ideology supportive of capitalism, and therefore fundamentalists should be economically conservative: "Fundamentalists continue into the present the Puritan justification of capitalism."[9]

Such arguments (found over and over in writings on the political role of religion) ignore the historical context. To be on the conservative side in twentieth-century ideological disputes between unfettered free market advocates and those advocating some kind of welfare state or public intervention is very different from the seventeenth- and eighteenth-century style of personal action that Weber calls the spirit of capitalism. One could argue more persuasively that the Puritans, if magically transported to our time, would find themselves a little left of center on economic issues, given their perception of our mutual responsibilities and the role of law and government. (Among the respondents, Joseph Krieger—even though he is a Catholic—is the one who articulates a social theory closest to that of the Puritans.) Modern-day Quakers, descendants of another group Weber discusses, are certainly on the left.

Theologically, furthermore, it is not plausible to say, as Tamney, Burton, and Johnson maintain, that traditionalist Protestants continue the Puritan heritage more than mainline Protestants. The Puritans were not biblical literalists in the contemporary sense, generally detested revivalism and most other methods of seeking conversions, opposed the Arminian theological assumptions rife among evangelicals, and felt themselves in full accord with the modern science of their time. One could argue that if anything modernist Protestantism is more in continuity with the spirit of Puritanism, as it would be expressed in a changed cultural context, than are contemporary evangelicalism and fundamentalism. Traditionalism, as we have seen, is not so "traditional."

A much more helpful appropriation of Weber's theoretical perspective is found in political scientist Michael Walzer's analysis of the Puritan Revolution, *The Revolution of the Saints*.[10] Walzer argues that certain versions of the Calvinist tradition provided a perspective that helped people undertake the first modern, ideological revolution. He identifies an important contrast between "a politics of conflict and competition for power, of faction, intrigue, and open war," on one side, and a politics of "radical ideology and revolution." The first exists wherever there is politics, but the second is characteristically modern. Intrigue can be carried on behind closed doors, but an ideological revolution requires a public language. Intrigue can rely on rational self-interest, but ideology and revolution must at least articulate something more: a set of transcendent goals with an ethical or religious basis. Intrigue can be carried on *ad hoc,* but the pursuit of ideological revolution requires methodical activity and the cultivation of the capacities to be a coherent individual capable of resisting outside pressures we have discussed in relation to asceticism.

Walzer draws from Weber a deep awareness of the potential social importance of religious commitments, and of the fact that people of faith can sometimes have the most practical impact when they are strongly otherworldly and not very interested in being practical. In Walzer's view, in the case of Calvinism (and other forms of what Weber called ascetic Protestantism), this impact was felt more in politics than in the private economic activities Weber studied in *The Protestant Ethic and the Spirit of Capitalism.*

Some of the themes noted by Walzer are echoed in the statements of the depth-interview respondents. William Westfield finds a basis for a highly non-conforming career line in his Quaker heritage; Philomena Jackson rejects both opportunities for personal profits and part of the ethos of American capitalism, on the basis of an otherworldly faith; Phyllis MacIntyre rejects what she sees as overly pragmatic politics; Linda Watson grounds egalitarianism in our filial relationship with God and in the reversal of earthly standards in the other world she sees promised in Scripture.

We have seen repeatedly that otherworldly thinking can, contrary to stereotypes but in full accord with the arguments advanced by Weber and Walzer, help ground liberal, radical, or change-facilitating views. Both modernist and traditionalist Christians draw on resources in Christian tradition that could be called non-rational in two senses. First, they place human life in the non-empirical framework of our relationship with God. Second, they involve a way of understanding and responding to life and the world that uses a different "methodology"—different kinds of statements, obtaining their plausibility by different strategies, and oriented toward different purposes—than used in cultural endeavors such as science, history, philosophy, psychology, or religious studies as pursued in universities.

This non-rational character of Christian faith is widely noted, although sometimes Christianity is taken to be a more or less rational system of ethics hooked up to a few supernatural propositions that perform functions such as making people feel that they cannot disobey its commandments with impunity. Jean-Jacques Rousseau wrote in this vein, articulating a civil religion to which he believed every citizen should subscribe or be "banish[ed] from the State." Among the principles of this religion are "the reality of the life to come; the reward of the just; and the punishment of evildoers. . . ."[11]

The assumption that the non-rational nature of Christian faith works primarily to support conservative views is found over and over again, among conservatives who welcome this support, leftists who decry it, functionalists who take religion to promote social integration and Marxists who analyze it using concepts such as "superstructure" or "hegemony." However, it is clear both from historical evidence and from what the depth-interview respondents say that religious faith can either legitimate or delegitimate existing institutions and ways of life, and promote either order or conflict. Faith can, as Rousseau believed, supplement the motivating power of earthly police and the intrinsic appeal of virtue, but it can also make the threats of earthly police less effective and define virtue in non-conforming ways. It can engage people's passion and energy, involving the whole person, heart and will as well as mind. This is a source of both potentials and dangers for political life.

These potentials and dangers are still with us, and not just among fundamentalists or traditionalists. Weber argued that what he called the disenchantment of the world in modern society, along with capitalism and bureaucracy, has resulted in a utilitarian worldview.[12] It is true that utilitarian views are widespread today, but this is not necessarily a consequence of declining belief in the supernatural. Theological modernists tend to give less emphasis than traditionalists to the supernatural, but traditionalists as well as modernists seem to have trouble sustaining the transcendence and independence of Christian values and eschewing utilitarian ideas about economic life. There is, indeed, something non-rational and non-"modern" that has to be maintained if people are to continue being otherworldly in any significant sense, but that thing is not supernaturalism per se. The ability of faith to sustain non-utilitarian views of economic life depends on qualities that crosscut theological and denominational lines.

American Exceptionalism

We have seen that there is no easy or plausible way, using public opinion data, to argue that American Christianity is a conservative force on economic issues. It is possible, however, to construct an argument in comparative terms: to argue, for instance, that the United States is the most Christian of Western nations and that is why it is the most conservative. This is the path taken by Alan Wolfe in ascribing the relative conservatism of U.S. economic politics to the influence of religion.[13]

This argument, however, presents several difficulties. First, the sense in which this is an exceptionally Christian or religious country needs careful examination, in light of the problems we have identified in any definition of religiosity. Second, the use of any single factor to explain our comparative economic conservatism is problematic. There is an enormous literature on American exceptionalism, or "why no socialism in the United States." In this literature, many different potential causes have been argued as the reason for the weakness of social democratic politics in the United States as compared with Europe. The American political situation is over-determined and the causes of the differences between U.S. and European trajectories of political development cannot be reliably disentangled.

Third, even if one is going to focus on religious factors, the relative traditionalism of the American religious scene (which may be what Wolfe has in mind when he says this country is exceptionally "rhetorically religious") may not be the key difference to focus on. (We have seen with regard to public opinion research the drawbacks of preoccupation with this one dimension.) Perhaps for example, the problem for the Left is the degree to which voluntaristic ways of thinking, descended from our strong Protestant and antinomian heritage, infuse American religious life, among both traditionalists and modernists.

Fourth, politically the United States is conservative in some respects, but hardly all, and the particular combination we have does not correspond to the exceptionalist model. This country is more conservative than most industrialized countries in terms of economic policy and in some other areas (treatment of criminals, for instance). In environmental policy and women's issues, however, it does better by liberal standards. Germany, to take one example, has a stronger welfare state but more restrictive abortion laws. Since a connection between religious traditionalism and conservative politics does often emerge in public opinion data with regard to women's issues, but not with regard to economic issues, Americans' comparative religious traditionalism might be expected to make the United States exceptionally conservative on gender issues but not affect economic politics—the opposite of the actual situation.

Finally, this whole literature is based on examining the sources of a *negative* condition: why the United States did *not* develop politically in the way Europe did. That can be an unfortunate basis for understanding, taking our attention away from the particular direction in which American politics *did* develop. The United States, to be sure, has very weak welfare state programs by European standards, but it is also different in many other ways, and these may be more significant for understanding America's political development and potential.[14]

Ideas of Privatization

In the United States, attendance at religious services, belief in God, and how important people say religion is to them are higher than in any other technologically advanced country, but the relevance of religion to public life is still much disputed.[15] Major studies of political behavior and attitudes in this country typically pay little attention to religious factors, and a number of commentators have argued that American Christianity has become increasingly "privatized": an important factor in providing people with meaning and solace in their private lives but irrelevant to larger spheres of life. Secularists may see this as a hopeful sign, church leaders as something distressing, but the description offered is the same.

However, the idea of privatization is murky and controversial; commentators are far from agreed on what would constitute privatization and whether in fact there has been any clear trend in this direction over the past few decades.[16] Furthermore, while it is clear that some changes in American religion have occurred and that American religion *is* privatized in some ways, the political implications are not so clear. The mainline churches do not have as easy access to the ears of authority as they used to (the evangelical churches, as denominations, never had it). In that sense, religion has less public presence than in earlier times. But Christians still affect politics in organized ways, perhaps as much as ever, through what Robert Wuthnow calls "special purpose groups," such as the Moral Majority or Witness for Peace.[17] American Christianity certainly is privatized (for Protestants, not necessarily more than in the past) in its focus on the individual as the font of authority and key seat of religious life. This means that churches as organizations cannot "deliver" their members as a unified voting or lobbying bloc. However, it can also mean that individuals feel *more* freedom and responsibility to think through the connections between faith and social issues personally; this kind of privatization can be empowering. On the other hand, we saw in chapter 3 that some Christians do focus purely on private life, compartmentalizing faith and politics, and for them faith is not connected to economic views. Most Christians, however, reject these forms of privatization in theory, however hard they may find it to make connections in practice.

When we discover that the religious variables used in public opinion research—with the exception of differences between White Catholics and Protestants—are generally unrelated to views on economic issues, the first interpretation that comes to mind is that people are secularized or at least privatized, that they vote and think—at least with regard to economic issues—on the basis of more secular concerns, such as their material interests.

The information coming out of my interviews, however, strongly suggests that this interpretation is mistaken. It is true that some of the respondents refuse to connect faith with economic issues; others simply fail to. Most, however, make at least some connections between faith and liberal economic views, conservative ones, or both; often these connections are strong. What is happening is that liberal and conservative uses of faith are of roughly equal strength (with perhaps a small advantage to the liberal side), both among mainline and evangelical Protestants. Among Catholics, where voluntaristic ideas are less influential, faith has more clearly liberal implications.

What this means is that Christianity, like the other contexts in which Americans articulate and discuss their values, is a terrain of debate where neither side is clearly winning. This is obvious with regard to religious leaders and movements—they cover a wide spectrum, from extreme left to extreme right. The same is true of rank-and-file church members. In addition to whatever a theologian or social ethicist might say Christian faith *ought* to imply socially, or what conclusions religious leaders draw, church members do their own thinking and draw their own conclusions, and their conclusions vary. Christian faith, then, is not irrelevant or privatized but has conflicting implications for the politics of economic life.

A Better Perspective on the Relationship between Religion and Politics

Having criticized an approach to understanding religion and politics that has failed in its own terms, and that makes some problematic assumptions, let us try to develop some starting points for a better approach.

As we have seen, there is no relationship between religious traditionalism and economic conservatism. This is not at all surprising, given what the depth-interview respondents tell us. In fact, their statements make sense of the findings without resort to the idea that Americans are hopelessly confused or privatized. The respondents tell us of the variety of economic views that can plausibly be grounded in either traditionalist or modernist faith, and show that the Christian themes by which they do so cut across the modernist-traditionalist dimension.

Perhaps some better religious variables could be found—variables that *would* be associated with economic liberalism-conservatism—but perhaps, instead, no variables would be much use. One fundamental problem is that the use of variables tends to go along with some kind of causal model. In the research we have been examining, one often finds an assumption that "ideas have consequences," and that religious ideas are a causal force, within individuals, molding their political ideas.[18] Religious ideas are a kind of motor within personality, capable of directing our thinking and activities in other areas, just as hunger can direct us. This idea is based on a correct intuition that religion often makes a difference in people's lives, including how they think and talk about politics. Furthermore, Americans tend to become aware of religious questions and make religious commitments earlier in life than they become politically aware and committed; therefore, it seems more logical to think of religion as the "cause" and politics the "effect" than the other way around. Also, their religious commitments are typically more important, more central to their identity, than their political ones, which again makes it more sensible to think of religious convictions as "causing" political views than vice versa. Nonetheless, there are serious problems with this way of looking at things.

First, although religious commitments do sometimes have motivating power, it is not plausible to argue that ideas are more than weak motors within personality, compared with other social, economic, and psychological forces influencing how people think.

Second, the theoretical basis on which one would expect one idea to be a causal force influencing another assumes that our minds are adaptively constructed to maximize cognitive coherence, enabling us to deal more accurately and easily with new situations than if our ideas were a wild jumble. But it seems clear that a variety of different patterns can be cognitively coherent. Coherence among ideas, furthermore, is largely culturally rather than psychologically constructed; it is developed by institutions and people who are employed full-time for that purpose, and communicated by practitioners such as clergy. Of course, people make individual choices, but most of the time they do so from among the range of previously constructed models of coherence with which they have come into contact. Any one of these models might meet needs for cognitive consistency, and yet people often come to different conclusions from similar premises. Hence, even if people were very logical and highly motivated by ideas, drives for cognitive consistency could not be expected to produce more than a weak and indeterminate motivational force that would make a person who has first adopted one idea then adopt a *specific* second idea.

Third, when a person holds two ideas that seem logically connected, and even experiences one to be an "implication" of the other, the reason that they are both held is not necessarily that one "causes" the other through some kind of mental process. It may easily be that they were learned together as a package, in the same setting, perhaps with the link between the two included as part of the package. Alternatively, they may both express an underlying personality characteristic, class interest, or way of establishing personal identity.[19]

Perhaps, then, an alternative, less "causal" approach that abandons the attempt to find religious variables associated with economic liberalism or conservatism would be better. A starting point for such an approach is suggested by three facts. The first is that those who call themselves Christians have about the same distribution of political views as Americans as a whole. This is true for arithmetic reasons, but it is also true for a more substantive reason: all Christians are both Christians *and* creatures of the social environment, influenced by both Christian and secular culture. It is very hard to disentangle, especially because Christianity is so dominant here, exactly what in a person's thinking is "Christian" and what is "American." In fact, efforts to do so are often controversial and polemical, as when the Right alleges that the secular influence of Marxism is distorting the faith of left Christians, or when left Christians return the insult by speaking of the Babylonian captivity to the status quo that they see distorting the faith of their conservative sisters and brothers.

A second fact, illustrated repeatedly by the depth-interview respondents, is that sometimes people put on their Christian hat and think or talk in Christian terms, and at other times they draw on other sources of ideas and values. Even if we define *Christian terms* very broadly here—to include any time when people use biblical images, speak of "God," refer to ethical principles couched in scriptural or theological language (for example, speak of the commandment to love our neighbors as ourselves), or mention what they have learned in church—most Christians probably speak or think in Christian terms much less than half the time. Instead, they mostly think in the ways described earlier with regard to the social implications of secular culture.

To put these two facts together: Christianity is a pervasive cultural context in America, and at the same time Christians are deeply influenced by non-Christian frameworks, so that they have two (or more) sets of frameworks in their minds, each of which can be used to support views on economic issues.

The third fact emerges from what we have seen among the depth-interview respondents: a single Christian is often quite capable of articulating quite varied, or even seemingly contradictory, political views. One view may be legitimated using the language of faith, another through secular language, or both may be grounded in faith, drawing on different Christian themes.

All these facts indicate that the implications of being a Christian for views on economic issues cannot be disentangled to any great extent by comparing the political views of different kinds of people (Christians and non-Christians, evangelicals and mainline Protestants), that is, by analyzing associations among variables. Better variables would not solve the problems we have been discussing. And yet, many of the depth-interview respondents clearly use the resources of Christian faith in coherent, intelligible, non-idiosyncratic ways to ground their views on economic issues.

To understand this coherence, we could ask what kinds of political and social ideas—conservative, radical, liberal—people favor *when they are thinking or speaking using a particular Christian theme.* The comparison here is not to other people, but to the views *the same people* favor when drawing on non-Christian values and beliefs, or on different Christian themes. What we are studying, if we take this approach, is not the individual but the cultural theme as an element in how people think and talk. The issue is not how religion, as a causal factor, alters people's thinking but what kinds of possibilities for talking about politics they acquire when they appropriate a particular theme out of Christian tradition. More broadly, the issue is how the terms of cultural struggle change, and what new possibilities for participation in political discourse develop, when people enter one of the various Christian cultural terrains.

People appropriate the themes in these terrains selectively, but not entirely as they please; assumptions, overtones, and implications tend to be built into cultural frameworks, and one can easily appropriate more than one realizes. Ideas and the structures that relate them to one another are "in the air," available without formal study. This is why we find respondents sounding like Aquinas, Augustine, Calvin, Leo XIII, Locke, Luther, Rousseau, or Roger Williams, even when they have never read any of the texts those people produced. The particular languages available to people are structured not in univocal ways but also not randomly; which languages are most readily available to which kinds and groups of people is also a far from random process. These factors do influence the potentials people have to appropriate various ideas about economic life, and it is in this weak sense (as a colleague has pointed out)[20] that we can properly speak of religion playing a causal role in how people think.

Using this approach excludes some of the questions raised when analysis of public opinion data uses religious "variables," but other questions can be reframed and asked within this approach. It is not helpful to compare the economic views of modernists and traditionalists, but it *is* possible to ask about the capacities for thinking about public issues that emerge when people talk in terms of a particular religious idea, such as the idea that God requires us to treat the needs of people who are very different from us as equal in importance to our own needs. Some Christian ideas, as we saw with universalism, can be used to support both liberal and conservative economic views, and many provide such general guidance that they can to support a variety of stances on particular economic issues, but many others tend to be used (when they are articulated and connected to economic life at all) in a fairly consistent way. Within the approach I am advocating, we do not try to compare individuals who do or do not adhere to a particular Christian idea, but rather examine what happens when people are using that idea, as opposed to the times when they are not. It is also possible to study the ways in which more general characteristics of Christian thinking, such as its non-rational and otherworldly side, help to ground economic views on implementation issues.

This approach means that we are studying not people's psychological functioning in its own right but cultural processes taking place within the thinking and speech of individuals. This avoids the problems of looking at religion as a causal force in a psychological sense, or of seeking associations between religious and political variables. This is the approach we have pursued in this book, supplementing public opinion data with an examination of the natural language people use when they talk about political issues, analyzing the occasions on which various themes drawn from Christian traditions come up, and discovering what political ideas these themes ground. This has required us to deal with the thinking of ordinary people using something of the methods, and certainly the same care and sensitivity, historians and cultural analysts use to analyze publicly available texts or the thinking of leaders and movements.

The Political Role of Religion and Ideology

Up to now, we have been concerned with the thinking and language of ordinary Christians. Clearly their contributions to public discourse are not the only way in which religion affects American politics. Churches issue social statements and lobby Congress; organizations and movements with a religious identity struggle in the political arena; and of course religion affects politics in less explicit and conscious ways as well.[21] Nonetheless, the thinking of ordinary people makes a difference, and not just because they vote. Let us see what can be said, without falling into an implausible reliance on the power of ideas as a historical force, about what this difference might be.[22]

First, a word about ideological thinking (a concept even fuzzier and more controversial than privatization).[23] People often think narrowly, holding many specific beliefs and options but not connecting them very much. On other occasions, people do connect their views on the particular issues of the day—whom to back in an election, whether a proposal for a new law is a good or bad idea—to larger visions, values, and assumptions about the world. These larger ideas are more general, in that they can be connected to a variety of particular issues and areas of life. They are also more basic in that they come from cultural traditions—ethics, religion, myths, commonsense ideas, ideals such as freedom—that people are usually more attached to than they are to their views on particular issues. When people make connections between particular issues and larger ideas, we could say that they are thinking or speaking ideologically. When the larger ideas have a strong ethical component, as they often do, we could say that they are thinking ethically.

Why is the ethical and ideological component of how people think and act politically important? Not because social change comes about primarily through education and consciousness-raising, or because ideas are the key determinants of the direction our country will move in, or because people are primarily motivated by ethical considerations rather than material interests. All such "idealist" assumptions deserve to be rejected. On the contrary: changes in consciousness often follow rather than precede changes in social structure or policy (the impact of civil rights laws in the South would be a good example); successful movements for social change require constituency building, organization, and institutional development; economic change is often produced by forces that lack consciousness, such as technology and the vagaries of international markets; and our position and experiences in the economic realm often have a large impact on how we think.

Nonetheless, ethical and ideological thinking are still important because of the contributions they make to the possibility of self-conscious political action and decisions that might affect economic life. (Here again, we might be said to be making an argument that is causal in a weaker sense.)[24] Political decisions clearly *can* affect economic life; it is sometimes possible self-consciously to change economic institutions and structures. Furthermore, although economic change resulting from technological change, the pressures of the world market, or other unself-conscious forces may be as frequent or far-reaching, self-consciously achieved changes have the important advantage that they can emerge from a democratic process in which we discuss together what kind of society we want and need. For the purposes of the Left, furthermore, there is the additional consideration that this kind of democratic, self-conscious process may offer more hope than other processes for movement in the direction of more equality and community.

Political decisions and self-conscious changes emerge from a political struggle that is not just a passive reflection of material forces but partly an independent, distinctively political process. That is not to say that it is a lovely, ethically high-minded process! It is full of power struggles and personal interests, but it is nonetheless a *political* process, involving organization, ideology, constituencies, and public institutions that operate in part according to their own principles. In the United States, this process has democratic features: leadership is elected in a process that provides some opportunities to put forward divergent political agendas; there are partly independent institutions (churches, universities, courts, corporations, and government) providing multiple bases for influence and power; political decision making is not totally controlled by unified, unaccountable elites working behind closed doors; and civil liberties are better protected than in most of the world. Furthermore, because of the size and complexity of our society and the diversity of sources of power, public means of communication that reach varying kinds of people, such as the mass media, are very important.

In this context, the political process includes debates that take place in public arenas—the media, Congress, universities, conventions of churches and labor unions, and so on—and one's success in these debates has some bearing on one's chances of influencing political decisions. Whatever one's true motives, it is essential to be able to articulate plausible grounds for one's proposals. Plausible grounds, very often, are ones that link specific proposals to more general values and concerns. In short, when people articulate the grounds for their proposals, they are often constructing ideology and using ethical arguments. Whenever people seek to organize others in new movements or voluntary associations, they have to articulate bases for unity and commitment, and again become involved in making ideology.

All of this is especially true for people who seek change. Such people need to organize themselves in new ways, developing and mobilizing constituencies. To do so, they must publicly articulate their proposals and the reasons that their proposals are valid and important, thus inevitably becoming involved in making ideology. They have a special need to connect their proposals to more general and basic values and assumptions, because they are not likely at the outset to have a broad base of support for proposals that go against the way things are now. By appealing to values that *do* have a broad base, they can hope to develop support for their proposals. Further, such people have a greater need for a broad, public base of support than do those they challenge, since they have less access to other means of influencing policy—inside contacts, economic resources, access to the media, and so forth.

On the other hand, people who believe that things are basically on track have less need of ideological appeals. They have the inertia of established practice on their side, greater control over existing institutions, and usually greater resources. This may be one reason that centrist political analysts take such pleasure in denouncing ideological politics.[25]

In sum, ethical and religious discourse is important because when it is connected with political discourse into "ideology" it provides ways of legitimating and articulating political proposals, and of organizing people together in associations and movements to advance these proposals. The key role of ideology is its public function within the "cultural" aspect of political life—that is, the part of political life in which meanings and values are constructed, articulated, and shared—more than whatever power it may have, as a causal force, to motivate individuals or influence events directly. And the most important political role of faith, within the thinking and language of ordinary Christians, is to provide resources for constructing and responding to ideological appeals, and thereby for participating in a fuller sense in the political life of our nation.

Practical Conclusions

9

What Is to Be Done? Implications for Left Politics and the Churches

Up to now, the arguments presented have been primarily descriptive rather than normative. To be sure, values enter into the definition of issues to explore, but the task has been to understand how people think rather than to say how they ought to think or what they ought to do. This kind of understanding is impersonal in the sense of being partially independent of the researcher's particular biography and values; the analysis of the views of American Christians presented here is meant to be valid and useful for people with a variety of religious and political perspectives.

To talk about the implications of the understanding we have arrived at, however, brings in values in a stronger sense. What one should do, if the analysis presented thus far is convincing, depends on one's purposes. Purposes differ; mine are defined by particular perspectives. I am a Christian (by conviction and conversion rather than birth) and find a Christian way of understanding history, life, and values both true and helpful. I am also a socialist-feminist and a pacifist and have been personally involved in a variety of social change organizations, giving me a special concern with why the work of the American Left has not met with more success, and how it could.

In this chapter, I will address people who share one or more of these perspectives with me, describing implications I see flowing from the descriptive argument made so far. That is, I will suggest what one might want to do to advance the purposes of the Left, or of Christian faith and churches. Of course, readers with different purposes are welcome to eavesdrop on this conversation, and may discover something interesting.

Implications for Liberal and Radical Politics

Liberals, socialists, and other people with left-of-center views can benefit in three key ways from the findings presented here. The first is to help the Left engage more American Christians in the struggle for economic justice and to work more effectively with Christian allies, thus enhancing the chances of success. The second is to clarify the values that leftists (a term I will use loosely, to refer to everyone to the left of the mainstream of the Democratic party) believe should inform economic life. The third is to refine thinking about ethical and cultural subjects. This involves reaching clarity on issues about relativism, public and private, individuation and community, and disentangling what in American culture and values one can affirm and what one must challenge.

Making Alliances on Economic Issues

In the past few years, secular people on the left have become increasing aware of the need and potential for alliances with people of faith. Michael Ferber, a prominent peace activist, has written recently in *The Nation* that "the religious left is the only left we've got."[1] Particularly in the movements for disarmament and for non-intervention in Central America, Christians have been key actors, and secular leftists have become accustomed to working with them. With regard to economic issues, such alliances are less visible on the national scene, but local economic justice movements around the country, concerned with issues such as housing, unemployment, hunger, and racial discrimination, frequently have a strong Christian component. However, the new openness to such alliances on the part of the Left is not always matched by enough sophistication about the ways in which Christian faith is connected with varying political stances, and a large part of the Left remains reflexively hostile to Christianity.

Given that almost nine out of ten Americans consider themselves Christians—and in most cases either belong to a church or in some other way manifest a significant connection to Christian faith—it is unlikely that the American Left will fare well if it manifests disdain for religious faith or fails to seek out common ground vigorously. However difficult it is to convert Americans to socialism, it would be far more difficult to convert them to atheism! If the latter is a precondition for the former, one might as well give up. Furthermore, as I have argued, if a large number of Christians were to lose their faith, the outlook for the Left would probably get worse rather than better.

It is evident from the depth interviews that there are clear and strong connections between central Christian values and the Left's economic justice agenda. To be sure, there are also strong connections between Christian faith and conservative views on economic issues, but this does not make it less possible or urgent for the Left to use the connections that facilitate its work. The conservative and liberal implications of faith work independently to a large extent; a Christian can adopt neither, one, or both. These differing implications tend to draw on different strands of Christian tradition, and often they are both found in the same person; a person can hold liberal views grounded in the value of love, for instance, and conservative ones grounded in voluntarism. Such a person has the capacity to adopt either liberal or conservative interpretations of faith.

Of particular importance for the Left is the fact that communal languages for economic life become much more available to Americans when they think in Christian terms. Since religious traditionalism is *not* connected to economic conservatism, this is all just as true for traditionalist Christians as for modernists. In some respects, traditionalist Christians may be better allies than modernists because they are more fluent in applying Christian language to many aspects of life, and have more resources for rejecting the relativism of the marketplace and asserting ethical standards for economic life. Catholics, as we have seen, are likely to be the best allies of all. If people on the left can overcome the distaste with which they often regard traditionalist Catholics and evangelical Protestants, they will find many Christians of all kinds who support a more egalitarian society and one less controlled by private enterprise. I am not sure how this can be achieved, given the deep cultural hostility many on the left feel for traditionalist Christians, but the hostility does appear to be diminishing, perhaps because of the experience of working together on shared projects in recent years.

On the other hand, many Christians are prone to what I have described as change-inhibiting views on implementation issues: for example, that conflict must be avoided at all costs, or that moral exhortation is enough to bring about social change. (This last is an attitude encountered often enough among secular leftists, too.) Traditionalist Christians, both Catholic and Protestant, are especially likely to think in these ways. Such views can lead to conflicts about political style and strategy, even when goals are held in common. Sometimes, alliances that look good in theory will not materialize in practice, or traditionalist Christians will be only passive supporters of economic change. Furthermore, we have seen that the resources of Christian faith can support conservative economic views almost as easily as liberal or radical ones; if faith comes to influence politics more, certain people may become more conservative. In short, people on the left need to avoid either stereotyping or romanticizing the views of Christians, instead looking for points of connection and ways to work together in spite of differences.

To forge the many alliances between Christians and the Left that are possible is not easy; if it happens at all, it will require work and tact. Issues on which there is no agreement may have to be excluded from the agenda for common action—but I hope not from discussion, for Christians and secular leftists have much to learn from each other. People on the left will need to be open to having their views modified by their encounters with Christians, rather than expecting to do all the converting themselves. They will have to take care with the language used in formulating their agenda. This does not mean dishonesty but simply removing cultural baggage—habits of speech and thinking—that are not intrinsic to the agenda. Liberals and radicals will have to get used to working in different organizational and cultural contexts—and with people who speak differently—from what they are used to. This will not be easy, given the well-educated, secular, White, middle-class character of most of the Left. But the difficulties should not be any greater than those encountered in efforts to build a multi-racial, multi-cultural Left. In fact, some of the difficulties will be exactly the same because African-American politics is more connected to the churches, and has more of a religious style, than White left politics.

Enriching Values to Apply to Economic Life

Alliances with Christians can strengthen the Left practically. In addition, I believe that dialogue with Christians can push the thinking of the Left in helpful directions. A typical leftist talking with Joseph Krieger would have an unsettling experience: they would have much in common, yet wide differences as well. Such a leftist might ask in exasperation, "How can a person who holds such good views on many issues be so conservative and closed-minded on others?" Because the key to Joseph's perspective is his consistently communal approach to life, such a dialogue might force those of us on the Left to confront the way in which we oscillate between communal and individualistic language. This does not necessarily indicate an inconsistency on the part of the Left, but it does indicate tensions leftists may need to be aware of, in order to clarify goals and articulate them in a convincing way.

The languages of economic rights and economic democracy have significant individualistic components, at least partly for good reasons. It is liberating for a person who is unemployed to be able to receive benefits as a matter of right rather than pleading for them. Social welfare programs have a communal dimension in that they bespeak our concern for one another, but their result is to allow us to live with less actual interaction and interdependence. This enhances individual autonomy in ways that are liberating but may also have negative effects. It would be liberating for many more Americans to have real opportunities to participate in making economic decisions that affect their lives. The idea of economic democracy builds on this hope, and it has both communal and individualistic components. Robert Bellah and his colleagues report that the economic democracy activist they interviewed had difficulty describing any substantive vision of social justice; his views could even be called relativistic in that he seemed to feel that a just society would be (approximately) the kind of society people talking together decided was just.[2] In sum, there are good reasons that the language of the Left has both individualistic and communal components, but the exact nature of the mixture and the reasons for it often remain inchoate; dialogue with Christians could motivate the Left to be clearer.

A related dilemma is that of relativism. As we have seen, Christian traditions provide resources that both encourage and combat the relativism of the marketplace. On the whole, liberals and radicals need to fight against relativism with regard to economic life. Yet this raises difficult questions.

The Left is often accused of wanting everyone to be alike, of seeking, in Stalinist fashion, to impose a gray uniformity that suppresses individuality and free choice. Although this is obviously an overstatement, we on the Left *do* want to argue that Americans have made a fetish of free choice, and that more communal decision making is required on behalf of justice and the common good. Yet there are surely some legitimate rights of free choice in economic life, and we do not have clear grounds for deciding which to support and oppose. Probably all socialists would be comfortable with relativism in some areas, considering these to be appropriate arenas for unaccountable personal choice and preference; even the most Stalinist are glad to let the market determine whether we should make more vanilla or chocolate ice cream! Some socialists in recent years have gone much farther, embracing the market and taking a more or less relativistic position about all consumer goods. But the gut instinct of many leftists would probably still be that there is something wrong if the resources that could be used to manufacture fishing boats for people who hunger are instead devoted to the production of luxury yachts for the private use of millionaires. This is a non-relativistic, counter-market ethical instinct, implying that commonly agreed upon, ethically grounded decisions rather than unaccountable individual choices should govern parts of economic life.

If one wants to implement such an instinct, does this require undemocratic means? Not necessarily. Leftists might advocate tax or other income redistribution policies to ensure that there would be no millionaires. Or, dealing more directly with the system of production, we might work toward a system that would limit the degree to which producers respond passively to consumer choice. Under central planning, this ethical instinct could be easily implemented, by allocating few resources to shipyards making luxury yachts. Within a democratic political system, such an allocation could result from public discussion of our common priorities rather than from the unaccountable rule of a bureaucrat. Many such decisions could be decentralized, made in cities or regions rather than nationally. One could easily argue that such a system would be *more* democratic than what we have now—one person, one vote rather than one dollar, one vote. The decision between allocating resources by a collective, self-conscious process and letting the market allocate resources is not a decision between Stalinism and democracy. Rather it is a decision between values best achieved by individual choice and those best achieved by public decision making, and there is an ethical question related to relativism involved in making this judgment.

In short, what needs to happen, and as yet has not, is for us of the Left to sort out our relativistic and non-relativistic ethical instincts and clarify the kinds of decisions we believe should and should not be publicly accountable. The language Joseph Krieger uses and the language of "pre-capitalist" moral economies in general, challenge the Left to clarify the issues of individualism and relativism. Doing so can benefit the struggle for justice, and raise the quality of political discourse in this country.

Ethics, Culture, and the Left

In addition to an economic justice agenda, the Left has non-economic aims, and also cultural perspectives and assumptions related to all its political goals. Of course, the Left is divided; socialists, communists, anarchists, populists, European-style social democrats, exponents of "feasible socialism," feminists, environmentalists, anti-interventionists, post-Marxists, post-modernists, and liberals (partly overlapping categories, to be sure) all hold different views. Some on the left are militantly "modernist" or "post-modernist," culturally, and others are somewhat "traditionalist"; differences within the Left on non-economic issues are if anything more serious than on economic issues. Christians, too, hold varied views on cultural issues. Some embrace much of the left agenda, but on issues such as sexual ethics the predominant views on the Left and among Christians are seriously divergent. Traditionalist Christians, especially, are apt to oppose the most common left agenda not only on sexual ethics but also on gay rights, feminism, abortion, and prayer in public schools. For issues of this kind, furthermore, the differences between theologically traditionalist and modernist Christians are significant in a way that they are not for economic issues.

The cultural differences between the Left and many Christians raise particularly serious problems because many of today's leftists, unlike the orthodox Marxists of the 1920s and 1930s, believe that "the personal is political," and are unwilling to leave cultural issues to be solved later, or to assume that forms of oppression not based on class, such as gender inequality, are secondary and will disappear once capitalism has been abolished. Feminist concerns, furthermore, are not just about what policies a left organization will work for in the public arena but also about how things are run internally, *within* the organization. To form an effective alliance, therefore, it is not sufficient to define the issues to be addressed narrowly, including only those on which there is full agreement. How leadership is selected and meetings are run can easily become bones of contention because of differences on cultural issues. Such differences affect the possibilities of working together even on economic issues—but also provide opportunities for dialogue that could benefit the Left in the long run. Furthermore, even on cultural issues there is some common ground.

It may be helpful to think of the Left as internally divided, culturally, along two dimensions. The first is whether people hold relatively "modernist" or "traditionalist" views about the family, sexual behavior, and so forth. Robert Westbrook has provided a helpful description of this dimension and the issues it raises for the Left. In a review essay in *Radical History Review,* he discusses some of the historical and political issues about the role of traditional culture and traditional community structures in American politics.

On the one hand, it is clear that American radicals have sometimes erred through insensitivity to the actual culture and loyalties of American workers, thinking that somehow these could be transcended by a radically universalistic appeal to class position (independent of all other identities) as a basis for solidarity, and that all existing, concrete loyalties—religion, region, ethnicity, language—are obstacles, irrational forces that must be destroyed for the Left to prosper. On the other hand, many radicals *have* been sensitive and responsive to these loyalties and drawn upon them in building radical movements. Scholars of American labor history or the history of radical movements (mostly sympathetic to the Left) have demonstrated that working-class culture has sometimes achieved a "relative autonomy," allowing it to be a resource for radical struggles.[3]

Recently, Westbrook says, a group of "radical traditionalist" intellectuals have emerged who, like some conservatives, criticize "radicals who fail to see the virtues of family, church and neighborhood and who call instead for a liberation of men and women from the constraints of these institutions, thereby trampling upon the sensibilities and deeply-held values of ordinary people." But, he says,

> radical traditionalists have not as yet been able to clearly distinguish the features of traditional mediating institutions which they find indispensable to human welfare from those that are not. Hence they have left themselves open to attack from "radical modernists" who fail to see what is so great about things like the nuclear family and religious authority. Radical modernists also accuse radical traditionalists of a mindless "populism" that fails to distinguish between those aspects of working-class culture that hold out the promise of radical social transformation and those that only legitimate "relative autonomy" within a larger context of oppression.[4]

The second dimension along which the Left is divided is less obvious; this is the split between those who are wholeheartedly pursuing the Enlightenment agenda and those who are more skeptical. Marx was an heir of that agenda, and although there are a variety of strands in his thought and a number of reasonable ways to interpret his writings, many of his followers and interpreters have used his ideas in a way that fits fully within the framework of Enlightenment convictions.[5] For instance, Marxists have often thought that their categories of class analysis had universal validity, a privileged status as a "scientific" framework by which to analyze false or irrational forms of consciousness. Such Marxists have been especially scornful of religion. Other strands of the Left have always existed, however, and have become increasingly prominent since the 1960s: strands that assign greater value to the non-rational element of life, criticize claims to objective or "privileged" knowledge, and in other ways question the Enlightenment agenda. Some reject it nearly totally, while others seek to disentangle what is of enduring value in this tradition—for instance, strong legitimation for free inquiry and civil liberties—from the parts that need to be rejected or revised.

These two dimensions of cultural division on the Left are to some extent unrelated. Many of those who question the Enlightenment agenda, are strongly modernist in their cultural preferences, and have no interest in the nuclear family, ethnic solidarities, or other things that "radical traditionalists" want to defend. Few leftists are both culturally traditionalist *and* strongly accepting of the Enlightenment agenda, but each of the other three possible combinations of positions on these two dimensions has been adopted by significant parts of the Left, and is briefly described below.

1. Secular people of the more old-fashioned Left, such as Michael Harrington and Irving Howe, represent the pro-Enlightenment/cultural modernist combination. Such people take a positive view of scientific and technological progress and hope for the eventual eradication of what they see as religious irrationalities. They tend to be deeply suspicious of politics that rely strongly on non-rational forces or give too much play to emotions, seeing these as threats to civil liberties; many opposed the New Left, and still try to counter what they see as New Left tendencies in contemporary left politics. They often distrust demagoguery to the point of seeming elitist, and are comfortable with hierarchy—especially if based on knowledge.

2. The non-Enlightenment/cultural traditionalist combination is seen in groups such as Just Life and Evangelicals for Social Action, and in leaders such as Jim Wallis; in secular circles, it is accepted by some who call themselves populists. (Harry Boyte and Jean Bethke Elshtain fit parts of this model.) Such people, if not personally religious and morally conservative, believe that the Left needs to be deeply respectful of the actual values and cultural particularities of non-elite Americans. Westbrook's description of radical traditionalists generally fits them: they emphasize the contributions traditional forms of culture can make to the struggle for justice.

3. The final possibility, cultural modernism combined with questioning of the Enlightenment agenda, is found among people who were influenced both by the New Left of the 1960s and by countercultural movements. Many environmentalists and feminists, especially many socialist-feminists, would fit here, as would some Marxist or politically radical post-modernists and deconstructionists.

It has probably not taken enormous discernment for the reader to figure out that my personal sympathies are primarily with the second and third positions; all three, however, have important things to contribute to the thinking and work of the Left.

Christians mostly hold views analogous to those of leftists in the latter two of these categories. That is, Christian faith can be interpreted in either a culturally modernist or traditionalist way (somewhat correlated with theological stances), but when people have their Christian hats on, they tend to speak in ways that cannot be subsumed within Enlightenment models of rational discourse.[6] Let us examine the issues raised by the relationship between each of these three left stances and these two versions of Christianity.

1. Because a style of thinking at variance with the Enlightenment agenda is a point of common ground for most Christians (when they have their Christian hats on), leftists in the pro-Enlightenment/cultural modernist camp will have trouble cooperating with Christians except on economic justice questions, and then only temporarily and in ways that do not require living within common organizations or discussing underlying values. Leftists of this kind could be described as cultural absolutists (though they reject the absolutism of others), in that they often read out of respectable discourse people they regard as irrational or intolerant. They implicitly say, if you will not engage in discourse that follows the norms of Enlightenment philosophy or social theory, there is no way to have dialogue. The perspectives of those who do not accept Enlightenment standards of truth are simply objectively wrong, and there is nothing one can learn from them. Some traditionalist Christians are equally absolutist, and the potential for dialogue between such Christians and this kind of leftist is almost nil.

When leftists of this kind and Christian traditionalists engage, I feel like running for cover. The debate over creationism is a case in point. Enlightenment-oriented leftists tend to view the movement to teach biblical accounts of Creation in public schools as a form of irrational absolutism, and want the door to such efforts to be legally closed. I believe that there are good reasons not to teach creationism in public schools, but I am struck by the elitist, statist, coercive, and anti-democratic character of the conversation I have heard from my friends on the left on this subject. They show little appreciation, in this context, for the idea that parents may experience school bureaucracies as unaccountable structures forcing an alien cultural perspective down the throats of their children—an experience that immigrant (especially Catholic) and low-status Americans have had over and over, and to which the Left is sensitive in many other contexts. They base their opposition on the idea that creationism is objectively false and evolutionism objectively true, and on adherence to the authority of science as interpreted by cultural elites. They sound as if they were unaware of the provisional and socially constructed character of all knowledge—which they speak of frequently in other contexts—and as if they were saying, "You *will* believe what expert scientists tell you!" The truth is that we are a society deeply divided over the issue of evolution, and to suppress one side of the debate—"objectively wrong" as it may be—is not the best approach.[7]

The dilemma this raises for cultural modernists on the left is how to be open to learning from dialogue with people—such as most traditionalist Christians and quite a few modernist Christians—who strongly disagree with their cultural agenda, while avoiding a relativistic approach to ethical language. (I will return to the issue of relativism in a moment.) As I remarked earlier, if we on the Left are to avoid being caricatured as Stalinist and repressive, we need to find ways of affirming some kinds of individual choice, even in the economic realm. We also need to avoid sounding like cultural elitists when in fact most of us are closer to being cultural democrats. This means that left language about culture needs to incorporate openness to other cultural frameworks in America, including the non-rational and sometimes seemingly zany ones that Americans are so talented at creating. This language needs to affirm diversity and choice in many realms of culture, without becoming relativistic.

2. Leftists who adopt the non-Enlightenment/cultural traditionalist perspective, even if not Christians themselves, are culturally compatible with Christianity. They can easily forge bonds and make alliances with Christians, not just on economic issues but on others as well. If anything, they are subject to the criticism raised by Westbrook, that they do not ask with enough clarity or critical distance what, given left values, one ought to affirm and disaffirm about the values and ways of life actually found among many Americans, such as a high value for the nuclear family, traditional sexual standards and gender roles; distaste for unconventional lifestyles; and fairly unconditional support for American foreign and military policy. Unlike leftists attached to the Enlightenment agenda, such leftists tend not to judge these mores by an external set of standards felt to be universal; to that extent, they are relativistic. And yet, what they accept are often rather intolerant and certainly non-relativistic perspectives.

The dialogue between the first group of leftists and Christians can hardly get started, and the dialogue between the second group of leftists and Christians is liable to be a bit boring (although the cooperation that is possible can be extremely important).

3. When we come to the non-Enlightenment, culturally modernist group of people on the left, the possibilities for both cooperation and dialogue become more ambiguous and interesting. Such leftists have differences with traditionalist Christians but also some important points of connection, even on cultural questions. They may not agree with evangelicals about homosexuality, but they have shared bases with all kinds of Christians for giving value to passion and the whole non-rational side of life, and for questioning

ideas of progress and attempts to impose a universal standard of truth constructed along Enlightenment lines.

As we have seen, traditionalist Christians and followers of the Enlightenment have one thing in common: both have a basis for absolute standards. In the first case, these come from God; in the second, from reason. In both cases they are much clearer than for those Christians who do not find either the Bible or the church a source of unequivocal, fully authoritative guidance, or for secular leftists who question the Enlightenment agenda. The latter kinds of Christians and leftists, therefore, have a special need to wrestle with the issue of relativism, which can, as we have seen, be a support both for free-market thinking and for social and political passivity. One important task for post-modernists and other people on the left who question the Enlightenment agenda is to counter the tendency, in criticizing universal standards of truth, to appear to be saying that all values are arbitrary and that there is no way for humans to have reasonable discourse together about the ends we seek as we act politically. The French social theorist Michel Foucault, a leading critic of Enlightenment thinking, is often interpreted in this way, although I do not think he really holds these views. If he did, or to the extent that his writings are understood in this way, they could serve to support a cynical, privatized, and purely self-aggrandizing approach to life, or the relativism of the marketplace.[8]

At their best, culturally modernist and non-Enlightenment thought on the left and theological modernism (including "post-liberal" theology) among Christians and Jews are manifestations of an ancient and honorable tradition: the critique of idolatry. All of these ways of thinking relativize claims to authority and universality, and deny claims for the finality, permanence, and ultimacy of the cultural artifacts—from golden calves to particular theological formulations, to theories of justice and sure foundations for scientific knowledge—we have constructed throughout our wonderfully imaginative history. These ways of thinking are strong resources for asserting human freedom and the possibilities for seeking social and cultural change, but in some respects they make it harder to articulate and to agree and act upon ideas of social justice. The struggle to do these things without falling into idolatry needs to continue, and this is a point of connection and fruitful dialogue between the Left and Christians, since the issue arises in both communities.

This is one way to place the issue of relativism: it has to do with negotiating the strait between idolatry of specific understandings of what is right, and the incapacity to argue and act on a coherent conception of what is right.[9] The Left is often incoherent on this issue, using highly relativistic and subjectivistic language on issues such as abortion and sexuality while rejecting this language on economic issues. (Conservatives sometimes do the reverse.) Liberals and radicals use the language of "choice" concerning abortion, for example, and often sound as if they felt that abortion decisions were of only private concern, and that even if abortion were unconditionally legal, nobody would have the right to ask a woman making an abortion decision to justify herself. (I am convinced that most pro-choice people do not really hold these views; I am only describing what pro-choice public language often sounds like.) Perhaps this use of different languages for dealing with different kinds of political issues is reasonable; if so, there needs to be a clear statement of why one should adopt such a subjectivistic ethical procedure with regard to abortion and not with regard to economic decisions. An even better course would be for the Left to defend the legality of abortion (and other important principles of liberty) without resort to subjectivistic ethical thinking.[10]

Another issue that divides both Christians and the Left internally has to do with the status of various kinds of "separations": of personal and political spheres, private and public, spiritual and material, church and state. American life consists of a variety of kinds of institutions—corporations, universities, churches, and so on—each operating according to its own criteria. Corporations are supposed to maximize profit and efficiency, universities to advance and transmit knowledge, and churches to foster the spiritual and ethical development of individuals and the community. Leaders of each kind of institution often resist pressures to use political criteria as part of their decision making: corporate managers oppose stockholder proposals trying to mandate particular versions of corporate social responsibility, universities want their faculty to do "scholarship," not "ideology," and churches tend to avoid involvement in controversial issues.

Within the Left, feminism and the influence of the counter-cultural currents of the 1960s have questioned these separations, in the effort to make cultural and "personal" issues part of the terrain of political debate. (Doing so makes the disjunction between the non-relativistic ethical language used for economic issues and the relativistic language commonly used for sexual issues even more striking.) Historian Eli Zaretsky has attacked these separations in a more academic vein, arguing that the difference between private and public spheres experienced as a reality (and valued by many) in modern capitalist societies is strongly related to the particular kind of economic structure we live in.[11] The Christian Right, meanwhile, has been attacking some of the same separations, making a political issue out of what is often considered the personal and private issue of abortion, and attacking the independence and religious neutrality of schools and other public institutions; some want to have the United States declare as a matter of public policy that this is a Christian nation. Within the Left, the more old-fashioned leftists have been deeply distressed not just by the Christian Right but also by the attack on traditional separations by the New Left, fearing (for example) that efforts to make courts and universities socially responsive will usher in new forms of tyranny. Many Christians, similarly, are frightened

by any attempt to connect faith to politics—whether with left or right implications—fearing that this will compromise either civil liberties and the
separation of church and state or the unity and well-being of the churches
(thought to depend on political neutrality, perhaps even on never discussing
political issues). Here again, there are points of connection between debates
going on among Christians and within the Left, between those who emphasize a concern for a more integrated and wholistic life, and those who
fear that the result might be conflict, instability, or diminished freedom.

In short, even on cultural issues, there are points of connection, as well
as many points of potential disagreement, between Christians and the Left.
On economic issues it is almost scandalous that more alliances have not
been forged, and they can be, if cultural differences can be overcome. This,
of course, is no easy task, but the fate of the American Left may well depend
upon it.

A final dilemma raised by the questions I have been discussing is the
ambiguous relationship of the left with American values and culture. American leftists are deeply American, and deeply committed to many core American values. Many are radical democrats, simply carrying further and into
new spheres principles of government "by the people" that are time-honored
and widely held in America. On the other hand, many on the left feel a
deep dislike for many aspects of American culture—toward what is felt to
be the reflexive tendency among Americans to think ourselves morally superior to the rest of the world and entitled to use violence to impose our
vision on it, toward American mass culture, or toward the commercialism,
homogenization, anti-intellectualism, and materialism that sometimes seem
to be dominant in American life. Sometimes leftists express this dislike more
loudly and clearly than they express admiration for the constant bubbling
up of new life manifested in this country—to take just a few examples—by
experimental theater and arts, humor, the publication of a great variety of
critical perspectives in books and magazines, and the constant creation of,
and widespread involvement in, an amazing diversity of voluntary associations oriented toward improving our common life.

What does this mean for the work of the Left? Sometimes it engages in
moral and cultural condemnation of the American mainstream, and this
tends to meet with hostility; it is not an effective political tactic, no matter
how valid the condemnations may be. On the other hand, one should not
be asked to accept uncritically aspects of American culture that may be in
urgent need of change, especially if—as may sometimes be the case—movement in the direction of social justice depends on cultural change. Effective
political organizing probably needs to be based on some kind of balance,
on critical love for our country and its culture. To be effective and to maintain
commitment for the long run, activists need some degree of faith that Americans possess great potentials for good and life-affirming values in their
hearts. Those of us who seek more equality and community need to be able

to believe that many times Americans reach unfortunate conclusions by combining good values with others less life-affirming, or with misinformation and inadequate understanding of how our society works. I call this all "faith" because data and experience could easily lead a person to a less hopeful view. With this kind of faith, we on the left can hope that with the right kind of organizing, experiences, struggles, and education more Americans might reach conclusions like ours from the core values we share. To do this kind of political work requires a kind of disentangling of the diverse perspectives and values Americans hold, in order to find the shared values and understand why they are not now yielding the desired implications. What the depth-interview respondents tell us is a contribution to this kind of disentangling, indicating the strength of values and views of life that can contribute to work for social justice, and of ways of thinking that sometimes negate these potential contributions.

Implications for the Churches

The purposes of the churches, and those implied by Christian faith, are even more varied, less clear, and more disputed than the purposes of the Left. As a starting point, however, let me articulate one: that individual Christians and the church manage to find ways to be both otherworldly and thisworldly. That means trying to present Christ and the gospel to the world in a wholistic way, relevant to politics and community needs but also to the personal and spiritual struggles each person faces. Such an approach genuinely engages with the world rather than seeking separation, but tries to maintain a distinctively Christian voice and message, not accepting the standard cultural frameworks of the social environment or confusing our message as Christians with any particular social agenda we may find ourselves struggling for in cooperation with people of other or no faith.

How can one be fully "in" the world? Many church members, ministers, and leaders want Christian faith to have an impact on American society, but there is little consensus on how this can happen. What do the statements of the depth-interview respondents tell us about the potentials and obstacles?

One key finding is the enormous variety of political perspectives that Christians can relate to what clearly are shared, historic elements of Christian tradition. Whatever the merits of the divergent interpretations of faith we have seen, Christians obviously are, in fact, capable of finding remarkably diverse plausible readings of our religious traditions and texts.

Another important fact is that there is no relationship between being religiously traditionalist (whether we measure that by personal beliefs or the denomination one belongs to) and holding conservative views on economic issues. The religious themes used to support conservative views, and those used to support liberal or radical ones, are the shared property of all kinds of Christians. The religious differences that matter politically crosscut denominational and theological lines.

A third fact is that there are significant strands within Christian faith that can support compartmentalization of religion and politics; many Christians make no connections between faith and social issues, and some believe that one should not do so. A larger proportion have serious reservations about church social action. Some worry even about *discussion* of social issues within the church, fearing the dissension this could generate. These views are based not just in political disagreements but also in ways in which some Christians interpret faith—ways that block or delegitimate such connections. In particular, interpretations that confine faith to an internal, private, or interpersonal sphere, or to purely "spiritual" concerns, can make economic issues seem irrelevant to faith.

Many of the people I interviewed also believe that any connection between faith and politics is liable to violate the principle of separation of church and state. Some of these people, I think, believe this simply for lack of an understanding of the distinctions among different meta-issues and different ways of connecting faith to politics. Some, also, take what seems to me an unduly restrictive view of what the non-establishment clause of the First Amendment means, believing that it bans the engagement of religious leaders and organizations in public debate.

A fourth fact, based on surveys of members and pastors of the Evangelical Lutheran Church in America, is that on the overwhelming majority of issues having to do with the social role of the church, there is *no relationship* between the views of the pastor and the views of the members that pastor serves.[12] I do not mean just that Lutheran pastors are on the average more liberal than their parishioners, although this is true, but that a liberal congregation (compared with other congregations) is no more likely to be served by a liberal pastor than a conservative congregation. This strongly suggests that in most congregations very little discussion of social issues goes on, and that members' loyalty to their congregations probably has little to do with shared beliefs and values, and more to do with shared history and experience, and a web of relationships. Congregations, in short, are typically quite non-ideological places.

These facts have practical implications, particularly for clergy and lay Christians who wish to have an impact on congregations. One is that there is no guarantee that if people are persuaded to accept a given theological position they will use it to support a particular set of political views. Another is that any Christian congregation, even if it is rather homogeneous in its theology or religious style, is likely to embrace almost as much political diversity as the community in which it is located.[13]

Therefore, clergy who take *any* clear political stance are likely to encounter opposition and to upset people who have a different reading of faith, or who believe in separating faith from politics. There is no least common denominator, no shared political position, to be found; there are shared basic principles, but they are few and general, and the moment one begins to discuss how to apply them, agreement ends.

Given all these facts, for churches or religious leaders—especially pastors of congregations, who deal with their constituency on a daily basis—to take positions or actions on substantive social issues is difficult indeed, and likely to have little impact other than to generate conflict. Instead, it might be worth pursuing two alternate strategies.

The first is for Christian churches—especially congregations—to try to become more of what James Gustafson has termed "communities of moral deliberation." That is, congregations could try to be studiously neutral corporately but to provide an environment that encourages and even challenges individual members to make their own connections between faith and politics. From the outset, leaders would admit that the connections would vary from one individual to another, but instead of trying to find a vague least common denominator, they would urge each Christian to make specific, personal connections. Furthermore, they might pursue this by creating occasions for discussion and debate where members could share perspectives, learn from, and argue with each other.

To be sure, this is not easy to do. Church members fear conflict and diminution of individual autonomy. Clergy in most mainline denominations are generally more liberal politically than members, and may have much to lose if the discrepancies between their views and those of their parishioners become more obvious. Many congregations find it much easier to focus on mutual support internally than on any activity (whether evangelism, social service, or discussion of social issues) directed toward the outside world.

The depth-interview respondents' statements indicate that there are many authentic, legitimate social interpretations of faith. That does not mean that one has to regard all interpretations as equally correct, but it does mean that people with differing interpretations are entitled not to be written out of Christianity, or told that their views result merely from the influence of secular currents of thought. When such charges are made, dialogue stops, and the possibility of changing and expanding the ways in which Christian language is used to understand the social world ends. If this principle is kept in mind, "moral deliberation" can take place in ways that encourage the expression of the full range of political views without undermining the solidarity of congregations. People can disagree with others politically, while affirming the faith, basic ethical values, and concern for the world felt by those with whom they disagree. With proper planning and leadership, dialogue within congregations can have this character. Pursuing this approach could help make Christian faith more of a force in the world.

The second strategy is to address head-on the meta-issues discussed in chapter 3. As long as Christians are in such disagreement on these issues, it is hard to address substantive ones, since many Christians deny the legitimacy of doing so. Meta-issues are not as emotionally loaded and have a more obvious theological component, and therefore it might be possible for religious leaders, churches, and congregations to articulate stronger positions, without disastrously divisive results, than on substantive issues. This can build on work already going on within the churches under labels such as "ministry of the laity" or "ministry in daily life," oriented toward persuading more Christians to take a wholistic view of faith. The Lutheran surveys discussed earlier indicate that although lay members are very divided on these issues, there is consensus among pastors; only a tiny percentage of pastors adopt the dualistic and voluntaristic positions favored by sizeable proportions of lay members. The possibility I am suggesting is for clergy and church leaders to try to persuade more of the laity to adopt the positions already held almost universally by their leaders. This will arouse much less upset than trying to take corporate positions and actions on substantive issues. Furthermore, I would argue that the "correct" Christian position is clearer on meta-issues than on substantive issues. It is easier to maintain, for example, that Christian ethical principles apply to material and public as well as spiritual and private concerns than that these principles mandate left-of-center economic policy positions. In other words, for both practical and theoretical reasons it makes more sense to take clear positions on meta-issues than on substantive ones. This will still arouse upset from Christians who wish to separate faith from politics and do not want such issues even discussed within their congregations, but the upset seems worth risking.[14]

It could also be valuable to address the First Amendment in church educational programs. The interviews revealed many respondents taking quite restrictive views, and such views appeared to be based partly on lack of information or perspectives to support a broader view rather than on real attachment to restrictive views.

Articulating an "integrating" perspective on meta-issues, assisting and motivating church members to think through their own political understandings of faith, and encouraging them to talk about these understandings with other members and with other people in their local communities should be high priorities for denominations and congregations. This kind of education and dialogue could be much more important than issuing social and political statements. Such statements play a role, but they are usually ignored by most congregations and members, and when they are noticed they may arouse opposition, in part because of disagreements on meta-issues; that is, because members have not accepted the validity of making the kinds of links between faith and social issues such statements typically imply, or the legitimacy of the church's taking corporate action. Social statements also play a quite limited external role, for the church as an institution has vastly less political power than its members have as citizens, voters, and potential activists. Nationally, religious bodies have little clout (with the possible exception of the Catholic church on abortion issues). Locally, congregations usually cannot expect to be major institutional factors affecting social change in their communities, but their members can play an important role if aroused by faith and encouraged to organize together with like-minded people inside and outside the congregation.

All of this is also to argue for taking seriously the views of ordinary members: the actual understandings of faith they hold, and the ways in which they link faith to economic issues. Opinion polls, including those conducted by denominations, indicate that members of denominations typically have little allegiance to the specific theological and social views of their denomination. Lutherans, for instance, are only slightly more likely than Presbyterians to accept a distinctively "Lutheran" perspective as understood by church leaders or theologians. Most of the differences in views, within broad families of denominations (such as the mainline Protestant ones), are *within* denominations rather than among them.[15] Members do not automatically or blindly follow the teachings of their churches, and most leaders of mainline Protestant denominations would not want them to.

Given this situation, dialogue between leaders or theologians, on one side, and rank-and-file members, on the other, is very important. If congregations are to become places where conversations on social issues informed by Christian faith can take place, and theologians and church leaders with liberal or radical views wish their perspectives to attain wider currency, they may need to concentrate less on fine-tuning theologies of liberation, or even on the theological education of future pastors, and more on opening up communication with the lay members of their churches. I believe that the new theologies linking faith to social issues that have developed over the past generation—especially liberation and feminist theologies—are important and hopeful developments, and need to continue to grow, but at this point broad forms of theological education and dialogue need more attention than they have received in the past.

In doing all this, people in the church need to realize the limitations of Christian faith.[16] Faith is multi-vocal, but it is also simply silent on many questions, particularly ones of social analysis and strategy. My own Chicago parish participates in a neighborhood alliance on housing issues. In discussions within the alliance it has become clear that even though all the people involved in the alliance share left-of-center political values, it is hard to discern the correct strategies. It is hard to tell how to affect city, bank, or corporate policies. Worse, it is sometimes hard to tell what policies would actually make the local housing situation better or worse. Our neighborhood is a fairly stable mixture of Anglo and Latino, rich and poor. With no investment coming into the neighborhood, it might deteriorate into a slum; with new investment, housing may be improved but rents may go up, making it unaffordable for many people who now live in the neighborhood. What, then, do we ask of banks? For the Christian participants in the coalition, faith helps us decide on our goals, the criteria for what a better or worse situation would be, and motivates us toward activism and concern, but faith has little to tell us about the many and complex forces that affect housing. Clergy have had training in ethical analysis but usually not much in social analysis. For churches, clergy, and lay Christians to be credible in their statements and actions, they need to operate within these limitations.

The Dilemma of Moralism

The difficulty in making alliances between Christians and the Left—even on economic issues, where there are strong points of connection—is not due just to the cultural disdain many on the left feel toward views they regard as backward and irrational. It is also due to the moralism that Christians, including modernists, sometimes manifest. In my experiences in the peace movement, working for a church-based organization, I often found Christians speaking of their secular allies as somehow morally inferior or suspect, less pure in their motives. Perhaps that is because a motive for some people's church involvement is to feel morally good about themselves. But perhaps, also, there are dilemmas built into the moralism (sometimes found on the right, sometimes in prophetic left Christianity) that has been so prominent in Christian history.

Certain readers, especially those who are not Christians, may find that some of the statements made by the respondents and quoted throughout this book—especially when respondents talk about avoiding selfishness and materialism—make them a little queasy. I have that reaction, on occasion. One frequent objection to Christianity is that it is death-dealing rather than life-affirming by being so "moralistic." If we constantly harp on the distinction between right and wrong, and the necessity for self-sacrifice, people can become rigid, repressed, and one-dimensional. Such "goody-goodies" are likely to be unrealistic in how they understand their own motives and feelings, and the way the world actually works.

According to this line of argument, left politics linked to religion can easily become based on guilt and self-hatred. This kind of politics will not have much staying power when we discover that the world is not going to get better fast and that the victims of injustice are not always ethically superior, as individuals, to those who benefit from the current situation.

Furthermore, Christian radicalism may portray itself as more radical than it really is. As Karl Marx put it in the *Communist Manifesto:*

As the parson has ever gone hand in hand with the landlord, so has Clerical Socialism with Feudal Socialism.

Nothing is easier than to give Christian asceticism a Socialist tinge. Has not Christianity declaimed against private property, against marriage, against the State? Has it not preached in the place of these, charity and poverty, celibacy and mortification of the flesh, monastic life and Mother Church? Christian Socialism is but the holy water with which the priest consecrates the heart-burnings of the aristocrat.[17]

Shifting from motives to outcomes, one important danger of a politics that focuses too much on moral principles is that it can distract us from what needs to be done politically. It is very easy to condemn the evils of the world, but harder to move on to political action to try to remedy them. Furthermore, we need to have a good social analysis of what is actually causing the social problems we wish to address, not just a moral analysis of how evil they are. Purely moral analysis easily leads into thinking that if only people (especially those in power) would reform, or we could get the right person into office, things would get a lot better.

Also, we can fall into thinking that we can change the world by appeals to people's understanding of what is just by showing them injustice and how to reduce it—a view of social change that I find implausible. Ideas are important, but they are never enough; we cannot depend on their persuasive power to make social change. It may be especially easy for those of us who are well educated to fall into this trap, since we good at constructing ethical arguments.[18]

A purely "moral" approach to politics, too, can lead people to look askance on the movements by which people with little power try to assert their interests and claims to justice. We saw this tendency in the corporatist thinking of Joseph Krieger and James O'Connell. A final danger is that because organizations and their leaders are never perfect and often far from it, a highly moralistic approach can lead people to give up on public life as an inherently "dirty" business.

Many Christians would agree with at least part of this critique. The traditional Christian doctrine of "justification by faith" focuses on how we are saved, not by following ethical laws but by God's free gift of grace. Our reaction to that gift should be to accept the forgiveness and reconciliation God offers, to move forward in joy and freedom to answer whatever God's call to us is, and to serve the world. Guilt and anxiety, like excessive attachment to possessions or to popularity, are obstacles, sources of unfreedom. As in the version of asceticism described earlier, the outcome is not intended to be that we pay no attention to our own well-being but, rather, that we remain free to answer whatever call we receive, even when that puts our comfort, possessions, social position, or normal way of living at risk. We need to chance giving up control and certainty, and that may mean giving up trying to be right with God by rigidly following a set of unambiguous ethical rules. This implies a politics of love and freedom, not guilt and moralism.[19]

From any of the perspectives just described, there may be problems with the views of some of the respondents. On the other hand, it is important to recognize the ways in which moralism in politics can be valuable. Let me list some of them:

- Self-interest is not necessarily an adequate motivation for the kinds of behavior required to make social change.
- Moral or ethical language is how we make arguments that can bridge the quite different interests of different groups, allowing us to appeal to many kinds of people. Moralistic thinking helps counter the idea that politics can or should be nothing more than a matter of brokering among competing "special interest groups," and gives us a handle for opposing the tendency for politics to degenerate into that kind of enterprise.
- Moralistic thinking can counter the relativism sometimes used to ground reliance on free markets. The market is a model of relativism; moralistic thinking helps some Christians think it is all right to "interfere" with market forces.
- Moralistic thinking reminds us that ethical questions, including questions about what situations are just and unjust, are not simply matters of subjective preference—no matter how hard we may find it to reach agreement on evaluations of particular situations. Moralism encourages us to argue with one another about the values that ought to inform public decisions and the way we organize our economic lives together.
- Such thinking can help us see collective institutions—the ways in which we put collective decisions into practice—as more than unfortunate makeshifts (which is the way Americans usually see them).

In short, there are many things right with moralism.[20]

The Communitarians

Some of the same issues come up in relation to the social theorists sometimes dubbed the "communitarians," especially Robert Bellah and his colleagues and the philosopher Alisdair MacIntyre.[21] These theorists are often criticized for being too moralistic (a criticism that has some things in common with Westbrook's critique of "radical traditionalists" on the left); Richard Rorty says they suffer from "terminal wistfulness," and Jeffrey Stout, while not so harsh, seems to agree.[22] Stout argues that Bellah and MacIntyre are utopian in that it is hard

> to imagine a full-blown alternative to our society that would be both achievable by acceptable means and clearly better than what we have now. No one has trouble imagining a way of life that, by their lights, would qualify as an improvement on the current order. But it always turns out to be a way of life in which everybody, or nearly everybody, comes to see the light. . . . The critics do succeed, at times, in articulating quite reasonable misgivings many of us feel concerning life in our society. Yet they rarely give us any clear sense of what to do about our misgivings aside from yearning pensively for conditions we are either unwilling or unable to bring about. When you unwrap the utopia, the batteries aren't included.[23]

The communitarians, in this view, rely on jeremiads, calls for conversion to republican or biblical language, to effect social change. Furthermore, Stout thinks our moral state is not as dire as the communitarians think. Americans, he says, are capable of "varied and supple" ethical languages; "we may parrot individualistic sayings on occasion," but these are by no means our first language, as Bellah and his colleagues maintain.[24] These non-individualistic ethical languages, however, are varied and specific, developed in different spheres of life, and are not as unified or theoretically articulate and other-regarding as the communitarians might wish. Some people, for instance, develop an allegiance to being skilled at playing baseball that goes beyond self-interest or even pleasure in any simple sense. It provides a language for making ethical judgments, disciplines their lives, involves them with others and in loyalties and obligations—for example, to their team— that are not individualistic, but it does not constitute even the embryo of a theory about public life or the economic order.

Stout makes some valid points. Many of the depth-interview respondents are capable, as individuals, of using multiple ethical languages, and many of these languages are indeed non-individualistic. Sermonizing is probably not a very likely strategy for social change (although I doubt that this is what Bellah and his colleagues are imagining). Furthermore, some of the individualistic themes found in the respondents' thinking—for instance, the use of such themes as part of the language of economic rights and equality— are morally reputable rather than reprehensible, and serve the cause of economic justice or articulate valuable principles of liberty. Again, Bellah and his colleagues would undoubtedly agree; what they criticize is the excessive focus on individual rights and freedom in our society, and the use of individualistic ideas to ground politics of meanness and self-interest; they have no desire to return to some imagined Puritan utopia.

Despite these positive points about the ethical languages spoken by Americans, it is clear from what is said both by the respondents in *Habits of the Heart* and by the respondents reported on here that there are strong individualistic components in the thinking of many Americans, and that these are hardly, as Stout would have it, just sayings that people parrot but do not mean. Stout's sense of American ethical thinking seems a bit optimistic.

It is also not clear how the "varied and supple" languages Stout speaks of could provide much of a basis for public discourse on how we should organize our economic order. When Stout finally starts articulating his own bases for talking about justice issues, his procedure does not look like one that ordinary people would arrive at inductively out of their engagement in sphere-specific ethical languages, without access to broader ones. Stout, after all, has fully available to him the languages developed by the tradition of social philosophy. For most Americans, that tradition is only available in fragmentary ways; Christian tradition, however, *is* available.

The respondents' statements indicate that when people appropriate the resources of the Christian linguistic community, they continue to have access to strongly individualistic themes but gain access to communal languages they do not use so readily in other contexts. They also gain an enhanced ability to reject commonsense definitions of practicality and in other ways manifest the potentials of the tradition of otherworldliness within Christianity. Moreover, when they use fairly "traditional" Christian forms of language, they show all these possibilities to an equal (and occasionally greater) extent as when they use "modernist" language. All this indicates the continuing importance of religion in America, and the value of some of the cultural traditions that can easily sound offputtingly moralistic or utopian. Christian faith—almost ignored by Stout, except as it appears in the thinking of a few theorists—still has a great deal to contribute to American public discourse. Like the "radical traditionalists," I think we can benefit from the contributions of "traditional" forms of culture in America—but, I would add, we can also benefit from modernism.

Remaining Otherworldly

Finally, however, for a Christian, considerations of the social utility of faith come second, for we are called to be as much "not of" the world as "in" it. The recent strand of Christian thinking called "post-liberalism" (or occasionally "post-modernism") might help us articulate a distinctively Christian perspective while fully engaging us with the contemporary world, its problems, joys, and sorrows.

Post-liberals characteristically wish to abandon attempts to justify Christian faith in terms of external, secular criteria. From this perspective, there are no universal experiences and truths that each religion expresses in a different way; rather, the common language and texts of a community, such as the Bible for Christians, provide a unique framework constitutive of our religious experience. In a way, this perspective is sociological and almost relativistic, in that it emphasizes the social construction of religious truth and experience, but in another way it harks back to neo-orthodoxy and the theology of Karl Barth, reasserting the primacy and specificity of a Christian worldview.[25]

Stanley Hauerwas is perhaps the leading social ethicist in this tradition. As he puts it, jumping off from the theology of George Lindbeck,

> Theology does not describe some universally available experience. Rather by our becoming members of a particular community, formed by Christian convictions, an experience not otherwise available is made possible. From this perspective Christian ethics does not simply confirm what all people of good will know, but requires a transformation both personally and socially if we are to be true to the nature of our convictions.[26]

Hauerwas wants Christians to be deeply involved in struggles for peace and justice but to do so as Christians. He criticizes both anti-nuclear and pro-nuclear intellectuals for using a common set of assumptions about the end of the world, and puts forward instead a Christian, scripturally based vision of God's promise for the future that leads him to a pacifism of an uncommon sort. "Liberals," he says, "often affirm what appear to be advances in the culture on the ground that they are advances toward the eschatological future, while the postliberal is committed neither to traditionalism nor progressivism."[27]

There are at least three important correspondences between this perspective and the arguments I have been making throughout this book. First, as we saw with regard to measures of religiosity and commitment, there is no way to define a common core of religious commitments common to all traditions (even within Christianity!), and the post-liberal perspective understands and accepts this.

Second, evolutionary thinking, relied on by those who call themselves "progressives," often by those who call themselves "traditionalists," and certainly by those who expect liberal politics and modernist beliefs to go together in a simple way, is a barrier to understanding how religion and politics are related. Post-liberalism rejects evolutionary assumptions—as we saw in the quotation from Hauerwas—not trying to justify faith within the criteria of modern secular culture but putting forward a Christian way of thinking in all its apparent oddity.

Third, we have seen that some of the most important resources Christians have for enriching public discourse are otherworldly commitments, which can give them (for instance) the ability to reject conventional justifications for inequality, or to follow lines of action that seem impractical or risky. A post-liberal perspective nurtures these capacities—for religious rather than political reasons. Hauerwas calls us to a style of life in which being practically effective in improving the world comes second to being faithful. He believes, however, that this can turn out to have more effect on the world than would more "practical" courses of action. He is often considered sectarian because of this stance, although in fact he is strongly committed to Christian social engagement.

I find most of this persuasive. We struggle for justice because that is our call, our response to God's gift of grace. We choose among possible religious perspectives, not on the basis of their social benefits but because we think we hear God's voice. As a Christian sympathetic to the aspirations of both modernists and traditionalists (although I belong to a modernist denomination), I hope that modernist Christians can learn from their traditionalist sisters and brothers. The fluency of traditionalists in the use of Christian language and the capacity of many to resist the hegemony of contemporary culture are commendable, and their criticisms of modernist Christianity have some basis. Yet it is clear, from what the depth-interview respondents say and from ordinary observation, that both modernist and traditionalist Christians can be genuinely otherworldly, and also that both can fall under the sway of the definitions of reality found in secular culture. Think of the images of Jesus as marketer and CEO found in some fundamentalist writings! The axis of religious commitment, in the sense of preserving what used to be called a saving difference from the world, is not theological traditionalism versus modernism; biblical literalism is neither a barrier nor much of a help in maintaining our capacity to be "not of" the world. Rather, the struggle to assert a distinctive Christian message needs to go on, perhaps in different forms, in both theological camps.

By adopting something like Hauerwas's approach—perhaps with a little more commitment to respectful dialogue with secular culture than he sometimes seems to advocate—one can also partly circumvent the dilemma of moralism. If moralism means feeling morally superior, it undermines the possibility of cooperation between Christians and others pursuing parallel social and political goals. Such a feeling is not only politically harmful but theologically unjustifiable; it manifests lack of trust in God's grace. The gospels and epistles tell us that God loves and cares for sinners, that being morally better than others is not a precondition—is if anything an obstacle— to receiving God's grace, and that we have no basis for this kind of pride. From a post-liberal point of view, we are not "better" people than others— which could mean only that we better live up to shared ethical standards that have no distinctively Christian quality. Rather, we partake of a social and linguistic community that molds our experience and calls us into witness and service for reasons internal to our perspective. If we do something useful for the world, it is almost an accident, or at least first and foremost an expression of God's grace, rather than because we are better than anyone else or have a special handle on universal standards everyone should accept.

The resources are there in Christian tradition, in short, to take a different route—to be ethically committed without being moralistic in the sense of feeling superior—and some of the time Christians manage to find it. With a great deal of help from God and one another, we Christians can be moralistic in the good sense—speaking with conviction and using ethical languages to resist what is wrong in the world; constructing ideological politics out of a framework of reality and values that take priority over the individualistic concerns American culture often celebrates—while avoiding the unlovely, socially harmful, and theologically unacceptable qualities of moralism. The reason for trying to do this is our trust in God, but its result can be to allow respectful dialogue and political cooperation with non-Christians while we maintain our ability to contribute something distinctive to public life.

If the respondents studied here are any indication, it is from Christian faith that many Americans acquire resources for egalitarian and communal images of how our shared economic life might be organized. Such images, I believe, are both badly needed and theologically well grounded. Our present economic arrangements alienate us from one another—and in a Christian view, from God—more than the contemporary human condition requires. My hope is that in coming years Christians and others who share egalitarian, communal, and democratic visions will join to support and assist in the creation of a better society and world: one where our capacities for love, community, creativity, self-determination, and participation in decision-making are nurtured; where human needs and relationships take priority over profits, market forces, and technology. People sharing these hopes will have varying views as to how they might become incarnate. In my view a quite radical—in some sense socialist—transformation of our economy will be required, along with non-economic changes in our lives and communities. Such hopes, in any case, constitute a vision at once political and religious. They tell us what God requires of us, and describe a society that offers more of the abundant life into which Christians and all the world are invited.

APPENDIX

Methods Used in the Research

When I set out to study the connections between faith and views about economic justice among ordinary Americans, I started by using public opinion data. It quickly became apparent that no interesting relationships among variables would be forthcoming, and that the variables used in public opinion surveys manifested a way of thinking about religion and politics that did not make sense to me—for reasons, described in chapters 7 and 8, of which I was not fully aware at the time. To this experience were added several other concerns.

First, because I believed that real connections between faith and politics were hidden behind the non-associations in the public opinion data, a method was needed that would allow people to explain how it was "logical" for each one to make connections between faith and economic opinions that might be quite different from one person to another—with one person grounding conservative views in faith, for instance, while another person grounded liberal views in faith.

A second concern (undoubtedly linked to my political inclinations as a radical democrat) was to bring to rank-and-file thinking the same care and sophistication routinely used to analyze texts and the writings and speeches of leaders, and to bring the real nature of the thinking of ordinary people to the attention of church leaders and political activists who often conceive of such people's thought processes in stereotypes. I assume, in other words, that rank-and-file members think independently and in ways that are not necessarily the ones theologians, ethicists, and church leaders wish but are also not simply ill-informed or poorly thought out. Since few church members give speeches or write for publication, the only way to determine their views is to ask them.

A third concern, linked to the others, was to be able to analyze people's thinking in terms of more subtle concepts than public opinion data on religion allowed, in order to understand better how and why people arrive at their differing appropriations of faith. To do this requires a degree of attention to the specific ways in which people connect their religious and political opinions that public opinion researchers, pressed by time and dividing limited resources among all the people in a large sample, cannot provide.

All these considerations led to the decision to undertake a depth-interview study. In a depth-interview study, one takes great care with each person. However, because people vary tremendously, it is important to speak with a fair number of people, and to select the people one interviews in a careful and systematic way. Many published depth-interview studies (for instance, *Habits of the Heart,* Jennifer Hochschild's *What's Fair?,* Craig Reinarman's *American States of Mind,* Robert Lane's *Political Ideology,* and Smith, Bruner, and White's *Opinions and Personality*) use somewhat informal methods.[1] Basically, one knows the kind of people one wants and inquires through appropriate networks until one locates suitable respondents. The difficulty with this procedure is not only that there are biases—that is, some kinds of people are more likely to be selected than others—but also that we do not know what the biases are; the procedure is not replicable and it is not clear to what degree, or to what part of the U.S. population, one can generalize from the results.

I used a method that compromises between informal methods and those used in survey sampling. All but ten of the forty-seven respondents were recruited in a fairly objective, replicable way; the other ten were recruited in the more typical fashion of depth-interview studies.

The largest group of respondents (thirty-one of the forty-seven) were selected from a random sample of the adult population of the San Francisco Bay Area that had been drawn two years earlier for a study of new forms of religious consciousness.[2] (I will call this group the New Religious Consciousness sample.) I first discarded all the respondents except the Christian church members from the sample. I then placed the remaining respondents on a two-dimensional grid defined by their views (as ascertained by the previous survey) on an index of religious traditionalism and an index of economic conservatism, and randomly (but in a controlled way) selected one person from each cell on the grid. (The control on this process was for two purposes. One was to get a useful denominational distribution; even though Catholics make up almost half of church members in the Bay Area, I allocated them only one-third of the slots in order to be able to represent a greater variety of Protestant denominations, and I made sure that no more than two respondents came from any one Protestant denomination. The second was to ensure demographic diversity; if a male was selected in one cell, for instance, a female would be selected from the next one if possible.)

I then tracked down the respondents and wrote them letters asking them to participate in the study, following up with a phone call. Some people refused,[3] and many had moved in the two years since they had been surveyed and could not be located. In such cases, the originally selected respondent was replaced by a new person from the same part of the grid, although some cells remained unrepresented.[4]

The reason for this procedure, similar to the "dimensional sampling" recommended by David Arnold,[5] was to use the very limited number of respondents one can manage in a depth-interview study with maximum efficiency to get respondents with a broad variety of perspectives and socioeconomic characteristics. With only about fifty respondents, I did not want to interview eight people with essentially the same views, or to get overwhelmingly college-educated people. Clearly this worked: the respondents are far more varied than those usually found in depth-interview studies. They come from seventeen denominations. Thirteen of them were under thirty years old when interviewed; seven were sixty-five or older; and less than half were (or, for students, were headed toward being) college graduates. This is a multi-class, multi-generational set of respondents! The procedure followed is also consonant with a cultural rather than a psychological approach, in the sense described in chapter 8; what it provides is more like a sample of the different perspectives or combinations of religious and political views that exist in America than a sample of the population.

There are three limitations of this procedure that one should be aware of. First, whatever correlation there might be between religious traditionalism and economic conservatism in the sample from which the respondents were drawn was wiped out. However, we have independent evidence from public opinion research (presented in chapter 7) that there is no meaningful association between traditionalism and conservatism. Second, the procedure I followed gave much more weight to the extremes, and less to the center, than would a sample giving every person equal probability of selection. On any economic conservatism index, for instance, people tend to clump near the center, with fewer people at the most liberal and most conservative points on the index. By contrast, given the way in which I selected my respondents, there are approximately equal numbers of people at each point, whether centrist or extreme. So my respondents are, on the average, probably somewhat more extreme than the population from which they were drawn. Quite likely, this means that they are also a little more systematic, consistent, and ideological than average. Third, refusals and my inability to track down some of the potential respondents who had moved introduce a bias in favor of getting the kinds of people who move less frequently— probably, older people with more settled and conventional lives—and the kinds of people more willing to subject themselves to this kind of interview— probably people with a greater interest in religious and perhaps political issues than average.

The population from which this sample was drawn was confined to Christian church members in the San Francisco Bay Area. The Bay Area is clearly not the same as the rest of the country, either politically or religiously. However, on economic issues (as opposed to drugs or sex) it is not greatly different. Furthermore, because I was dealing only with Christian church members, the unconventional religious phenomena of the Bay Area were largely excluded. Church members in the Bay Area are not greatly different from church members in other northern, urban areas—just scarcer. Religious perspectives particularly characteristic of the South and of rural areas may be under-represented. However, since one of the effects of my procedure was to oversample the extremes, if the main difference between southern and northern Christians is that southerners tend to be significantly more religiously traditionalist, then the kinds of views characteristic of southerners should be better represented among my respondents than they would be in an equal probability sample. Finally, since secular and unconventionally religious perspectives are stronger in the Bay Area than elsewhere, it is possible that repeating my study elsewhere in the country would show even stronger connections between faith and politics.

Six more respondents were chosen in a parallel way from two Presbyterian churches (one suburban, one inner city) that I had surveyed in an earlier phase of the project. Thus thirty-seven respondents were chosen using the same basic method. Among the seven respondents profiled in chapter 1, Susan Wainwright comes from the Presbyterian sample, and the other six from the New Religious Consciousness sample. All of the other respondents mentioned by name, except for those listed below, come from one of these samples.

As mentioned in the text, the chances of any perspective with a significant presence among American Christians *not* appearing among my respondents is low. If they had constituted an equal-probability random sample, and a given view were shared by only 5 percent of American Christians, the probability of finding at least one of the thirty-seven respondents chosen in the sample holding it would be $(1 - .95^{37})$ or .85; for a perspective held by 10 percent of American Christians the probability would be .98.[6] (The expected number of respondents with such perspectives would be about two in the first case and four in the second; however, when one draws samples of thirty-seven people from a population, one gets random fluctuation, with some samples containing more or fewer people with this characteristic.) Given that extreme perspectives are scarce in the population and therefore in samples, and that I gave augmented chances of selection to people with extreme perspectives, the odds of finding any perspective with a significant following should be even better. If one is concerned to locate and study perspectives, as opposed to measuring accurately their distribution in the population, a small sample—if chosen in a replicable way—can be quite adequate.

The remaining ten respondents were recruited through networks—pastors, people in religiously based political organizations, and so on—in much the same way as in other major depth-interview studies. Three were African-

Americans. One came from a predominantly African-American mainline Protestant congregation, and two—one politically liberal, the other centrist (Philomena Jackson)—from an evangelical African-American congregation. I had been able to obtain only one African-American respondent from the two samples, and so this provided at least a taste of the perspectives found in African-American churches.

The final seven respondents were selected to represent "extreme types"; the idea was to get some idea of the boundaries of the political-religious playing field I was studying, some reference points to which to compare other respondents. One was a Quaker (William Westfield), and two each were mainline Protestants, evangelical Protestants, and Catholics. In each of these pairs, one was radical and one was extremely conservative (George Hoffman was the conservative mainline Protestant).

One interview was done, in Spanish, by a male sociology graduate student born in Guatemala, six by a male sociology graduate student with a southern evangelical background, eight by a female Catholic theological student, and the other thirty-two by me. There was a fixed sequence of topics, a checklist of information to be obtained, and several required questions for each topic, with the rest of the questioning left to the interviewer's discretion. The interviews typically lasted about three hours, divided between two sessions. They were conducted at the location of the respondent's choice (usually a home, but occasionally a church or workplace), from June through November 1976.

This raises another question of generalizability, with regard to time. Some of the specific issues and candidates discussed in the interviews have left the political landscape. However, the interviews really had little to do with the specific issues of the day; these were occasionally discussed, but mostly to get at views on fundamental questions about equality, private enterprise, the role of government, economic rights, and so forth. These more fundamental questions have not changed in any major respect since at least the New Deal; they are essentially the same today as they were in 1976, and equally controversial. To be sure, the way religious leaders, movements, and organizations are involved in politics has changed since 1976, but this is primarily the case with regard to abortion, homosexuality, nuclear weapons, and Central America. Even on such issues, change in grass-roots sentiment happens more slowly than one might think from journalistic accounts of "new" political and religious developments, but on economic justice issues, there is no sign of change in the relationships between religion and politics. In sum, I am confident that interviews today would find the same Christian themes being used in the same range of ways to ground economic views.

The interviews were tape-recorded, with the respondents' permission (none refused), and then transcribed verbatim. (The interview in Spanish was also translated into English.) The result was the data set actually used in this book; physically, it consists of a large file drawer full of transcripts. The transcripts were subjected to a systematic content analysis in which statements manifesting particular themes (for example, giving high value to being "non-judgmental") were marked and recorded. The codings were quantified to a limited degree (we know how many times each respondent made a statement expressing each of five major kinds of themes), but the main use of the content analysis was to organize the statements of the respondents in a coherent way for a qualitative, essentially textual analysis.

The statements from the respondents quoted here are verbatim when in quotation marks, and paraphrases when not. The only editing done to the verbatim quotations is to correct the kind of simple grammatical errors (usually of tense or number) that are normal in conversation; to add explanatory words when required to make a statement comprehensible in the context of this book; and to omit unnecessary or repeated words without ellipsis. Paraphrases are used extensively, in most cases because the respondent, struggling to articulate positions on complex issues without preparation, has talked in a roundabout, imprecise, or repetitive way that does not, if quoted verbatim, do justice to the ideas being expressed.

"Methods" as I have spoken of them so far may sound like ways of enhancing objectivity, perhaps even of keeping a safe distance between myself and what I study. There is some truth to this impression, in that I desire (in this research) to understand more than to judge, and to explain what I found in ways which are publicly accessible: persuasive to people with a variety of perspectives, and understandable to those who have not walked in my shoes.

However, the interactions among me, my subject matter, and my audiences have also been a major part of how I have learned. The respondents have affected my understanding of the connections between religion and politics, as have the political and religious events and writings of the thirty-five years since I became politically active as a ten-year-old wearing Adlai Stevenson buttons and explaining my position in a solidly Republican town. These events and writings, and my own spiritual and political development, can be regarded as parts of the research process. I have also learned a great deal through the process of explaining what I found, in person and in writing, to people in the churches and on the Left. In a sense, these interactions have been another method of research, casting new light on what the respondents told me. Methods of research, I hope, can be wholistic (just as I hope faith and politics will be wholistic), with a wide range of experiences and interactions contributing to the process by which human understanding grows.

Notes

Introduction

1. Robert N. Bellah, Richard Madsen, Ann Swidler, William M. Sullivan, and Steven M. Tipton, *Habits of the Heart: Individualism and Commitment in American Life* (Berkeley: University of California Press, 1985).

2. In chapter 7 we will supplement the statements of the depth-interview respondents with data from public opinion polls.

3. Non-economic issues, which are only very weakly related to economic ones within the thinking of most Americans, and are related to religious faith in a quite different way, will be left aside.

Chapter 1

1. See Wade Clark Roof and William McKinney, *American Mainline Religion* (New Brunswick, NJ: Rutgers University Press, 1987), for a recent analysis of differences among Protestant denominations. They distinguish among theologically liberal, moderate, and conservative "families" among white Protestants. The theologically liberal and moderate denominations are what I am calling modernist here; the conservative ones are what I call traditionalist. An older description of the situation is found in Rodney Stark and Charles Glock, *American Piety* (Berkeley: University of California Press, 1968); essentially, the divisions were the same. Stark and Glock note, however, that the differences *within* denominations are more important than all but the biggest differences *between* denominations; Robert Wuthnow's *The Restructuring of American Religion* (Princeton: Princeton University Press, 1988), makes the same point about the situation today.

2. One classical statement of liberation theology is Gustavo Gutiérrez, *A Theology of Liberation* (Maryknoll, NY: Orbis Books, 1973; originally published 1971).

3. *Rerum Novarum* (originally issued in 1891) can be found in Etienne Gilson, ed., *The Church Speaks to the Modern World* (Garden City, NY: Doubleday, 1954), pp. 205–240; the "Bishops' Program of Social Reconstruction," in *American Catholic Thought on Social Questions,* ed. Aaron I. Abell (Indianapolis: Bobbs-Merrill, 1968),

pp. 326–348. For one example of John Paul II's thought, see *Laborem Exercens* [On Human Work] (Washington, DC: United States Catholic Conference, 1981).

4. The fragmentation of her thinking has some parallels to the fragmentation of her time and activities as a housewife—constantly interrupted by the needs of her children and husband, and by myriad miscellaneous involvements. Quite a few of the housewives interviewed showed a similar fragmentation in their thinking, and perhaps this is not an accident.

Chapter 2

1. Robert N. Bellah, Richard Madsen, Ann Swidler, William M. Sullivan, and Steven M. Tipton, *Habits of the Heart: Individualism and Commitment in American Life* (Berkeley: University of California Press, 1985). The authors argue that the ethical languages most available to Americans are individualistic. Since my study is primarily of *religious* frameworks used to ground political views, whereas *Habits* is concerned most of all with the impact of frameworks that are not explicitly religious, I will rely on *Habits* when I need to make comparisons to the ways in which non-Christian perspectives ground Americans' views on economic issues.

2. For an analysis of some of the political meanings of relativism, see my article "Ethical Relativism, Left-Wing Politics," *Dissent* (Fall 1982): 483–486.

3. Privatized ways of thinking about churches can have both favorable and un-favorable impacts on churches as organizations. For an analysis of the meaning and implications of privatization, see my article "Privatization in American Religion and Society," *Sociological Analysis* 47 (Winter 1987): 319–334.

4. On the economic side, Max Weber's *The Protestant Ethic and the Spirit of Capitalism* (New York: Scribner, 1958; originally published 1904–1905) is the classical argument. Michael Walzer's *Revolution of the Saints* (Cambridge: Harvard University Press, 1965) makes a parallel argument with regard to the first modern, ideological revolution, the English Revolution of 1640. And several scholars have pursued the connections between Protestantism and the emergence of modern science.

Weber's perspective is most often understood from *The Protestant Ethic,* but he actually stated it in more general terms elsewhere. One important statement is in *The Religion of China* (New York: Macmillan, 1951; originally published 1920), where Weber contrasted Puritanism and Confucianism. Puritanism, he says,

> creates and systematically orients conduct toward one internal measure of value. In the face of this the "world" is viewed as material to be fashioned ethically according to the norm. Confucianism in contrast meant adjustment to the outside, to the conditions of the "world." A well-adjusted man, rationalizing his conduct only to the degree necessary for adjustment, does not constitute a systematic unity but rather a complex of useful and particular traits. (p. 235)

Whether or not Weber understands Confucianism correctly, he makes clear the nature of a voluntaristic perspective: that it seeks to organize the individual in a way independent of the environment, around a set of transcendent commitments. The world is basically secular—a place to do holy works but not holy in itself. It does not provide the values to organize a Christian self; rather, these values come from a "within"—a conscience—which is at the same time the only and best representation one can find of the utterly "without"—of God and God's laws.

5. For a description of the idea of citizenship, see T. H. Marshall, "Citizenship

and Social Class," in his collection *Class, Citizenship and Social Development* (Garden City, NY: Doubleday Anchor, 1965). At one point, Marshall mentions the non-achieved quality of citizenship, making the parallel to Christian universalism even stronger. Durkheim's argument is found in various places, but most strongly and clearly in his defense of the pro-Dreyfus camp in the essay "Individualism and the Intellectuals" (1898), found in English in *Emile Durkheim on Morality and Society*, ed. Robert N. Bellah (Chicago: University of Chicago Press, 1973). The universalism of Marx's vision is expressed in almost all his writings.

6. Michael Walzer, "Teaching Morality," *The New Republic*, June 10, 1978, p. 13.

7. John Paul II, *Laborem Exercens* [On Human Work] (Washington, DC: United States Catholic Conference, 1981).

8. The ideas presented in historical characterizations of the next few paragraphs and the description of universalism presented earlier are deeply indebted to Robert Bellah's seminal article, "Religious Evolution," *American Sociological Review* 29 (June 1964): 358–374. Many people do not feel comfortable with an evolutionary perspective, and Bellah's own views have changed significantly in the nearly thirty years since he wrote this article. Nonetheless, many of the contributions of this article stand regardless of one's stance on evolutionary thinking. The article can be taken as a way of categorizing religious frameworks; a study of the social implications—especially for freedom—that tend to come from different kinds of religion; and a meditation on how our past still affects us. On the last point, Bellah shows that the world-acceptance that now characterizes Christianity has a different meaning because Christianity (along with the other religions of the same era) was so radically world-rejecting at one point—and retains important, if reinterpreted, aspects of world-rejection—than it would if that heritage of world-rejection were absent.

9. Note that contrary to the stereotype of otherworldliness as anti-modern and anti-rational, in this respect the tradition of otherworldliness made and still makes a contribution to modernity, helping desacralize existing customs and prejudices, and facilitating rational examination of nature and human life. The iconoclasm inherent in otherworldliness also supports voluntarism, as we saw in the first section of this chapter.

10. In a sense, one could say that the Reformation made the distinction between religious and secular purposes less "concrete" and more "analytical": the distinction is now not between the church and the world, or religious and secular vocations, but between those activities in any sphere or vocation that are carrying out God's purposes versus those that reflect worldly values and concerns. This shift is part of a process—sometimes termed generalization of values—that is found in various trends of cultural change over the past few centuries.

11. Heiko A. Oberman, *Luther: Man between God and the Devil* (New Haven: Yale University Press, 1989; originally published 1982).

12. *Book of Common Prayer* (Greenwich, CT: Seabury, 1928), p. 277.

13. *Book of Common Prayer* (Greenwich, CT: Seabury, 1977), p. 302.

14. The themes or tendencies described in this chapter present some shared characteristics in various combinations. Voluntarism, universalism, and love all involve the dilemma of the relationship between individual and community; thisworldliness and otherworldliness present the dilemma of how to live in but not of the world. Universalism, love, and, to some extent, thisworldliness tend to support human

solidarity and connectedness, while voluntarism, universalism, and otherworldliness
all enhance our capacity to assert our individuality. Universalism and love are principles with clear, substantive ethical content. The other three are more "meta-
ethical," by which I mean that they concern basic conditions, or the correct process
or criteria, for making ethical decisions. Universalism and love are also ideas that
respondents hold explicitly and self-consciously; the other three building blocks are
less consciously held by rank-and-file Christians and have a more abstract quality.
Voluntarism, universalism, and thisworldliness, finally, are the three themes that
have a relatively "modern" feel to them; the others have a more old-fashioned tone.
To present these shared and varying characteristics schematically:

	Theme				
Characteristic	Volun- tarism	Univer- salism	Love	This- world- liness	Other- world- liness
Individual/community dilemma	✔	✔	✔		
In but not of the world dilemma				✔	✔
Source of solidarity		✔	✔	✔	
Enhances individuation	✔	✔			✔
Substantive ethical content		✔	✔		
Consciously, explicitly held		✔	✔		
Modern (vs. traditional) tone	✔	✔		✔	

Chapter 3

1. It is important to keep the two issues just mentioned distinct; church social
action, it can well be argued, need not infringe on the separation of church and
state. Many respondents did confuse these two issues, and opposed church social
action under the banner of keeping church and state separate.

2. One classical exposition of the idea of structural differentiation (seen as an
evolutionary direction, not necessarily a value) is found in Neil Smelser's *Social
Change in the Industrial Revolution* (Chicago: University of Chicago Press, 1959).
It is important to note that differentiation, as applied to ideas, is not necessarily the
same as compartmentalization. In fact, it is compatible with integration. Here is a
possible model (essentially, that found in what is called "functionalism" within sociology): People may have more or less well-developed ideas by which to understand
how social structure works, how inequality gets created, and what impact different
possible public policies would have. They may also have religious perspectives placing
human life in an ultimate context and defining central values to guide human life.
Social structure is seen as non-sacred and part of nature; faith refers to realities of
a different kind; the languages used in talking about God and in talking about society
are largely different. Yet one can integrate these differentiated discourses by using
religious faith to define the most general principles on the basis of which one will
determine the values one wishes to govern the economic order. Such an integration

takes place only at the "highest," most general level of political discourse; the rest of political discourse takes place using secular language, but is governed by these general principles. Compartmentalization, within this model, could be seen as a failure to perform such an integration. This model has a certain plausibility, and yet the more "integrated" of the Christians interviewed in this study want a more robust and variegated integration of faith and politics, one with much more day-to-day impact, than this model would countenance. This might sometimes include fairly specific value judgments, and even images of reality (which, in the model just described, would be derived naturalistically)—for instance, political action, as the left-of-center evangelical journalist and preacher Jim Wallis describes it, based on trusting in the promises of God.

One can detect a religious history in views about structural differentiation. Historically, the issue of church and state has been by far the most important arena for discussions of where and how institutional spheres should be separated, and this issue largely defined the terms of debate for all the others. Furthermore, there are important links between our religious history and the issue of structural differentiation. The British historian Christopher Hill depicts social conflicts in sixteenth- and seventeenth-century England, showing how Puritans came to be aligned with forces pushing for various forms of differentiation—for instance, the independence of the legal system from the immediate wishes of the Crown, as well as from the church and church law. The Puritans took this stance partly because it served the economic interests of the kind of people who tended to be Puritans, but partly also because it fit their model of human personality and society. (Christopher Hill, *Puritanism and Society in Pre-Revolutionary England,* 2d ed. [New York: Schocken Books, 1967]).

3. An elegant yet simple formulation of this dilemma and example of how it works in practice are found in Edmund Morgan's biography of John Winthrop, *The Puritan Dilemma* (Boston: Little, Brown, 1958).

4. This respondent is probably referring to Acts 5:1–11, the story of Ananias and Sapphira, who sold land but gave only part of the proceeds to the Christian community. According to the story, both fall dead when Peter berates them. The community does not change its communistic ways (described just before, in Acts 4:32–35) in response to this event, and so it could be argued that the story does not really support this respondent's case.

5. There are other surveys from which data are available that do not have this denominational limitation—notably, the General Social Survey conducted every year by the National Opinion Research Center—but these surveys are broad, multipurpose instruments and do not usually ask questions that allow one to get at issues of compartmentalization and integration. The General Social Survey is useful, however, for getting at associations between religious and political attitudes, and will be used to address that issue in chapter 7.

6. The 1982 survey is reported in "Summary of Results: The Lutheran Listening Post—Panel II, Questionnaire 3: Christian Living and Ministry and Financial Support of the Church," by the Department for Planning, Research and Evaluation of the Lutheran Church in America (1983); the 1988 survey is reported in "Faith, the Church, and the World: How ELCA Members See the Connections," by the Office for Research, Planning, and Evaluation of the Evangelical Lutheran Church in America (1990). These reports contain information on the methods used in each survey and a full account of the findings.

7. A third survey explored (among other things) the prevalence of "two-kingdoms" thinking, in the context of national defense issues. This kind of thinking seems less prevalent than the barriers to integrating faith and politics we have been discussing. The research is reported in my article "Christian Faith and Nuclear Weapons: Rank-and-File Opinions," *Journal for the Scientific Study of Religion* 26 (March 1987).

8. Thomas Luckmann's *The Invisible Religion: The Transformation of Symbols in Industrial Society* (New York: Macmillan, 1967) is the classical statement of this position.

9. To respond to this difficulty, the 1988 survey mentioned earlier used what is called a vignette technique. The "vignettes" consisted of computer-generated specific cases of church social action, specifying an actor, an action, an issue, and a position; for example, "The pastor of Redeemer Lutheran Church spoke at a rally to oppose the death penalty." These allowed the people surveyed to respond to something fairly concrete. There were about 1,700 such vignettes generated, and each respondent got a random sample of eleven of them; this method allows one to see whether there are systematic differences, with social action more approved on some issues than others, for instance. The methods and results are described in "Faith, the Church, and the World: How ELCA Members See the Connections," by the Office for Research, Planning, and Evaluation of the Evangelical Lutheran Church in America (1990).

Chapter 4

1. E. P. Thompson, *The Making of the English Working Class* (New York: Vintage, 1963); see especially chap. 11, "The Transforming Power of the Cross," pp. 350–400. There is an extensive literature on the question of work motivation and the role of religion in creating it, particularly in the context of economic development. A sampling of this research is found in an anthology edited by S. N. Eisenstadt, *The Protestant Ethic and Modernization* (New York: Basic Books, 1984). Controversies over "moral incentives" in China (before it took a capitalist turn) and over "parasitism" in the Soviet Union are concerned with similar issues. Thus the issue of work motivation crosscuts the division between capitalism and socialism; one could even argue that internalized work motivation and responsible individuals are actually *more* needed to make a socialist than a capitalist economy work.

2. In *Habits of the Heart: Individualism and Commitment in American Life* (Berkeley: University of California Press, 1985), Robert N. Bellah, Richard Madsen, Ann Swidler, William M. Sullivan, and Steven M. Tipton criticize even their most radical respondents for not having a substantive vision of social justice; instead, they have what might be called a "contentless" concern for freedom. In a different sense, there is something contentless, also, about the perspectives we have just been discussing. Joseph Krieger wants more social justice, to be sure, but he wants harmony even in the absence of justice; the principle of solidarity is "contentless" in that Joseph desires to maximize it *in any society,* without regard to its characteristics. Radicals, by contrast, would say that some social arrangements do not deserve such allegiance. Similarly, the views of work described here are "contentless" in that they make work a value regardless of the conditions under which it is performed, the social order in which it takes place, the purposes to which it is put, or the remuneration. One simply tries to do the best job one can.

All of these three instances of "contentless" thinking bear some relationship to what the social philosopher Max Horkheimer, a member of the Frankfurt school of culturally oriented Marxists, calls "instrumental rationality." Horkheimer uses this term to describe a pattern he argues is characteristic of contemporary society: the never-ceasing pursuit of the most technically effective means for achieving goals that are not themselves examined because they are felt to be agreed upon, the result of subjective choices, unchangeable, or for some other reason "given." (*Critique of Instrumental Reason* [New York: Seabury, 1974; originally published in German in 1967].) Christians like James O'Connell and Joseph Krieger would not approve of this pattern, but their views toward work bear a family resemblance to it.

3. The social philosopher and sociologist Karl Mannheim used usury as a central example of "false consciousness"; that is, of a norm "with which action in a given historical setting, even with the best of intentions, cannot comply." Such inapplicable standards, Mannheim thinks, serve the "ideological" function of "conceal [ing] the actual meaning of conduct rather than reveal [ing] it." Once social life is no longer "based upon intimate and neighborly relations" the condemnation of usury takes on an ideological character. *Ideology and Utopia* (New York: Harcourt Brace, 1936), p. 95.

It would be hard to quarrel with the assertion that lending without interest is impractical (except within family units, or as an exceptional practice) under capitalist conditions, in any social order that does not create *gemeinschaftlich* communities extending beyond the family, and perhaps in any complex, differentiated society. (Kibbutzim and other intentional communities might be exceptions. These do, of course, have *gemeinschaftlich* qualities, but they are also capable of being quite modern institutions.) Philomena's condemnation of usury, however, need not be understood as a practical proposal that ignores these "facts," and certainly not as a view that conceals reality.

The classical sociologist Max Weber also discussed the issue of usury, arguing that changes in the traditional Christian prohibition on usury were not a critical factor in the emergence of modern capitalism. Nonetheless, he sees that prohibition as reflecting the tension between an otherworldly ethic of love and the nature of modern economic life. *Sociology of Religion* (Boston: Beacon Press, 1963; originally published 1922), pp. 252ff.

4. Jeffrey Stout's *Ethics after Babel* (Boston: Beacon Press, 1988) contains a strong critique of the idea that we once had but now have lost a kind of unity in our moral discourse. However, the arguments on the other side are strong, also.

5. There is an extensive literature about the interplay between market and non-market aspects of life in capitalist societies. Some of this literature argues that while in theory non-market behaviors often seem to be motivated by values contrary to those of the market, in practice the workings of these non-market spheres (family, religion, and so on) make the market system function better, not worse. The classical sociologist Emile Durkheim, for instance, argues that there are social, collective principles—of social justice, for instance—that produce solidarity and without which a market system would sooner or later break down. This argument is found in the chapter "Organic Solidarity and Contractual Solidarity," in *The Division of Labor in Society* (New York: Free Press, 1964; originally published in 1893). It is also possible to argue that capitalist economies operate better, even for the capitalists, when there is a considerable degree of government intervention in the economy.

Such an argument is made, to take one example, by the Swedish sociologist Goran Therborn in *Why Some Peoples Are More Unemployed Than Others* (London: Verso/ NLB, 1986).

6. Robert J. Shiller, Maxim Boycko, and Vladimir Korobov, "Popular Attitudes towards Free Markets: The Soviet Union and the United States Compared," unpublished paper, August 1990 (copy provided by Professor Shiller of Yale University), p. 39. Some related research on Canadian attitudes toward pricing decisions (including setting rents and wages) is reported in Daniel Kahneman, Jack L. Knetsch, and Richard Thaler, "Fairness as a Constraint on Profit Seeking: Entitlements in the Market," *American Economic Review* 76 (September 1986): 728–741.

7. Transcript of "All Things Considered" for September 24, 1990 (Washington, DC: National Public Radio, 1990), p. 8.

Chapter 5

1. There are many versions and forms of equality. Douglas Rae's *Equalities* (Cambridge: Harvard University Press, 1981) rigorously disentangles the different dimensions on which such versions can differ. For discussing the depth-interview respondents' views of economic life, a rough distinction (much less sophisticated than those Rae proposes) among equality before the law, equality of opportunity, and equality of conditions or outcomes will do. It is evident, however, that there are several versions of each of these views of equality. Sometimes the boundaries among them even become unclear, as in arguments in favor of affirmative action—in theory a radical approach to achieving equality of opportunity, but in practice partly a way to reduce inequalities of outcome that are felt to be unjust but have not gone away in response to less radical steps. (This is not a criticism of affirmative action; as a radical egalitarian, I believe in it strongly, but I think those of us who favor affirmative action should be forthright about the fact that we regard the current extreme disparities of *outcomes* between races in the United States as unjust, and that many of us would continue to feel this way even if we were convinced that full equality of opportunity had been achieved.)

2. "Liminality and Communitas," *The Ritual Process* (Ithaca: Cornell University Press, 1977), pp. 94–130.

3. Karl Marx and Frederick Engels, *The Communist Manifesto* (New York: International Publishers, 1948; originally published in 1848), pp. 11–13.

4. This description of Jung's ideas comes partly from her article, "Lenin, Glasnost, and the Jewish Labor-Bund" (*Jewish Spectator* [Winter 1991]), and partly from personal conversations.

5. For one example of such a critique, see Michael Novak, *The Rise of the Unmeltable Ethnics* (New York: Macmillan, 1972).

6. Charles Reich, "The New Property," *Yale Law Review* 73 (April 1964).

7. The lyrics for the song read:

> He is an Englishman!
> For he himself has said it,
> And it's greatly to his credit,
> That he is an Englishman!
> For he might have been a Roosian,
> A French, or Turk, or Proosian,

Or perhaps Itali-an.
But in spite of all temptations
To belong to other nations,
He remains an Englishman!

Ian Bradley, ed., *The Annotated Gilbert and Sullivan* (Harmondsworth, United Kingdom: Penguin, 1982; first performed 1878), p. 69.

8. A basic document expressing the aspirations of the New Left is the Port Huron statement, written in 1962. This statement enunciated the goal "that the individual share in those social decisions determining the quality and direction of his life," in the economic just as much as the political sphere. Thus one can see the voluntaristic, radically democratic side of its aspirations. The communal side is equally real: an aspiration to overcome the "estrangement" the authors of the Port Huron Statement saw in America and to promote social arrangements in which "love" and "community" could grow; a positive view of politics as the place for shared decision-making; and a desire that people be provided the channels by which "private problems . . . [can be] formulated as general issues." Reprinted in *Socialist Review* 17, nos. 3–4 (May–August 1987): 105–140.

9. For instance, critics of the kind of "populist" approach promoted by Harry Boyte—which is similar to "economic democracy"—say that he overemphasizes democracy and underemphasizes equality. For such a critique, see Manning Marable, "The Contradictory Legacy of American Democracy," *Socialist Review* 9, no. 1 (January–February 1979): 114–120. Another important essay on issues about democracy as they arise on the left is David Plotke, "Democracy, Modernization, democracy," *Socialist Review* 14, no. 2 (March–April 1984): 29–53.

10. For an example of this historical literature, see Richard Bushman, *From Puritan to Yankee* (New York: Norton, 1970), pp. 183–195.

11. Geoffrey Hawthorne, *Enlightenment and Despair* (Cambridge: Cambridge University Press, 1976), pp. 192–193.

12. There is some research indicating that the cognitive frameworks within which people understand social life have an important influence on their views. Sociologist Charles Glock, in particular, has pioneered a line of research into people's assumptions about what causal forces determine human events. For instance, what are the causes of human suffering, of racial inequality, and of economic inequality? Glock describes a set of "explanatory modes" people use to answer such questions—ones focusing on supernatural forces, on genetic endowments, on individual skill and "will-power," and on social factors—and argues that people's choices of explanatory modes strongly influence their views on public policy questions. For an example of this line of research, see Richard A. Apostle, Charles Y. Glock, Thomas Piazza, and Marijean Suelzle, *The Anatomy of Racial Attitudes* (Berkeley: University of California Press, 1983).

13. For this passage, the text in the old Revised Standard Version is used because of its elegance.

Chapter 6

1. John Paul II, *Laborem Exercens* [On Human Work] (Washington, DC: United States Catholic Conference, 1981).

2. Weber formulates this idea in his essay "Politics as a Vocation," originally

published in 1919 and found in English in *From Max Weber: Essays in Sociology,* ed. Hans Gerth and C. Wright Mills (New York: Oxford University Press, 1946).

3. This is approximately the position, for instance, of John Cort, in *Christian Socialism* (Maryknoll, NY: Orbis Books, 1988), pp. 277–278. An even stronger attack is offered by Bill Kellerman, in "Apologist of Power: The Long Shadow of Reinhold Niebuhr's Christian Realism," *Sojourners* 16 (March 1987): 15–20.

4. For a classic analysis of such a secular perspective, and how it is entirely different from selfishness, see Emile Durkheim, "Individualism and the Intellectuals," in *Emile Durkheim on Morality and Society,* ed. Robert Bellah (Chicago: University of Chicago Press, 1973; this essay originally published in 1898).

5. For a parallel argument about evangelical thinking on social issues, see Richard Quebedeaux's *The Young Evangelicals* (New York: Harper and Row, 1974). He says that even for the new breed of socially concerned evangelicals his book is describing, the first task is always to convert the individual; social action is expected to follow from individual regeneration (pp. 33, 38).

6. For an elegant analysis of how this kind of universalism actually uses parent-child symbolism to make the bonds between biological parents and children weaker than they are in many non-Christian cultures, see Robert Bellah, "Father and Son in Christianity and Confucianism," originally published in 1960 and reprinted in his collection *Beyond Belief* (New York: Harper and Row, 1970).

7. Such coordination ideally requires that people make a long-term commitment to an organization or institution rather than making a decision on each occasion as to whether it is right or wrong. This is more likely if one sees the organization not just as a means to achieve one's individually defined social goals but also to some extent as an end in itself. That is, the organization needs to be viewed more than instrumentally, and perhaps even given a certain amount of sacredness. For a more detailed analysis of this issue, see my article "Privatization in American Religion and Society," *Sociological Analysis* 47 (Winter 1987).

8. It is not possible satisfactorily to resolve the question of whether there is such a connection by using public opinion data because the questions needed have not been asked in major surveys. In the 1988 Lutheran survey used here and in chapter 3, we can relate the answers on implementation issues to a question on biblical literalism that was asked on a survey sent a year later to two-thirds of the 1988 respondents. Only a small minority of these Lutherans are literalists, however, and this reduces the chance for associations to emerge. In any case, the results are inconsistent. For instance, 60 percent of literalists and 43 percent of non-literalists believe that we are responsible for trying to improve our society and not only for living ethically; about 60 percent of both groups believe that one should use laws in addition to persuasion; 42 percent of non-literalists, compared with 35 percent of literalists, believe that we need to change policies and structures rather than just individual behavior. That is, in the first case literalists hold more change-facilitating views than non-literalists, in the third more change-inhibiting views, and in the second identical views. On questions of conflict within the church, the results are more consistent: the literalists are somewhat more concerned than non-literalists to avoid social and political issues that might lead to conflict, on both questions dealing with this topic.

Chapter 7

1. Important literature reviews include Robert Wuthnow, "Religious Commitment and Conservatism: In Search of an Elusive Relationship," in *Religion in Sociological Perspective,* ed. Charles Glock (Belmont, CA: Wadsworth, 1973); Stephen Hart, "Survey Literature on Religion and Economic Attitudes," in "The Social Meanings of Faith" (Ph.D. dis., University of California at Berkeley, 1979; available from University Microfilms, Ann Arbor, MI), pp. 56–90; and Donald R. Ploch, "Religion as an Independent Variable: A Critique of Some Major Research," in *Changing Perspectives in the Scientific Study of Religion,* ed. Allan Eister (New York: Wiley, 1974), pp. 275–294.

2. Nineteen-eighty-four was chosen as the starting point because that was the first year in which the General Social Survey employed a precise denominational breakdown. The survey involves around fifteen hundred people each year, drawn randomly (by probability sampling methods) from the U.S. adult population. The sampling procedure gives people in large households a smaller chance of being selected than people in small households, and in certain years African-Americans had greater chances of being selected than Whites (in order to obtain a large enough number of African-Americans to make racial comparisons). Weights are used to correct for these procedures, and therefore the results presented here are generalizable to the U.S. adult population.

3. Andrew Greeley, *The American Catholic* (New York: Basic Books, 1977); Kenneth D. Wald, *Religion and Politics in the United States* (New York: St. Martin's Press, 1986).

4. In some cases, confirmation would be impossible because the variable used has never been used by any other researcher. Research projects using such idiosyncratic variables, however, have typically been highly restricted denominationally and geographically, and have often used sampling methods that do not permit generalization to *any* significant population (not even, for instance, the population of a metropolitan area, or the membership of a denomination). Such research can provide a basis for developing hypotheses or issues to be explored in more breadth or depth later but cannot establish trustworthy findings. Furthermore, in many cases *ad hoc* measures seem to be basically tapping how theologically modernist or traditionalist the respondents are, and so the results can be checked against other studies using that same general dimension. In two cases where variables developed by particular researchers that seem to be quite independent of that dimension have been used in subsequent research, the findings were not confirmed. Andrew Greeley has pioneered a "grace scale" concerned with images of God, and has found these to be powerful predictors of many kinds of social attitudes, for instance in "Evidence That a Maternal Image of God Correlates with Liberal Politics," *Sociology and Social Research* 72 (Spring 1988). Peter Benson and Dorothy Williams (*Religion on Capitol Hill* [New York: Oxford University Press, 1982]) have had similar results with variables they created measuring different kinds of religious orientations. But Michael Welch and David Leege ("Catholic Sociopolitical Attitudes," *Journal for the Scientific Study of Religion* 27 [1988]: 536–552) have used the Greeley and Benson/Williams variables and found little predictive power.

5. There are, as described in the text, data collected in the years 1984 through 1989; the results presented here are part of a more extensive analysis currently under

way. The data collection was done by the National Opinion Research Center at the University of Chicago, and the data and documentation are publicly available. James Davis and Tom Smith, *General Social Surveys, 1972–1989*, machine-readable data file (24,893 logical records) and codebook (Chicago: National Opinion Research Center, 1989).

6. Other questions deal with economic life, but either fall outside the dimensions of concern in this book—for instance, questions about environmental issues—or do not clearly distinguish liberals and conservatives. In the latter group are such questions as one on price and wage controls; in the present political climate, it is not clear which stances on this issue are more liberal or conservative.

7. Question 120A, found in Davis and Smith, *General Social Surveys 1972–1989: Cumulative Codebook*, p. 168. The General Social Survey has also used an alternate literalism question (120B), but this has been used only for some of the respondents and only in a few years, and therefore the responses are not of much help.

8. The denominational categories used here are slight modifications of those employed by Wade Clark Roof and William McKinney in *American Mainline Religion* (New Brunswick, NJ: Rutgers University Press, 1987). The categories have been renamed to avoid the use of "liberal" and "conservative" to describe religious orientations, since this contributes to the confusion between religious and political dimensions, and the respondents have been divided in a slightly more precise way than Roof and McKinney used, employing the more refined breakdown of denominational affiliation the General Social Survey has employed in recent years—a breakdown that was not available for many of the years of data used by Roof and McKinney.

9. This was done through a procedure called "multiple classification analysis." In essence, this procedure calculates the average response in each denominational group on an economic issue, adjusts the group averages to take into account the influence of other factors, and then determines whether reliable group differences remain and, if so, of what magnitude.

10. Question 442F, found in Davis and Smith, *General Social Surveys 1972–1989: Cumulative Codebook*, p. 506.

11. The African-American Protestants and Jews in this table are few in number, and so the percentages reported here are subject to a large sampling error. However, these percentages, relative to those for the larger groups, are very similar to the ones resulting from many other questions, increasing their plausibility.

12. "The Retreat of the Right," *The Nation*, October 23, 1982, p. 400. Wolfe's newest book, *Whose Keeper? Social Science and Moral Obligation* (Berkeley: University of California Press, 1989), argues that social science is the key locus of moral reasoning today. Social science is a good exemplar of a secular, scientific approach to human life, and so this argument, in combination with the one in *The Nation*, manifests his commitment to the proposition that left-of-center politics on economic issues are encouraged by secular thought and discouraged by religious faith.

13. Given this attitude and the realities of journal publishing, it is likely that the findings of the literature reviews cited earlier would be even stronger if unpublished findings were included. Researchers who find relationships between what they consider religiosity and political conservatism may be more likely to publish their findings than those who find no associations, since the absence of an association seems less interesting and important, and contradicts the assumptions under which the research

is conducted. Editors of journals, similarly, may be less likely (everything else being equal) to publish articles showing no associations, since the results may not seem to demonstrate anything important.

14. Robert Wuthnow, "Religious Commitment and Conservatism: In Search of an Elusive Relationship," in *Religion in Sociological Perspective,* ed. Charles Glock (Belmont, CA: Wadsworth, 1973).

15. Leo Driedger, "Doctrinal Belief: A Major Factor in the Differential Perception of Social Issues," *Sociological Quarterly* 15 (1974): 66.

16. Jeffrey Hadden, *The Gathering Storm in the Churches* (Garden City, NY: Doubleday, 1969), p. 81.

17. Joseph Tamney, Ronald Burton, and Stephen Johnson, "Christianity, Social Class, and the Catholic Bishops' Economic Policy," *Sociological Analysis,* vol. 49 supplement (December 1988), quotations from pp. 81s–82s.

18. It is sometimes hard to determine the theoretical position of public opinion research because many of the studies of religion and politics are quite atheoretical, stating no theoretical stance beyond an expectation that religiosity will be related to political conservatism.

19. Question 206G, found in Davis and Smith, *General Social Surveys 1972–1989: Cumulative Codebook,* p. 249. Because the question followed so many other questions on abortion, it could be that the responses are less pro-choice than they would be if the question had been asked by itself or in another context. But that should not affect the relationship between answers to this question and religious factors.

20. There is a large literature on the question of whether political views are uni- or multi-dimensional, tending toward the conclusion that they are multi-dimensional. For a classic, early argument for multi-dimensionality, differentiating an economic dimension from one concerned with intolerance and racial bigotry, see Seymour Martin Lipset and Earl Raab, *The Politics of Unreason* (New York: Harper and Row [Torchbook], 1973), pp. 452–456. Without explicitly dealing with the question of multi-dimensionality, Herbert McClosky and John Zaller, in *The American Ethos* (Cambridge: Harvard University Press, 1984), similarly define two distinct dimensions, one concerning economic issues (a "capitalism" scale) and the other civil liberties and tolerance issues (a "democracy" scale). They argue that in some respects the more consistent position would be to be conservative or liberal on both, but in other respects to be conservative on one and liberal on the other, since capitalist and democratic values are partly congruent and partly in tension. On the other hand, Norman Nie, Sidney Verba, and John Petrocik, in *The Changing American Voter* (Cambridge: Harvard University Press, 1976), use a liberal-conservative measure that includes both economic and non-economic issues, and find meaningful patterns. However, when they deal with the politics of Catholics and give data on the single items, it becomes clear that Catholics are relatively liberal on the two economic issues but not on the two non-economic issues in the scale.

This issue cannot be resolved in any final way empirically, but because the relationship of religious variables to economic issues is so different from the relationship to many non-economic issues (especially those concerning sexuality), it seems wisest to start with more specific and focused dimensions for measuring political attitudes rather than using global liberal-conservative scales.

21. The General Social Survey asks respondents to place themselves on a contin-

uum from "extremely liberal" to "extremely conservative," and I checked on the relationship between how people described themselves here and their views on a series of particular issues. On sixty-four economic issues, the average of the correlation coefficients was .11, and on seventeen non-economic issues, it was also .11. These weak correlations are another piece of evidence against assuming that most people are operating out of a political philosophy organized around the conservative-liberal continuum as understood by journalists and elites.

There is a long tradition of research on the ways in which political opinions are not "consistent" among the general public, and the degree to which people structure their views into coherent, ideological patterns. One pioneering, highly influential study is Philip Converse's chapter "Attitude Structure and the Problem of Ideology," in *The American Voter,* ed. Angus Campbell et al. (New York: Wiley, 1960), pp. 188–215. Converse argued here and in his article "The Nature of Belief Systems in Mass Publics" (found in *Ideology and Discontent*, ed. David Apter, [New York: Free Press, 1964]) that most Americans are not very coherent thinkers. His argument has been attacked on a number of grounds, and the debate is still raging. Part of the problem has been inadequate or controversial ways of conceptualizing and measuring what it might mean to be "ideological." In much of the research, the only way for respondents to be recognized as ideological is to connect their attitudes explicitly to what journalists would define as a consistent liberal or conservative political philosophy. This is unfortunate because clearly some coherent political philosophies result in taking conservative positions on economic issues and liberal ones on many non-economic ones.

The most sophisticated study dealing with this issue, W. Russell Neuman's *The Paradox of Mass Politics* (Cambridge: Harvard University Press, 1986), uses depth interviews to measure respondents' levels of political conceptualization more plausibly than other studies, and also allows respondents to be categorized as ideological whenever they use abstract organizing principles—whether or not they are "liberal" or "conservative." Neuman finds that somewhat under a third of his respondents are ideologues or near-ideologues, making at least some reference to abstract organizing principles to which they connect specific statements. (Another third use ideas about different group interests to organize their thinking, while the remainder either do their thinking in terms of the specific successes and failures of leaders or policies—with no broader organizing principle—or do not really respond to political issues at all.)

22. W. Russell Neuman shows a clearly different structure in the correlates of "economic distribution issues" and "political culture issues" in *The Paradox of Mass Politics,* pp. 79–81. Similarly, Herbert McClosky and John Zaller, in *The American Ethos* (Cambridge: Harvard University Press, 1984), show how political sophistication is related to liberal views on civil liberties but to mixed views on economic issues.

23. As one might expect, those of higher status—especially higher income—tend to be more conservative. However, the predictive power of these variables is less than one might imagine on the basis of a pure economic/class interests model of ideology. For instance, 52 percent of the respondents in the bottom third of the income distribution take a liberal position on the question about unemployment benefits, compared with 25 percent of those in the top third. This is a clear relationship (the Pearson correlation coefficient is .24) and may seem fairly strong, but from a

statistical point of view income explains only 6 percent of the variation in views on this issue.

Three factors may explain this. The first is that there is a fair amount of consensus in this country on economic issues, as for instance, Herbert McClosky and John Zaller's analysis of attitudes toward capitalism (*The American Ethos*), Peter Rossi's work on judgments of fairness of income levels (for instance, Rossi and Guillermina Jasso, "Distributive Justice and Earned Income," *American Sociological Review,* 42 (August 1977): 639–651), and Jennifer Hochschild's depth-interview study of views about income distribution (*What's Fair?* [Cambridge: Harvard University Press, 1981]) show. Apparently, Americans tend to believe that differences in income to reward different levels of skill and work are justified, but that the current differences are somewhat too large. The second factor is that subjective factors—values and beliefs, such as the ones we have been examining—seem to have some effect on the economic views Americans express. The third is that the cultural processes by which issues are presented to Americans and the ways Americans characteristically think about political issues give enormous scope to individual choices that are based on personally constructed, somewhat idiosyncratic perspectives. This is not a psychological but a social and cultural assertion; if there were more class-based institutions in the United States, disseminating perspectives that had class interests as an organizing principle, and Americans had strong bonds to such institutions, people's issue positions on economic issues would probably be more predictable and less random. Instead, the most important sources of information and perspectives about politics are the mass media and political parties, which try to be trans-class institutions.

24. "Religious Commitment and Conservatism: In Search of an Elusive Relationship," in *Religion in Sociological Perspective,* ed. Charles Glock (Belmont, CA.: Wadsworth, 1973), pp. 119–120.

25. *National Catholic Reporter,* December 14, 1990, p. 24.

26. Wade Clark Roof and William McKinney, *American Mainline Religion* (New Brunswick, NJ: Rutgers University Press, 1987), p. 57.

27. These figures are based on General Social Survey data, and are found in Stephen Hart, "Religious Giving: Patterns and Variations" (Paper presented at the annual meeting of the Religious Research Association and Society for the Scientific Study of Religion, Virginia Beach, November 9, 1990).

28. Roof and McKinney, *American Mainline Religion,* pp. 83–84.

29. Also, the respondents were chosen in a way designed to maximize the range of perspectives represented in the study rather than our ability to assess associations between religious and political attitudes, or to generalize quantitatively from their responses to the population of Christians in the United States. The Appendix describes the selection procedure in detail.

Chapter 8

1. Robert Bellah, Richard Madsen, Ann Swidler, William M. Sullivan, and Steven M. Tipton, *Habits of the Heart: Individualism and Commitment in American Life* (Berkeley: University of California Press, 1985).

2. Douglas Rae, in *Equalities* (Cambridge: Harvard University Press, 1981), analyzes the forms that the idea of equality can take and demonstrates their immense

variability. The radical potentials of the idea, he argues, can be blunted extremely easily and plausibly, and not by opposing other ideas to equality but by using the conservative or moderate potentials of the idea to oppose the radical ones. In political discourse the idea of equality acts something like a "rhetorical screen": for proposals to be acceptable, the people presenting them need to be able to show that they are compatible with at least one interpretation of the idea of equality (p. 148). This is not hard to bring off, but that does not mean that appeals to equality are a sham and that the idea has no influence. Particular people become passionately committed to particular versions of equality, and this can be a powerful factor in how they think and speak. Rae's argument could be applied to the idea of constructing a set of shared values to which any reasonable person would agree; such a set of values would have the same kind of variability as the idea of equality, and might operate in the same way, as a rhetorical screen.

3. The issues dealt with here are related to fundamental axes of debate within modern philosophy and theology; they come up in philosophy of science, the analysis of language pioneered by Ludwig Wittgenstein, the debate engendered by John Rawls's *Theory of Justice* (Cambridge: Harvard University Press, 1971), in post-liberal theology, and in postmodernism and deconstructionism. A good review of issues about foundations for ethics, as related to religious issues, is found in William C. Placher's *Unapologetic Theology* (Louisville: Westminster/John Knox Press, 1989).

4. James Davison Hunter, *American Evangelicalism* (New Brunswick, NJ: Rutgers University Press, 1983), pp. 6, 14.

5. Ibid., p. 15; emphasis in original.

6. Ibid., p. 134.

7. For an incisive critique of the idea of progress, from a Christian perspective, and an insightful analysis of how that idea has penetrated many aspects of Western thought, see Bob Goudzwaard, *Capitalism and Progress,* English second edition (Toronto: Wedge, 1979; the same edition first published in Dutch in 1978). In the Jewish Left circles represented by the magazine *Tikkun,* similar perspectives are being expressed. For an argument against the evolutionary assumptions on which Jürgen Habermas bases his attempt to construct a rational, naturalistically based social philosophy, see Placher, *Unapologetic Theory,* pp. 74–81.

There is also a strand of Western thought which might be called "negative evolutionism," in which our recent history is seen as having a coherent direction, but one inimical to human well-being. Such a view is far from rosy hopes for progress, but its description of historical tendencies, and of the connections among economic, political, and religious change, is essentially the same.

8. Max Weber, *The Protestant Ethic and the Spirit of Capitalism* (New York: Scribner, 1958; first published in German in 1904–1905).

9. Joseph Tamney, Ronald Burton, and Stephen Johnson, "Christianity, Social Class, and the Catholic Bishops' Economic Policy," *Sociological Analysis,* vol. 49 supplement (December 1988). Another example of this argument is found in Herbert McClosky and John Zaller, *The American Ethos* (Cambridge: Harvard University Press, 1984).

10. Michael Walzer, *The Revolution of the Saints* (New York: Atheneum, 1974); quotation from p. 1.

11. Jean-Jacques Rousseau, *The Social Contract*, found in *Social Contract*, ed. Ernest Barker (New York: Oxford University Press, 1962), pp. 305, 306; originally published in French in 1762.

12. A clear statement of Weber's position on utilitarianism is found in his *The Protestant Ethic and the Spirit of Capitalism*, pp. 180–182.

13. Alan Wolfe, "The Retreat of the Right," *The Nation*, October 23, 1982.

14. For a parallel critique of a literature pursuing in similarly single-minded fashion a similar negative question–why the rest of the world *did not* develop economically in the way Europe did—see Robert Bellah, "Reflections on the Protestant Ethic Analogy in Asia," found in his *Beyond Belief* (New York: Harper and Row, 1970; originally published in 1963).

15. Kenneth Wald, in *Religion and Politics in the United States* (New York: St. Martin's Press, 1986), presents data on the relationship—across countries—between economic development and the proportion of people in each country who say that religion is very important to them. Given the general pattern, and the level of economic development in the United States, that proportion would be predicted to be 5 percent. Instead, it is 51 percent!

16. For a skeptical analysis, disentangling various meanings of privatization and assessing the evidence for their reality, see my article "Privatization in American Religion and Society," *Sociological Analysis* 47 (Winter 1987).

17. Robert Wuthnow, *The Restructuring of American Religion* (Princeton: Princeton University Press, 1988).

18. This particular phrase is from the article quoted earlier by Leo Driedger, "Doctrinal Belief: A Major Factor in the Differential Perception of Social Issues," *Sociological Quarterly* 15 (Winter 1984): 66–80.

19. A somewhat parallel situation was noted over thirty years ago, in a different area, in M. Brewster Smith, Jerome Bruner, and Robert White, *Opinions and Personality* (New York: Wiley, 1956). This book's criticisms of the research literature seeking correlations between personality traits and attitudes (for instance, the literature on authoritarianism) was one of the inspirations for the approach taken here. They show that such research had made little progress, and argue that the reason is a lack of theoretical fit between attitudes and personality. Political opinions are psychologically heterogeneous; for instance, the same opinion may be a way to fit in socially for one person, a rational expression of class interest for another, and a neurotic projection for a third. Psychological processes, similarly, are politically heterogeneous; using political opinions as a tool for establishing solidarity with one's social environment, for instance, can lead to either left- or right-wing views, depending on the environment.

The situation is similar for religion and economic issues. Therefore, it is unlikely that any "purely religious" variable—that is, a variable having to do with an issue that does not already have some political or social overtones—would predict economic attitudes very well. And if one uses (as many researchers have) a variable that does have such overtones, there is a conceptual overlap between independent and dependent variables, and any associations one may find are meaningless from a causal standpoint.

20. Personal communication from Benton Johnson, November 20, 1990.

21. For a lucid summation of various religious influences on politics, including explicit ones but also such factors as the history of religio-ethnic groups, see Seymour

Martin Lipset, *Religion and Politics in the American Past and Present* (Berkeley: Survey Research Center, 1964).

22. In constructing such an argument, we need to be mindful of the dangers Jeffrey Alexander has described in "strong" theories of culture: that they either become idealist, or are kept from becoming so by asserting indeterminacy or bringing in more "material" factors in an *ad hoc* way. The multi-vocality noted over and over in how the depth-interview respondents use the resources of Christian faith may sound like this kind of indeterminacy. It manifests the diverse possibilities structurally available to individuals in a complex, culturally heterogeneous society. The choices individuals make, however, are not necessarily indeterminate in some ultimate sense; people choose among structured alternatives, in patterned ways, and ultimately the particular choice of a particular individual might be explainable in terms of that person's biography and characteristics. For the purposes of this book, there is no need to try to be able to explain the particular choices of individuals, and so we have not tried to move from multi-vocal cultural forms to determinate choices— which would require taking into account non-cultural factors. Then the analysis would become "multi-dimensional" in Alexander's sense. Such multi-dimensionality is essential for a fully adequate account of particular outcomes but is not in order to understand the contributions Christian frameworks make to public discourse about economic life. (See Jeffrey Alexander, *Twenty Lectures* [New York: Columbia University Press, 1987], particularly his analysis of Clifford Geertz.)

23. For a related but not identical conception of ideology, see Clifford Geertz, "Ideology as a Cultural System," reprinted in his collection, *The Interpretation of Cultures* (New York: Basic Books, 1973). Another discussion that has enlightened me was a paper on culture as a force in historical processes presented by Ann Swidler at the August 1987 meeting of the American Sociological Association. There are many other conceptions of ideology, from Marx, Mannheim, Shils, and so forth, and the way I use the term here should not be confused with any of these other usages. In terms of public opinion literature, the controversies over the concept of ideology are well summarized in W. Russell Neuman, *The Paradox of Mass Politics* (Cambridge: Harvard University Press, 1986), especially pp. 73–81.

24. I am indebted to Benton Johnson for arguing to me that this is the case, in a personal communication.

25. Geertz describes some polemics against ideology in his essay "Ideology as a Cultural System." Many more contemporary examples could be found. The basic idea is that ideological politics threatens democracy and individual freedom, can overload political institutions by placing too many demands upon them, and undermines the efficacy and independence of other institutions (universities, business, and so on) upon which it hopes to place political demands.

Chapter 9

1. Michael Ferber, "Religious Revival on the Left," *The Nation,* July 6–13, 1985, p. 10.

2. Robert Bellah, Richard Madsen, Ann Swidler, William M. Sullivan, and Steven M. Tipton, *Habits of the Heart: Individualism and Commitment in American Life* (Berkeley: University of California Press, 1985). The respondent in question is called Wayne Bauer.

3. The work of Yudit Jung, described in chapter 5, has the same agenda, although it deals with European historical materials.

4. Robert Westbrook, "Good-bye to All That: Eileen Kraditor and Radical History," *Radical History Review,* no. 28–30 (1984), pp. 69–89; quotations from p. 86.

5. There is an extensive tradition of writings on this subject, with many different interpretations of Marx and suggested stances for the Left. For one view, see Michael Ryan's *Marxism and Deconstructionism* (Baltimore: Johns Hopkins University Press, 1982), particularly chap. 9. Ryan argues for an appropriation of Marx that is complementary to deconstructionism; the feminist and environmentalist critiques of Leninism, in his view, are in this vein.

6. The tradition of natural theology and natural law thought within Christianity (which I take to be an influence on recent "revisionist" theology) has some analogies to Enlightenment thought in assuming that universal values are accessible to everyone through reason and conscience. However, there are still significant differences between these traditions and that of the Enlightenment. We might, similarly, draw an analogy between the non-Enlightenment/culturally traditionalist stance and the focus on revelation among Christian traditionalists, and between the non-Enlightenment/culturally modernist stance and the Christian perspective recently articulated by what is called "postliberal" or "postmodern" theology. For a more systematic treatment of these issues—one that has influenced my views—see William Placher, *Unapologetic Theology* (Louisville: Westminster/John Knox, 1989), p. 61.

7. For a similar analysis of the intolerance found among those who come out of the Enlightenment tradition, and even of some who consider themselves relativists, see Placher, *Unapologetic Theology.*

8. Scott Lash, in an analysis of the debates between Jürgen Habermas (a German social philosopher who comes out of the Frankfurt school of critical social theory, and continues the Enlightenment tradition, trying to construct a universal, rational basis for social values on the basis of a theory of discourse) and contemporary French theorists, argues that the latter really do give up on having any basis for discourse in pursuit of shared values. He may be right in terms of the logic of their argument, and yet thinkers such as Foucault and Jean-Jacques Lyotard (a leading "postmodernist" philosopher) do not absent themselves from debate on issues of values. They believe themselves to be speaking and acting for justice and liberation, if not for a theory (or fixed principles) of justice and liberty. Perhaps they cannot make accountable, theoretically, why they would not be cynical and nihilistic, but in fact often they are not. And Lyotard's critique of Habermas's attempts to construct a universally demonstrable basis for social values, as Lash agrees, is quite persuasive. So they do make a contribution to developing a more adequate ethical language for seeking liberty and justice, whatever the faults in their thinking may be. (Scott Lash, "Postmodernity and Desire," *Theory and Society* [January 1985]: 1–33. See also Lyotard's *The Post-Modern Condition* [Minneapolis: University of Minnesota Press, 1984; originally published in French in 1979] and Foucault's "What Is Enlightenment?" in *The Foucault Reader,* ed. Paul Rabinow [New York: Pantheon, 1984], pp. 32–50.)

9. There are, of course, other ways to frame the issue of relativism; see, for instance, the formulations given by Jeffrey Stout in *Ethics after Babel* (Boston: Beacon Press, 1988).

10. Such a defense of legal abortion can be constructed on two bases. The first is that there are circumstances in which an abortion is the ethically life-affirming choice, and that the decision about whether this is the situation in any particular case is too ethically complex and too dependent on circumstances that can be weighed only by the woman who is pregnant to regulate by law. The second is that the rights of the fertilized ovum/embryo/fetus and the interest of the community in protecting them are not clear and critical enough to justify the demonstrable and severe consequences for women's equality, self-determination, economic and physical well-being, and freedom of conscience (and, of course, the harm to the integrity, fairness, and efficacy of a legal system faced with "victimless crimes" not believed to be crimes by a sizeable part of the community) that would result from taking away the right to a legal abortion. Neither of these arguments assumes ethical relativism, makes "choice" an absolute, asserts an absolute constitutional right of personal privacy, or stops debate about the *ethics* of abortion. In fact, if we decide to keep abortion unconditionally legal on grounds like these (and, I hope, restore public funding for abortions for women on Medicaid, so that they are not treated like second-class citizens), the ethical debate can be much more vigorous. If nobody fears that saying that some abortions may be ethically illegitimate will be used as ammunition for establishing legal restrictions, some people who now refrain from expressing ethical reservations they feel may speak up. Practical issues of legal restraints and affordability (the latter because of the ban on using public funds for abortions) distort and partly suppress the ethical debate that should be happening.

11. Eli Zaretsky, *Capitalism, the Family, and Private Life* (New York: Perennial, 1976).

12. Details can be found in a report entitled "Faith, the Church, and the World: How ELCA Members See the Connections," issued in 1990 by the Office for Planning, Research, and Evaluation of the Evangelical Lutheran Church in America.

13. The exceptions would be the very few cases where a congregation has a strong political identity—for instance, is known locally as a place where there is a lot of Christian left or Christian right activity—and even in such cases there are likely to be many people who became members before this identity was established, or joined for other reasons, and are therefore politically diverse.

14. The implementation issues are somewhere between substantive and meta-issues with regard to the concerns we have been discussing; some of them are less potentially divisive than substantive issues, while others (such as using conflictual means to try to make social change) are equally so.

15. This was noted a generation ago, in an essay by Charles Glock and Rodney Stark entitled "The New Denominationalism," found in *Religion and Society in Tension,* by Glock and Stark (Chicago: Rand McNally, 1965). More recently, Robert Wuthnow's *The Restructuring of American Religion* (Princeton: Princeton University Press, 1988), and Wade Clark Roof and William McKinney's *American Mainline Religion* (New Brunswick, NJ: Rutgers University Press, 1987) make similar points, arguing that denomination has become an even weaker force since the 1960s.

16. From the standpoint of some people influenced by a Lutheran "two-kingdoms" perspective, the whole approach taken in this book, and especially here, may seem unfortunate. Such a perspective opposes what it sees as attempts to baptize particular social values as "Christian," and emphasizes making decisions about what public policies one will favor on the basis of our natural ethical and rational capacities

shared with all human beings. Personally, I believe that it is possible to make common cause and enter into dialogue with non-Christians but still articulate an actual Christian perspective on social justice. But in any case, evidence from Lutheran surveys I have conducted indicates that few Lutherans adopt a two-kingdoms view. Most American Lutherans, at their hearts, appear to be, as one Lutheran staff person, commenting in some dismay on my findings, put it, a bunch of "Calvinist realists" in the spirit of their thinking about how to connect faith to political issues. This was even true of many of the pastors! If Americans separate faith from politics, it is for reasons different from an attachment to two-kingdoms thinking.

17. Karl Marx and Frederick Engels, *The Communist Manifesto* (New York: International Publishers, 1948; originally published in 1848), p. 33.

18. That does not mean that people who are more educated in fact behave more ethically; they are only more adept at articulating reasons for their actions. The links among ethical reasoning, cognitive skills, moral character, and ethical behavior are complex and disputable. For one view, see Lawrence Kohlberg, "Moral Development," in *International Encyclopedia of the Social Sciences,* ed. David Sills (New York: Macmillan, 1968), 10:483–494.

19. This view is similar to that found in some of Paul Tillich's work, particularly *The Courage to Be* (New Haven: Yale University Press, 1952), and also reflects themes found in sermons given by Frank T. Griswold III, now Episcopal Bishop of Chicago, from 1982 to 1985, at the Church of St. Martin-in-the-Fields, Philadelphia.

20. For a more extensive discussion of issues about relativism and moralism, see my article "Ethical Relativism, Left-Wing Politics," *Dissent* (Fall 1982): 483–486.

21. The key work by MacIntyre for this debate is *After Virtue* (South Bend: Notre Dame University Press, 1984).

22. Richard Rorty, unpublished manuscript quoted in Stout, *Ethics after Babel.*

23. Stout, *Ethics after Babel,* p. 229.

24. Ibid., p. 271.

25. A key work articulating post-liberal theology is George Lindbeck's *The Nature of Doctrine* (Philadelphia: Westminster, 1984); a good treatment of post-liberalism and the perspectives that compete with it is found in Placher, *Unapologetic Theology.*

26. Stanley Hauerwas, *Against the Nations* (San Francisco: Harper and Row, 1985), p. 2.

27. Ibid., p. 3.

Appendix

1. Jennifer Hochschild, *What's Fair?* (Cambridge: Harvard University Press, 1981); Craig Reinarman, *American States of Mind* (New Haven: Yale University Press, 1987); Robert Bellah, Richard Madsen, Ann Swidler, William M. Sullivan, and Steven M. Tipton, *Habits of the Heart: Individualism and Commitment in American Life* (Berkeley: University of California Press, 1985); Robert Lane, *Political Ideology* (New York: Free Press, 1962); M. Brewster Smith, Jerome Bruner, and Robert White, *Opinions and Personality* (New York: Wiley, 1956).

2. This survey is reported most fully in Robert Wuthnow's *The Consciousness Reformation* (Berkeley: University of California Press, 1976). In this survey, youth were oversampled, but weights can be used to compensate.

3. The overall refusal rate was 28 percent, but within the New Religious Con-

sciousness sample it was 35 percent. Requesting an appointment in advance by mail and phone, asking for two appointments and three hours with no payment, and making a more low-pressure approach than usual in surveys (this was mandated by the Committee for the Protection of Human Subjects) account for the refusal rate, which is high compared with in-person surveys but low compared with mail surveys.

4. In making replacements and controlling the selections, there was a certain amount of handpicking of respondents, but the handpicking was based on specific criteria and limited, objective data on the potential respondents, and so the scope for subjective biases was relatively small.

5. David Arnold, "Dimensional Sampling: An Approach for Studying a Small Number of Cases," *American Sociologist* (May 1970): 147–149.

6. Considering only the thirty-one respondents from the New Religious Consciousness sample, these probabilities would be .80 and .96, respectively; if we included all forty-seven respondents, they would be .91 and .99.

Index

Abortion, 244n.10. *See also* Liberal-conservative dimension
Affirmative action, 232n.1
Alexander, Jeffrey, 242n.22
Alinsky tradition of community organizing, 174
American exceptionalism, 180–81
Anti-materialistic views, 18, 25, 36, 136
  and critique of American life, 137
Antinomian thinking, 48
Apostle, Richard, 233n.12
Arminian views, 120, 121, 178
Arnold, David, 221, 246n.5
Asceticism, 133–34, 135–36, 179
Atomistic view of society, 75, 120–22, 143–44
  rejection of, 149

Barth, Karl, 215
Bellah, Robert, 5, 45, 227n.8, 234n.6, 241n.14. *See also Habits of the Heart*
Benson, Peter, 235n.4
Biblical literalism. *See* Modernist-traditionalist division
Book of Common Prayer (Episcopal), 58, 227nn.12–13
Boycko, Maxim, 232ch.4n.6
Boyte, Harry, 200, 233n.9
Bruner, Jerome, 220, 241n.19, 245n.1
Building blocks in Christian faith, 43–61, 227–28n.14 (table showing varying characteristics)
Burton, Ronald, 163, 178, 237n.17, 240n.9

Bush, George, 96
Bushman, Richard, 233n.10
Butros, Michael (respondent), 53, 73, 74, 77, 90, 100–102, 103, 105, 111, 138, 149

Calvin, John, 57
Calvinism, 57. *See also* Puritanism
Caring and sharing, language of, 84, 91–98
Carter, Jimmy, 4, 71
Catholic-Protestant differences. *See* Protestant-Catholic differences
Christian hat (comparisons between what happens when using Christian themes and other frameworks), 59, 70, 71, 96, 98, 125, 126, 127, 138, 184, 201. *See also* Fluency in Christian language
Church and state, separation of (First Amendment), 65, 116, 204, 207, 209, 228n.1
Church social action. *See* Social action by churches
Churches, issues confronting
  difficulties of church social action, 206–8
  dilemmas of moralism, 211–13, 217
  importance of addressing meta-issues, 208–10
  importance of dealing with rank-and-file views, 210
  observing limits to expertise, 210–11
  remaining otherworldly, maintaining transcendence and distinctiveness, 215–217
Citizens for Community Values, 146–47